FAMILY ASSESSMENT IN EARLY INTERVENTION

Donald B. Bailey, Jr.

University of North Carolina at Chapel Hill

Rune J. Simeonsson

University of North Carolina at Chapel Hill

D1304681

Merrill Publishing Company

A Bell & Howell Information Company

Columbus / Toronto / London / Melbourne

Published by Merrill Publishing Company
A Bell & Howell Information Company
Columbus, Ohio 43216

This book was set in Bookman

Administrative Editor: Vicki Knight
Production Coordinator: Carol S. Sykes
Art Coordinator: Patrick Welch
Cover Designer: Cathy Watterson

Library of Congress Catalog Card Number: 88-60676
International Standard Book Number: 0-675-20996-X
Printed in the United States of America
1 2 3 4 5 6 7 8 9 – 92 91 90 89 88

Preface

Special educators, psychologists, social workers, therapists, and other personnel are increasingly becoming involved in the provision of early intervention services to infants and preschoolers with handicaps. In recent years, the focus and scope of intervention services have been expanded to include the family of those infants or preschoolers. This expanded focus is evident in the central role of families affirmed in Public Law 99–457, in the growing interest in family issues in early intervention research, and in the increase of family services in infant and preschool programs.

Although there is wide support for providing family services in early intervention, its implementation is hampered by conceptual, measurement, clinical, and practical limitations. This text examines issues related to the systematic assessment of family strengths and needs, describes characteristics of various family assessments, identifies considerations in selecting and using family assessments, and proposes an approach to the development of family goals. Focus is placed on family assessment for clinical purposes, drawing on a variety of issues and measures. The text thus provides practitioners with the information necessary to design and implement a comprehensive family assessment and to engage in collaborative goal-setting with parents.

The stimulus for this text is drawn primarily from our work in the F.A.M.I.L.I.E.S. Project, a five-year study of families with young handicapped children enrolled in a home-based intervention network in North Carolina. The project was a part of the Carolina Institute for Research on Early Education for the Handicapped, an early childhood research institute awarded to the Frank Porter Graham Child Development Center of the University of North Carolina at Chapel Hill. A major purpose of the project was to develop and field-test a model for assessing family needs and planning family goals in early intervention.

The contribution and support of many individuals to this project must be recognized. Dr. James Gallagher, Principal Investigator of the institute and, at that time, Director of the Frank Porter Graham Child Development Center, provided the support and leadership necessary for the project to achieve its goals. Colleagues and graduate students in the F.A.M.I.L.I.E.S. Project provided immeasurable support throughout the project and over the years have contributed to the project's activities and products in a substantive fashion: Kris Huntington, Pam Winton, Marilee Comfort, Trish Isbell, Jim Helm, Karen O'Donnell, and Ed Arndt. Duncan Munn, of the North Carolina State Department of Human Resources, provided important statewide support and encouragement. We also extend our sincere thanks to the manuscript's reviewers for their excellent suggestions, which aided us in developing this text: David W. Anderson, Lock Haven University of Pennsylvania; Mary Lynne Calhoun, University of North Carolina at Charlotte; Kent Gerlach, Pacific Lutheran University; Frances T. Herrington, Radford University; Janice Jipson, University of Oregon; Ann P. Kaiser, Vanderbilt University; Evelyn C. Lynch, Moorhead State University; and Helmi Owens, Pacific Lutheran University.

The project would have been impossible, however, without the support, time, and commitment invested by the professionals in North Carolina's Early Childhood Intervention Services system. These individuals are too numerous to name individually, but their involvement is greatly appreciated. This text is dedicated to them.

Contents

Rationale and Model for Family Assessment in Early Intervention

The assessment of family needs is not a new phenomenon in early intervention. Since 1968, when federal legislation established the Handicapped Children's Early Education Program, interventionists have recognized the importance of parental involvement and have attempted to incorporate parent services. Recent advocacy efforts, research, and legislation, however, have highlighted the importance of individualized *family* support and services in early intervention (Bailey et al., 1986; Dunst, 1985). Comprehensive assessment of family strengths and needs is a necessary prerequisite for such individualized services. This text describes approaches and procedures for conducting assessments with families of young handicapped children. This chapter provides a rationale for conducting such assessments, discusses barriers to effective collection and analysis, describes characteristics of appropriate assessment, and provides a functional model.

This chapter was contributed by Donald B. Bailey, Jr., University of North Carolina at Chapel Hill.

WHY CONDUCT FAMILY ASSESSMENTS?

Ascertaining the needs of very young children with handicaps is often a lengthy and complex activity; so much so that the addition of a comprehensive family assessment would constitute a considerably demanding effort. However, at least five reasons exist for making this effort:

1. To meet legal mandates
2. To understand a child as part of a family system
3. To identify families' needs for services
4. To identify families' strengths that promote family adaptation
5. To expand the base for evaluating services

Legal Reasons

Public Law 94-142 did not require that goals or services be specified for families. It did require parental involvement in a written individualized education plan (IEP) for each handicapped student and provided for due process rights if parents disagreed with goals or services for their child.

The passage of Public Law 99-457, however, represented a fundamental change. The law mandated that by the school year 1990–1991, all states must provide a free and appropriate education to handicapped children ages 3 to 5. In addition, the legislation offered states grants to serve handicapped infants and toddlers from birth through 2 years of age.

Significantly, the report accompanying the legislation states that the IEP for preschoolers should include, when appropriate and desired by parents, instruction for parents. The law also states that parents of infants and toddlers should help develop their own individualized family services plan, with assistance from a multidisciplinary team. This plan would focus on how family strengths could enhance the child's development and would state the family's goals. A "case manager" must be designated for every family to help them on the plan and to help coordinate with other agencies and service providers. In addition to services for children, the plan may also include family training and counseling services. The key word in the law is *individualized*, thus requiring an analysis of individual family needs.

A Child as Part of a Family System

We now recognize from modern theorists that a child is part of a larger family system. As such, the child both influences and is influenced by the family. Thus, changes in the family affect the child, and changes in the child alter the family. Many researchers have conceptualized this idea. Bell (1968), in discussing research on social development, emphasized this bidirectional nature of interactions. He argued against the traditional one-way interpretation of maternal effects on children's behavior and suggested that children may exert an equally powerful effect on their parents' behavior. Sameroff and Chandler (1975) proposed a transactional theory in which children and caregivers change one another in repeated interactions over time. Bronfenbrenner (1977) described the importance of an ecological view of development in which the child is nested within a family, which in turn is nested within a broader neighborhood or community system.

Such conceptualizations of how children and families interact have these implications for assessment:

1. Intervention with a child is likely to affect the family, too. These effects may be helpful (e.g., as when a child is taught to perform a self-help task) or stressful (e.g., where a consistent application of behavior-management principles is required). Family assessment will help the professional gain insight into potential family reactions.
2. Interventions with *one* family member may have subsequent effects on others in the family. These effects may be helpful (e.g., as when father attends a fathers-only support group and subsequently provides increased assistance in caregiving at home) or stressful (e.g., as when a mother who is encouraged to participate in advocacy groups reduces the time she spends with her family). Family assessment will help predict the influence of such interventions on others in the family.
3. Families must interact with the larger community. Assessment clarifies how families view children and the services provided for them, and how families view and interact with service systems. Recognition of system-level influences can enhance the effectiveness and efficiency of services.

Family Needs

Many families of young handicapped children have unique needs, some of which can be met by the early interventionist or preschool teacher. These families have only recently learned of their child's disability and may need information about the handicap. They may be stressed by the shock of having a handicapped child (Drotar, Baskiewicz, Irwin, Kennell, & Klaus, 1975). Caregiving demands often exceed expectations (Beckman-Bell, 1981); parents may need help in locating day care, babysitting, or respite services. Parents may be uncertain about the future and need to find other appropriate professional services. They may also need assistance in interacting appropriately with their child or in helping siblings deal with a handicapped brother or sister (Simeonsson & Bailey, 1986). Furthermore, parents of handicapped infants and preschoolers may feel that they have lost some degree of control over their lives and may lose confidence in their ability to parent.

Certainly not all families with handicapped children experience high levels of need or stress. Many families have or develop natural support systems that allow them to adapt to their child and continue to accomplish important family functions. As a group, however, families with handicapped children have needs over and above those associated with caring for nonhandicapped children (Farber, 1959; Gallagher, Beckman, & Cross, 1983; Murphy, 1982). Assessing individual family needs can lead to the provision of services most likely to be successful and acceptable for families. Wynne, McDaniel, and Weber (1987) emphasize the role of "consultative stocktaking" before initiating family therapy. This involves a series of meetings between families and therapists in which all parties jointly explore issues and needs. This approach can help determine whether therapy is needed and improve therapeutic potential. It also communicates the therapists' genuine concern and interest in families, thereby strengthening the relationship between parents and professionals.

Family Strengths

Just as all families have needs, so too do they all have strengths. Dunst (1985) argues that traditional approaches are often based on a deficit model, which assumes that all families with handicapped children have problems. Early intervention programs operating under this model aim to remediate family deficits. Others have argued that too much emphasis has been placed on pathology in families with handicapped children, with inadequate attention given to the healthy side of family functioning. For example, Turnbull and Turnbull (1986) state that the professional literature contains many biased statements indicating "pervasive negative generalizations" (p. 110) about families with handicapped children and a tendency to discount any indication that a handicapped child may, in fact, exert a positive influence on family members. Citing preliminary research findings, Turnbull and Turnbull emphasize the importance of such positive outcomes because

> (a) it is consistent with the principle of empathetic reciprocity (a principle requiring others to attempt to understand how another person views the world), since it will fairly ascribe the benefits that persons with disabilities contribute to others as well as the drawbacks that have already been documented, (b) it has the potential of decreasing the stigma that accrues when persons are viewed as wholly negative, and (c) it has the potential for providing intervention strategies aimed at supporting persons with disabilities and their families to accentuate the positive aspects of their circumstance. (p. 112)

Therefore, another rationale for family assessment is to identify, build on, and reinforce potential family strengths and resources.

Dunst (1985) has operationalized this notion in an approach referred to as Proactive Empowerment through Partnerships (PEP). In this model, families and professionals work together to determine family needs. Decision making is controlled by families rather than by interventionists or teachers to "empower families with skills, knowledge, and competencies that allow them access and control over resources that can be used to meet family needs" (p. 168). Central to the PEP model is a focus on family strengths and resources. Bronfenbrenner's (1977) ecological model is used as a framework to assess support from immediate family members, extended family, friends and neighbors, social organizations, human service agencies and professionals, and policy makers. These social support systems are assumed to contribute significantly to the broad effects of early intervention, and the preschool teacher's job becomes one of enhancing family support systems. The overall goals of the program are accomplished

> through provision and mediation of supports that strengthen families as well as other normal socializing agents (relatives, friends, neighbors, the church, etc.) but which neither replaces or supplants them. The process of strengthening families consists of imparting information, knowledge, skills, and competencies through provision or mediation of support that proactively influences child, parent, and family functioning. (Dunst, 1985, pp. 181–182)

Strategies for assessing family roles and supports are described in Chapter 7 of this text.

A Basis for Evaluating Services

A final rationale for family assessment relates to the ultimate goals of early intervention. Traditionally, early intervention has been justified on the basis of child needs, and researchers have striven to prove its effects on children (Casto & Mastropieri, 1986; Dunst & Rheingrover, 1981; Simeonsson, Cooper, & Scheiner, 1982). Recent publications, however, have argued that family outcomes may be as important as child outcomes (Bailey et al., 1986; Bailey & Simeonsson, 1984; Dunst, 1985). If so, interventionists should periodically gather data to assess changes in family needs and strengths resulting from participation in early intervention programs. Such monitoring of progress should help interventionists recognize when interventions and services for families are effective and when they need to be changed. A recent meta-analysis of formative evaluation procedures concluded that in classrooms where teachers frequently measured and analyzed child progress, significant improvements were noted (Fuchs & Fuchs, 1986). Although such research has not been conducted with regard to family outcomes, similar results might be expected. Periodic family assessment *plus* child assessment also demonstrates a program's accountability. Finally, including family assessments as part of a program's overall evaluation system makes a public statement regarding program goals and objectives. It forces policy makers and the public to recognize that early intervention is not simply a child-oriented service. Issues and considerations in evaluating family services are described in Chapter 12.

BARRIERS TO EFFECTIVE FAMILY ASSESSMENT

Despite the strong reasons supporting family assessment in early intervention, many barriers make assessment difficult. An analysis of prevailing approaches to family services reinforces this point: Most programs do not assess family needs at all. Instead, identical services are offered for all families, regardless of their individual needs. For example, a center-based program might offer a parent support group and a series of workshops on behavior management. A home-based program might use a specific curriculum that requires all parents to engage in specific teaching activities (e.g., Shearer & Shearer, 1977). Or a program may embrace a particular model of family functioning and emphasize that approach for all families. For example, Affleck, McGrade, McQueeney, and Allen (1982) describe a relationship-focused early intervention program that concentrates on enhancing the quality of relationships between parents and their young children with handicaps.

Occasionally services are individualized. However, this strategy is based on the interventionist's clinical judgment about family needs derived from informal family contacts and discussions. Although clinical judgment is important in any service-delivery system, used alone it is insufficient. Its usefulness rests entirely on the skills, knowledge, and experience of the interventionist in the area of family needs. Furthermore, its use tends to vary according to aspects of family functioning that the interventionist personally deems important; other dimensions may be omitted, and opportunities for systematic monitoring and evaluation, except on a subjective basis, are lost.

Why is systematic family assessment rarely incorporated in early intervention? At least five kinds of barriers can be identified: (1) conceptual, (2) measurement, (3) interventionist, (4) institutional, and (5) family.

Conceptual Barriers

One barrier to effective family assessment has been the lack of functional models for conceptualizing families and their needs. Most early intervention programs adopt a developmental model for conceptualizing children's needs and a learning theory model for enhancing skill acquisition (Bailey & Wolery, 1984). These models embody specific assumptions about children and the way they acquire skills, and lead to specific decisions regarding intervention goals and strategies. Although a host of family models have been described in the professional literature, they have not been very useful in prescribing services. Tseng and McDermott (1979) suggest a triaxial model, with three dimensions of family functioning: developmental changes, family subsystems, and whole-family problems. McCubbin and Patterson (1983) propose an ABCX model that emphasizes the role of stressors, family perceptions of those stressors, and family resources for adapting to stress.

Crnic, Friedrich, and Greenberg (1983) describe a model demonstrating the ecological influences that mediate possible stress and coping associated with having a handicapped child. Turnbull, Summers, and Brotherson (1984) incorporate family systems theory to propose a model of family functioning consisting of family functions, family interactions, family supports, and family development.

Each of these representative models can advance our understanding of families and how they function. None, however, has led to specific procedures for assessing family needs and strengths in a fashion that leads to the specification of family goals and services. This problem means not that the theories are incorrect, simply that if used alone they are insufficient as guides for clinical practice. A model is needed that identifies important domains of family functioning and provides guidance for assessing each domain and generating relevant family goals and services.

Measurement Barriers

Teachers of young handicapped children can choose from a host of assessment tools to identify children's strengths and weaknesses and subsequently to plan objectives and services. A comparable battery of family assessment tools has not been developed for early interventionists. Thus, a second barrier to effective family assessment is a lack of functional assessment tools.

Although many instruments are available for assessing various aspects of family functioning, most suffer from several limitations. Many measure hypothetical constructs such as stress or locus of control. Just as intelligence tests have limited utility in identifying objectives and planning services for children, so are these family measures limited in their usefulness in planning family services. Knowing that a family is experiencing great stress is important, but it is also important to understand the sources of stress and how to deal with it. Many instruments are deficit-oriented, value-laden, or intrusive, asking personal questions about lifestyle, spouse support, personal values, and feelings. Not only are such questions of little use in program planning, but they may actually be counterproductive by creating resentment and mistrust.

Owing to the lack of available measures, many interventionists have resorted to developing their own instruments. Although such measure may be useful at times, their statistical properties, reliability, and validity are unknown.

Interventionist Barriers

Characteristics of early interventionists and preschool teachers may also constitute barriers to effective family assessment. Most teachers and related service professionals have received extensive training in child development, child assessment procedures, handicapping conditions, and effective teaching practices. In contrast, they typically receive limited training in working with families and are often unfamiliar with family assessment tools or strategies for working with families. Fostering change and coping in adults requires strategies different from those for children. Communicating effectively with families, including interviewing and negotiating values and priorities, requires unique skills, most of which are not taught or practiced in university training programs. Intervention programs providing practicum sites are generally unwilling to let students work with families except in the most superficial fashion. Furthermore, many early interventionists are young, unmarried, and childless. These factors are often barriers because some families question whether the professional understands the complexities of married life with children.

Institutional Barriers

Programs themselves can pose barriers to family assessment. Most emphasize child services; some administrators regard any work with families as nice but above the call of duty. Supervisors may lack skills in family assessment and intervention and thus be unable to assist staff who seek advice and support in family-related issues. In some areas, families with handicapped youngsters are served by multiple agencies and professionals, and family stress can increase when uncoordinated services are fragmented or duplicated. Programs may give lowest priority to hiring a social worker or other professional with extensive training in working with families. Finally, the time- and resource-consuming demands of child care impose very real constraints on serving families in center-based programs.

Family Barriers

Finally, family characteristics may act as barriers to assessment and subsequent services. Some parents may be uninterested in having their needs, relationships, or support systems assessed, viewing such assessments as intrusive and possibly irrelevant to their child's needs. Families operating under economic hardships may be unable to focus on aspects of family functioning that, for them, are of lesser priority; these families may do poorly when participating in early intervention (Brassell, 1977). Parents who have only recently learned of their child's handicap or who are otherwise depressed may be unable to respond adequately to family questionnaires and surveys and may be less likely to engage in planned program activities (McMahon, Forehand, Griest, & Wells, 1981). Dumas and Wahler (1983) found "insularity" of mothers (those with a pattern of negative interactions with relatives, friends, and professionals) to be negatively related to successful parent training. Occasionally, family members may deny their child's disability and refuse services, even when confronted with a serious handicapping condition (Pollner & McDonald-Wikler, 1985). Finally, some parents may have limited skills of expression or insight, restricting their ability to communicate adequately with professionals.

CHARACTERISTICS OF EFFECTIVE FAMILY ASSESSMENT

The barriers described suggest that family assessment is not simple. It is critical, however, because the approach taken and the measures used in assessing family needs and strengths will significantly shape the professionals' views of the family, communicate messages to family members about the values and priorities of the professionals, and ultimately influence family goals and services. Consider, for example, an analogy in child assessment. Suppose a teacher chose to assess a child using an intelligence test and a personality test. The results would likely provide an interesting picture of the child, lead to diagnostic interpretation of the child's developmental status, and result in a plan for intervention. The focus of the child's goals and the nature of the intervention provided would probably be quite different, however, if the child had been assessed in areas of adaptive and social functioning, and if both testing and naturalistic observations had been incorporated.

Likewise, the selection of family assessment measures will influence subsequent decisions. Assessing stress, marital relations, and locus of control is likely to result in a very different conceptualization of a family and a different plan for service than assessing family needs and parent-child interactions.

An effective approach to family assessment should incorporate the following functions:

1. Cover important family domains
2. Incorporate multiple sources and measures
3. Recognize the importance of family values and traditions
4. Determine family priorities for goals and services
5. Vary according to program type and demands
6. Evaluate family outcomes on a regular basis

Domains for Family Assessment

Teachers planning to assess children know that each child should be evaluated in the basic domains of communication, motor, self-help, cognition, and social skills. Is there a corresponding set of fundamental domains necessary for a comprehensive family assessment? Because much less is known about family structure, development, and needs, this question cannot be answered definitively. Even a brief review of the literature suggests a long list of family dimensions that could be assessed, areas that include parent teaching behaviors, parent-child interactions, parental stress, locus of control, parents' sense of competence, acceptance of the handicapped child, attachment, stress, coping, support, stages of grief, needs, marital relations, and sibling reactions, to name but a few. Although research has documented each of these as a potential area of need for some families, it would be not only impossible, but also intrusive and unnecessary, to assess each area.

Bronfenbrenner (1977) proposed an *ecological model* of human development that emphasizes how individuals live and function within systems of varying degrees of complexity. A series of levels of child and family assessment drawing on this model and those proposed by others is presented in Table 1.1. The table briefly describes each level and shows examples of assessment concerns. Although historical emphasis has focused almost exclusively on the handicapped child's abilities, contemporary theorists argue that other components of the child's world must be assessed to make clear the context within which the child and family must function and to provide services uniquely tailored to that context.

Selecting an assessment tool for families must be based on individual program philosophies and individual family needs. However, based on our own work (Bailey et al., 1986), that of Dunst (1985), and our best reading of the clinical and research literature, five domains emerge as potentially important areas of family assessment:

1. Child needs and characteristics likely to affect family functioning
2. Parent-child interactions
3. Family needs
4. Critical events
5. Family strengths

Of course, the actual areas assessed should be determined on an individual family basis. Other domains, such as the home environment (see Chapter 8), may also be important for some families.

Child Characteristics.   One reason parents of handicapped children differ in their reactions and coping styles is that their children vary in behavioral and personality characteristics. Traditionally, early childhood special educators and therapists have conducted comprehensive assessments of children's language, cognitive, social, self-help, play, and motor skills. These assessments are essential and require specialized knowledge and training (Bailey & Wolery, in press). An additional aspect of assessment important for both child-centered intervention and family-focused services is the documentation of behavior or temperament characteristics of children. Beckman (1983), for example, examined the relationship between maternal stress and specific child characteristics. She found child responsiveness, temperament, repetitive behavior patterns, and the presence of unusual caregiving demands to be significantly related to maternal stress. The spe-

TABLE 1.1
Levels of Child and Family Assessment

Level	Description	Focus of Assessment
1	Individual clients: handicapped or at-risk infants and preschoolers, and individual members of their families	Children's skills in socialization, communication, thought, self-help, play, and motor ability. Children's behavioral characteristics (e.g., endurance, consolability, ability to deal with frustration, reactivity) Characteristics of individual family members
2	Demographic and environmental characteristics of families	Family size and membership Home environment
3	Interactions that occur within families	Parent-child interactions Relations between spouses Family roles and functions Family cohesion and decision-making strategies
4	External forces that directly create stress *or* provide support for families	Family needs Family resources Critical events Professional services
5	External factors that indirectly affect families or have the potential for providing support	Legislation Untapped state and community resources Agency policies

cific domain most likely to result in high levels of stress was the number of additional caregiving demands. Hinde, Easton, Mella, and Tamplin (1982) documented a significant relationship between children's temperament style and how their parents interacted with them. Other child variables likely to affect families include characteristics such as consolability, regularity, responsiveness to others, endurance, and motivation. Issues and considerations in assessing child behavioral characteristics are discussed in Chapter 3.

Parent-Child Interactions.   The relationship between parent and child in the infant and preschool years is critical. During this time, emotional bonds between children and parents are established—bonds that lay the foundation for a lifelong relationship. Also, through social interactions with parents, children learn and practice cognitive, language, self-help, social, and motor skills.

Many parents with young handicapped children develop and use adaptive, warm, and appropriate interactional styles with their children. However, well-documented potential problems in parent-child interactions and relationships warrant the inclusion of an interaction component in a comprehensive family assessment. Research suggests that some families need assistance in learning how to teach their child specific skills (Filler & Kasari, 1981; McCollum, 1984) or how to read and respond appropriately to the communication cues their child presents (Als, Tronick, & Brazelton, 1980; Crawley & Spiker, 1983; Goldberg, 1977; Yoder, 1987). Other studies have shown that some families need help in interacting positively with their children (Kelly, 1982; Kogan, 1980; Stoneman, Brody, & Abbott, 1983) or in developing and maintaining strong emotional bonds with their children (Blacher & Meyers, 1983; Cicchetti & Serafica, 1981). Issues and considerations in assessing parent-child interactions are described in Chapter 4.

Family Needs.   The needs of families are incredibly diverse. The early interventionist is in a position to help families meet certain needs; to refer families to other professionals, agencies, or resources to meet needs; and to help family members build and reinforce their own resources for meeting needs. As a group, families with handicapped children often express frustration in obtaining services such as babysitting, pediatric care, dental care, or day care (Blackard & Barsh, 1982). They may have increased financial responsibilities owing to medical complications, necessary adaptive equipment, or specialized respite care. They may experience isolation from friends and neighbors (Darling, 1979) or extended family members (Gabel & Kotsch, 1981). Some families need and want information about their child's handicap, future services that may be available, or strategies for teaching their children. Others may experience personal crises or difficulties in family relations because of stress. Thus, one important dimension of family assessment is the documentation and identification of specific needs with which each family would like assistance. Strategies and considerations in assessing family needs and stress are described in Chapter 5.

Critical Events.   Effective family assessment should anticipate events likely to cause stress or problems. Several studies have documented such events (Bray, Coleman, & Bracken, 1981; Wikler, Wasow, & Hatfield, 1981; McKeith, 1973). The most frequently discussed event in the professional literature has been the family's response to the initial diagnosis or realization of a handicap. Stages of parental reactions and adjustment to the diagnosis and strategies for helping parents cope with it have been described (Blacher,1984; Drotar et al., 1975). However, other important events include medical crises, transitions from one program to another, and a child's failure to achieve highly visible developmental milestones such as smiling, talking, or walking. Documentation of these critical events as part of a comprehensive family assessment may help the interventionist to understand families' present feelings and reactions and to plan specific coping strategies for families. Considerations in assessing critical events are discussed in Chapter 6.

Family Strengths. Family strengths and resources constitute powerful components of any family coping system (Dunst, 1985; McCubbin & Patterson, 1983; Schilling, Gilchrist, & Schinke, 1984). Strengths and resources generally fall into three categories. *Personal resources* are characteristics that give meaning to life and allow individuals to address problems constructively. These resources may include an outgoing and assertive personality, a strong sense of competence and control over life, and religious or philosophical beliefs. *Within-family resources* are obtained within the nuclear or extended family—from a spouse, sibling, parents, or in-laws. Both instrumental support (help with specific tasks such as child care, housework, or respite) and socioemotional support (love, caring, listening and responding empathetically) are important within-family resources. *Extra-family resources* come from outside the family—from neighbors, friends, church members, professionals, agencies, and other public or private sources.

All too often we assume that families with handicapped children have tremendous needs but few resources. In fact, many families have done a remarkable job of adapting by drawing on personal, family, and community resources. The assessment of these resources is important to prevent duplication of services and, more importantly, to prevent the erosion of family resources by providing unneeded services. Professionals are often prone to offer services that families can provide for themselves. Although in the short run this may be simpler than having families assume these responsibilities, the resources that families themselves bring to bear on a problem are more important and enduring over time.

A final rationale for assessing family resources is to identify the families for whom few personal, family, or community resources are available or who have not accessed these resources. These families are at greatest risk for problems and are probably in greatest need of early intervention services that either provide resources or build and reinforce the few resources that do exist.

Issues and considerations in assessing family roles and supports are discussed in Chapter 7.

Multiple Sources and Measures

A second characteristic of effective family assessment is that it draws on multiple sources and measurement strategies to gather information. When assessing children, for example, most teachers would use a combination of direct testing, naturalistic observation, and parent interview to determine a child's skills and the situations or settings in which these skills are typically displayed. Likewise, a comprehensive family assessment should use multiple approaches to gather information (Hetherington, 1984; Mott et al., 1986; Odom & Shuster, 1986).

Tests, Survey Instruments, and Rating Forms.   Tests are useful to compare the responses of parents to a standard set of questions or stimuli, or to responses obtained from a normative sample. For example, a standardized inventory could be used to assess variables such as stress (Abidin, 1986; Holroyd, 1974), spouse relations (Spanier, 1976), parental perceptions of children's characteristics (Carey & McDevitt, 1978), perceptions of support from spouse (Gallagher, Scharfman, & Bristol, 1984), locus of control (De-Villis et al., 1985), parental satisfaction with services (Larsen, Attkisson, Hargreaves, & Nguyen, 1979), or family needs (Bailey & Simeonsson, 1987).The advantage of such instruments is that they provide a common set of stimuli to which all families respond, thereby giving a sense of how an individual family's responses compare with those of other families. They may even stimulate parental responses to issues they have not considered or have avoided. Furthermore, they circumvent the problems that may occur if interventionists rely solely on clinical judgment and other informal procedures for gathering information. Those problems include the possible omission of important domains for assessment, a focus only on issues of interest to the interventionist, and considerable variability in interventionists' approaches to assessing family needs. A final advantage of standardized measures is their potential use for program evaluation through periodic reassessment of parental responses.

Naturalistic Observation.   The methodology for direct observation to determine precise patterns of behavior has been described in many sources (e.g., Gentry & Haring, 1976). In the context of family assessment, naturalistic observation can be used to document the warmth and quality of parent-child interactions (Farran, Kasari, Comfort, & Jay, 1986), parental teaching behaviors (Rosenberg, Robinson, & Beckman, 1984), specific child behavioral characteristics (Simeonsson, Huntington, Short, & Ware, 1982), or sibling interactions (Brody & Stoneman, 1986). Direct observation provides a mechanism for documenting the actual use of parent skills, and the rate, duration, and intensity of child behaviors. It is an objective procedure based on actual behavioral performance, not on perceptions of that performance.

Interviews.   Sometimes the interventionist wants to determine how a parent perceives events, services, or resources (Winton & Bailey, in press). An interview provides an open-ended format, through face-to-face discussions, in which families and interventionists can elaborate on issues and concerns. The interview allows for the emergence of unanticipated areas of concern not addressed in standardized measures or naturalistic observations, and provides a context in which parents' priorities for service can be determined.

Effective assessment should not only incorporate multiple approaches to data collection; it should also elicit the same information from multiple sources. In family assessment, for example, an important strategy is to ask mothers and fathers to complete selected measures independently; another is to conduct separate observations of mother-child and father-child interactions. Several studies have documented similarities and differences in mothers' and fathers' perceptions of needs and resources, and the desire for specific services (Bailey & Simeonsson, in press; Cummings, 1976; Stoneman, Brody, & Abbott, 1983; Wandersman, Wandersman, & Kahn, 1980). Following the principle of individualization, separate assessments of fathers and mothers allow interventionists to tailor services to the needs of each. Discrepancies and agreements in maternal and paternal perceptions of the child, and of events, resources, and stressors, can be the basis for fruitful discussion and can also highlight system-level issues. For example, a mother may feel that she needs more instrumental support from her husband, while the father may feel he is doing all he can. This information could be used to discuss alternative sources of support.

Issues and considerations in conducting interviews with families are discussed in Chapters 9 and 10.

Family Values and Traditions

Effective family assessment and provision of services must consider family values and customs. Lynch (1986), for example, suggests that cultural values and beliefs influence family goals and responses to early intervention. Aponte (1985) describes the role that values play in family therapy, a description that seems equally applicable to early intervention:

> Values frame the entire process of therapy. They are the social standards by which therapists define problems, establish criteria for evaluation, fix parameters for technical interventions, and select therapeutic goals. All transactions between therapist and family or individual about these aspects of therapy involve negotiations about the respective value systems that each party brings into the therapeutic relationship. These values, whether moral, cultural, or political, are the standards by which a person directs his actions and defines, interprets, and judges all social phenomena. A person's values are drawn from family life, social networks, educational experiences, and community and sociopolitical organizations. These multiple standards converge into the complex configurations that become the dynamically evolving value systems of the therapist and the families and individuals in treatment. (p. 323)

If early interventionists fail to recognize strong family values and attempt to implement services or goals that conflict with those values, the inevitable result is mistrust and failure to follow through.

One source of variability in values is cultural differences. Lynch (1986) suggests a number of strategies for improving cultural awareness, including having a multicultural staff, providing in-service training about different cultural practices, accepting and working within cultural values, developing links with cultural advisory groups, using multicultural materials, focusing on family priorities, listening and watching, and pairing families of similar cultures for treatment or other services. For example, parents could be encouraged to teach or provide support for other parents from similar cultures (Bruder & Bricker, 1985). Weber, McKeever, and McDaniel (1985) describe *joining* as the skill of "accommodating to the style of family members and creating an environment in which family members will feel supported" (p. 358). Finally, Aponte (1985) suggests that interventionists should not try to influence family values except when a problem cannot otherwise be addressed. Rather, goals and services that are consistent with family values and traditions should be identified. The role of values in the goal-setting process is further discussed in Chapter 11.

Family Priorities for Goals and Services

Systematic assessment of family needs and face-to-face interviews or discussions with family members enhance the involvement of families in decision making. Although effective and appropriate assessment extends beyond asking a family to provide information, interventionists must use parents' priorities as the primary basis for determining goals and services. Several studies have documented that parents and professionals do not always agree on priorities (Blackard & Barsh, 1982; Cadman, Goldsmith, & Bashim, 1984; Wikler et al., 1981). These discrepancies are a useful context for discussing issues with parents. Whenever possible, the interventionist should address parent priorities first, because asking parents to pursue goals in which they are not interested or with which they disagree is likely to be counterproductive (Bailey, 1987). Further, this practice usurps parental empowerment and ownership of goals, and in the long run may have negative effects, such as parental mistrust of professionals or overdependence on professionals (Dunst, 1985). Brinckerhoff and Vincent (1986) found that when parents were involved in assessing their child's developmental status and presented their goals and concerns first in the IEP meeting, they were more likely to contribute to programming decisions and made more decisions themselves. Parents who were less involved were more likely to have decisions made by school staff. In a study of decision making that led to compliance with recommendations, Cadman, Shurvell, Davies, and Bradfield (1984) identified several factors that increased client follow-through on goals and recommendations: time and care spent in listening to clients, client agreement with recommendations, client belief that he or she had the skills to follow through on the recommendation, and client belief that the recommendation was feasible. Thus, effective family assessment focuses heavily on parental priorities.

Program Type

Effective family assessment also depends on family, child, or contextual variables likely to affect family outcomes. One source of contextual variability is the type of program in which children and families are enrolled. An example of unique family needs as a function of program type is reflected in home-based versus center-based programs. Such programs provide very different kinds of services, and thus are likely to result in different issues (Bailey & Simeonsson, 1988). For example, home-based programs by their very nature provide no respite for parents and focus heavily on parent teaching skills and parent-child interactions, because the parent must be the child's primary teacher. Thus, assessing parent teaching and interactional skills and locating respite services may be of first importance. Center-based programs provide respite and direct instruction. Family assessments may need to focus more on parental skills in fostering generalization or other family issues.

A second example of variability in family needs associated with program type is observable in comparing mainstreamed and self-contained programs (Bailey & Winton, 1987). Families in mainstreamed programs observe their child interacting with nonhandicapped children and are constantly reminded of their child's abnormalities. Furthermore, they must interact with families of nonhandicapped children and may therefore feel excluded or isolated. Bailey and Winton describe a rating scale to determine the hopes and concerns of parents of both handicapped and nonhandicapped children in mainstreamed preschool programs. Such an assessment addresses unique family issues encountered in a specific intervention environment and provides information useful in working with families in that environment.

Periodic Evaluation

Finally, effective family assessment is not a one-time process conducted at program entry. Rather, it is periodic and ongoing, for at least two reasons. First, family needs are not static; they consist of peaks and valleys as a function of new events and stressors as well as developmental changes in the family (Solomon, 1973; Wikler et al., 1981). To be responsive to parents' needs, interventionists must conduct periodic assessments. Second, periodic assessment is important for program evaluation. By documenting family changes or accomplishments, programs can demonstrate effectiveness and accountability for appropriate services. A part of this process should include periodic assessment of parents' satisfaction with services. Issues and considerations in evaluating family services are discussed in Chapter 12.

A MODEL FOR FAMILY ASSESSMENT

As an outgrowth of providing services and conducting research with families, we have developed a model for assessing family needs and writing family goals in the context of early intervention programs (Bailey et al., 1986). The model, referred to as *family-focused intervention*, draws on the characteristics of effective family assessment, and is based on the "goodness-of-fit" concept described in the longitudinal research of Thomas and Chess (1977). Goodness-of-fit assumes that services must be individualized. Furthermore, it assumes that a particular goal or service is appropriate only if it "fits," or matches with, parents' perception of need for that service. Outcomes cannot be predicted by a simple analysis of program, child, or family variables, but rather on the degree to which these components mutually interact. An example of the importance of such a match was reported in a study of family routines and infant rhythmicity (Sprunger, Boyce, & Gaines, 1985). The authors found that family adaptation to an infant was better predicted by the match or congruence between family routines and infant rhythmicity than by either family routines or infant rhythmicity alone. Arrhythmic, unpredictable infants were less likely to be a problem for families with less predictable family routines than for families with more predictable routines.

Goals of Family-Focused Intervention

Family goals, of course, must be individualized. However, it is important for early interventionists to have a set of principles or programmatic goals that reflect the ultimate intention of the program's efforts. These principles guide decision making both for programs and for individuals. Furthermore, they make a public statement of program purpose and philosophy.

Professionals and program staff should engage in active decision making relative to their program's goals and philosophies. Fundamental disagreements among staff must be resolved if family services are to be effective and coordinated. Because the new federal legislation mandates individualized family assessment and services but does not state the goals of such services, decision making becomes even more important. We have described four basic goals of family-focused intervention:

> *(1)* To help family members cope with the unique needs related to caring for and raising a child with a handicap. The needs may range from the very specific (e.g., How do I teach my child to feed himself?) to the very global (e.g., How can I cope with the stress and worry associated with raising this child?).

(2) To help family members grow in their understanding of the development of their child both as an individual and as a member of the family. Activities related to this goal range from providing information about handicapping conditions or child development to organizing and running a support group for siblings.

(3) To promote parent-child interactions which are (a) of sufficient quantity, sensitivity, and warmth, (b) mutually enjoyable, and (c) appropriately stimulating at the child's developmental level.

(4) To preserve and reinforce the dignity of families by respecting and responding to their desire for services and incorporating them in the assessment, planning, and evaluation process. This requires active efforts to avoid creating dependency or learned helplessness in families by teaching, encouraging, and reinforcing advocacy and independent decision-making skills. (Bailey et al., 1986, p. 158)

Steps in Family-Focused Intervention

The goals of family-focused intervention were originally operationalized in a sequence of assessment and planning activities. Six steps, displayed in Figure 1.1, were followed. First, a comprehensive assessment of family

FIGURE 1.1
Steps in Family-Focused Intervention Model

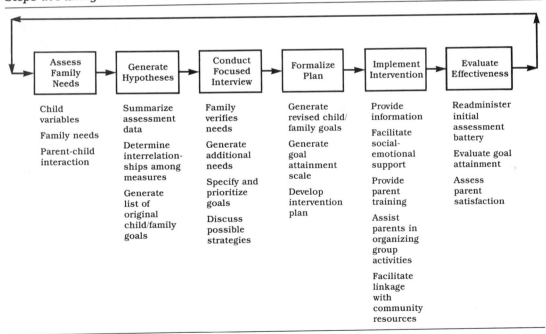

From D. B. Bailey, R. J. Simeonsson, P. J. Winton, G. S. Huntington, M. Comfort, P. Isbell, K. J. O'Donnell, & J. M. Helm. Family-focused intervention: A functional model for planning, implementing, and evaluating individualized family services in early intervention. *Journal of the Division for Early Childhood*, 1986, *10*, 156–171. Reprinted with permission.

needs and resources is conducted, using assessment procedures and instruments in the domains of child variables, family needs, parent-child interaction, and critical events likely to influence family functioning. Second, the information gathered from the assessment is summarized and organized. Areas of concern common to both spouses are noted, and hypotheses about major family needs and resources are generated. Third, a focused interview is conducted in which interventionists and parents engage in face-to-face discussions about needs and priorities for services. Fourth, a formalized plan is developed containing child and family goals. The goals are weighted according to priority, and strategies for achieving those goals are specified. Fifth, services are provided based on the individualized plan. Finally, effectiveness is evaluated through the readministration of measures, determination of goal attainment, and assessment of parent satisfaction. This information is then used to plan subsequent child and family activities.

Since the publication of the original model, we have modified several components, for three reasons. First, we wanted to reduce the length of time required in the initial family assessment phase. Second, there was a clear need to include an assessment of family strengths. Finally, a multidisciplinary team meeting was not a part of the original model. A revised version of the model is displayed in Figure 1.2. In the first phase a brief assessment addresses family needs and strengths. In addition, basic family demographic information is gathered and the occurrence of critical family events is documented. This is followed by the focused interview, a meeting in which an interventionist and family members discuss needs and strengths and identify other areas in which further assessment is needed. The third phase consists of any additional follow-up assessments identified in the focused interview. The fourth phase is the multidisciplinary team meeting,

FIGURE 1.2
Family-Focused Intervention Model (Revised)

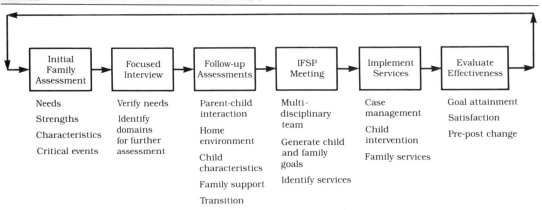

followed by the final two phases—implementation of services and subsequent evaluation to determine service effectiveness and identify new goals.

Although the model is conceptually straightforward, its implementation is complex, requiring a skilled interventionist who can combine systematic assessment procedures, clinical judgment, and skills in interviewing families, discussing problems, and resolving differences in priorities in such a way that parents feel a real sense of ownership in determining appropriate services for themselves and their children. This text addresses five of the six steps of the model having to do with assessing needs, planning goals, and evaluating the effectiveness of services. We have intentionally omitted a discussion of the services to be provided to families; that topic covers a broad array and could not be addressed adequately in this text, although it is indirectly addressed in our discussion of family goals.

SUMMARY

Family involvement is increasingly being urged in early intervention because of diverse family needs. Recent federal legislation greatly increases the responsibility of infant specialists and preschool teachers working with handicapped children to include individualized services for families. To fulfill this mandate, professionals will need to conduct *individualized* assessments of family needs. Unfortunately, barriers to such assessment include a lack of appropriate measures, a lack of appropriate training, and institutional and family resistance.

This text addresses the assessment of family needs and specification of family goals and services. This chapter argues that an effective family assessment (1) is comprehensive, covering all important family domains, (2) is based on multiple sources and measures, (3) considers family values and traditions, (4) draws on family priorities for goals and services, (5) varies according to program type, and (6) regularly evaluates family outcomes. A functional model for individualized assessment and planning with families is described.

REFERENCES

Abidin, R. R. (1986). *Parenting stress index* (2nd ed.). Charlottesville, Va.: Pediatric Psychology Press.

Affleck, G., McGrade, B. J., McQueeney, M., & Allen, D. (1982). Promise of relationship-focused early intervention in developmental disabilities. *Journal of Special Education, 16,* 413–430.

Als, H., Tronick, E., & Brazelton, T. B. (1980). Affective reciprocity and the development of autonomy. *Journal of the American Academy of Child Psychiatry, 19,* 22–40.

Aponte, H. J. (1985). The negotiation of values in therapy. *Family Process, 24,* 323–338.

Bailey, D. B. (1987). Collaborative goal-setting with families: Resolving differences in values and priorities for services. *Topics in Early Childhood Special Education, 7*(2), 59–71.

Bailey, D. B., & Simeonsson, R. J. (1984). Critical issues underlying research and intervention with families of young handicapped children. *Journal of the Division for Early Childhood, 9,* 38–48.

Bailey, D. B., & Simeonsson, R. J. (in press). *Assessing the needs of families with handicapped infants. Journal of Special Education.*

Bailey D. B., & Simeonsson, R. J. (1988). Home-based early intervention. In S. L. Odom & M. B. Karnes (Eds.), *Early intervention for infants and children with handicaps: An empirical base.* Baltimore: Paul H. Brookes.

Bailey, D. B., Simeonsson, R. J., Winton, P. J., Huntington, G. S., Comfort, M., Isbell, P., O'Donnell, K. J., & Helm, J. M. (1986). Family-focused intervention: A functional model for planning, implementing, and evaluating individualized family services in early intervention. *Journal of the Division for Early Childhood, 10,* 156–171.

Bailey, D. B., & Winton, P. J. (1987). Stability and change in parents' expectations about mainstreaming. *Topics in Early Childhood Special Education, 7*(1), 73–88.

Bailey, D. B., & Wolery, M. (1984). *Teaching infants and preschoolers with handicaps.* Columbus, Oh.: Merrill Publishing Company.

Bailey, D. B., & Wolery, M. (Eds.) (in press). *Assessing infants and preschoolers with handicaps.* Columbus, Oh.: Merrill Publishing Company.

Beckman, P. J. (1983). Influence of selected child characteristics on stress in families of handicapped infants. *American Journal of Mental Deficiency, 88,* 150–156.

Beckman-Bell, P. (1981). Child-related stress in families of handicapped children. *Topics in Early Childhood Special Education, 1,* 45–53.

Bell, R. Q. (1968). A reinterpretation of the direction of effects in studies of socialization. *Psychological Review, 75,* 81–95.

Blacher, J. (1984). Sequential stages of parental adjustment to the birth of a child with handicaps: Fact or artifact? *Mental Retardation, 22*(2), 55–68.

Blacher, J., & Meyers, C. E. (1983). A review of attachment formation and disorder of handicapped children. *American Journal of Mental Deficiency, 87,* 359–371.

Blackard, M. K., & Barsh, E. T. (1982). Parents' and professionals' perceptions of the handicapped child's impact on the family. *TASH Journal, 7,* 62–70.

Brassell, W. R. (1977). Intervention with handicapped infants: Correlates of progress. *Mental Retardation, 15,* 18–22.

Bray, N. M., Coleman, J. M., & Bracken, M. B. (1981). Critical events in parenting handicapped children. *Journal of the Division for Early Childhood, 3,* 26–33.

Brinckerhoff, J. L., & Vincent, L. J. (1986). Increasing parental decision-making at the individualized educational program meeting. *Journal of the Division for Early Childhood, 11,* 46–58.

Brody, G. H., & Stoneman, Z. (1986). Contextual issues in the study of sibling socialization. In J. J. Gallagher & P. M. Vietze (Eds.), *Families of handicapped persons* (pp. 197–218). Baltimore: Paul H. Brookes.

Bronfenbrenner, U. (1977). Toward an experimental ecology of human development. *American Psychologist, 32,* 513–531.

Bruder, M. B., & Bricker, D. (1985). Parents as teachers of their children and other parents. *Journal of the Division for Early Childhood, 9,* 136–150.

Cadman, D., Goldsmith, C., & Bashim, P. (1984). Values, preferences, and decisions in the care of children with developmental disabilities. *Developmental and Behavioral Pediatrics, 5,* 60–64.

Cadman, D., Shurvell, B., Davies, P., & Bradfield, S. (1984). Compliance in the community with consultants' recommendations for developmentally handicapped children. *Developmental Medicine and Child Neurology, 26,* 40–46.

Carey, W. B., & McDevitt, S. C. (1978). Revision of the infant temperament questionnaire. *Pediatrics, 61,* 735–738.

Casto, G., & Mastropieri, M. A. (1986). The efficacy of early intervention programs: A meta-analysis. *Exceptional Children, 52,* 417–424.

Cicchetti, D., & Serafica, F. C. (1981). Interplay among behavioral systems: Illustrations from the study of attachment, affiliation, and warnings in young children with Down's syndrome. *Developmental Psychology, 17,* 36–49.

Crawley, S. B., & Spiker, D. (1983). Mother-child interactions involving two-year-olds with Down syndrome: A look at individual differences. *Child Development, 54,* 1312–1323.

Crnic, K. A., Friedrich, W. N., & Greenberg, M. T. (1983). Adaptation of families with mentally retarded children: A model of stress, coping, and family ecology. *American Journal of Mental Deficiency, 88,* 125–138.

Cummings, S. T. (1976). The impact of the child's deficiency on the father: A study of fathers of mentally retarded and/or chronically ill children. *American Journal of Orthopsychiatry, 46,* 246–255.

Darling, R. B. (1979). *Families against society: A study of reactions to children with birth defects.* Beverly Hills, Calif.: Sage Publications.

DeVillis, R. F., DeVillis, B. E., Revicki, D. A., Lurie, S. J., Runyan, D. K., & Bristol, M. (1985). Development and validation of the child improvement locus of control scales. *Journal of Social and Clinical Psychology, 3,* 308–325.

Drotar, D., Baskiewicz, A., Irwin, N., Kennell, J., & Klaus, M. (1975). The adaptation of parents to the birth of an infant with a congenital malformation: A hypothetical model. *Pediatrics, 56,* 710–717.

Dumas, J. E., & Wahler, R. G. (1983). Predictors of treatment outcome in parent training: Mother insularity and socioeconomic disadvantage. *Behavioral Assessment, 5,* 301–313.

Dunst, C. J. (1985). Rethinking early intervention. *Analysis and Intervention in Developmental Disabilities, 5,* 165–201.

Dunst, C. J., & Rheingrover, R. M. (1981). An analysis of the efficacy of infant intervention programs with organically handicapped children. *Evaluation and Program Planning, 4,* 287–323.

Farber, B. (1959). Effects of a severely mentally retarded child on family integration. *Monographs of the Society for Research in Child Development, 24* (2, Serial No. 71).

Farran, D. C., Kasari, C., Comfort, M., & Jay, S. (1986). *Parent-child interaction scale-II.* Honolulu: Center for Development of Early Education, Kamehameha Schools, Kapalama Heights.

Filler, J., & Kasari, C. (1981). Acquisition, maintenance, and generalization of parent-taught skills with two severely handicapped infants. *Journal of the Association for the Severely Handicapped, 6,* 30–38.

Fuchs, L. S., & Fuchs, D. (1986). Effects of systematic formative evaluation: A meta-analysis. *Exceptional Children, 53,* 199–208.

Gabel, H., & Kotsch, L. S. (1981). Extended families and young handicapped children. *Topics in Early Childhood Special Education, 1,* 29–36.

Gallagher, J. J., Beckman, P., & Cross, A. H. (1983). Families of handicapped children: Sources of stress and its amelioration. *Exceptional Children, 50,* 10–19.

Gallagher, J. J., Scharfman, W., & Bristol, M. (1984). The division of responsibilities in families with preschool handicapped and nonhandicapped children. *Journal of the Division for Early Childhood, 8,* 3–12.

Gentry, D., & Haring, N. G. (1976). The essentials of performance measurement. In N. C. Haring & L. Brown (Eds.), *Teaching the severely handicapped* (vol. 1, pp. 209–236). New York: Grune & Stratton.

Goldberg, S. (1977). Social competence in infancy: A model of parent-infant interaction. *Merrill-Palmer Quarterly, 23,* 163–177.

Hetherington, E. M. (1984). Stress and coping in children and families. In A. Doyle, D. Gold, & D. S. Moskovitz (Eds.), *Children in families under stress* (pp. 7–33). *New Directions for Child Development,* no. 24. San Francisco: Jossey-Bass.

Hinde, R. A., Easton, D. F., Mella, R. E., & Tamplin, A. M. (1982). Temperament characteristics of 3–4 year-olds and mother-child interaction. *Temperament differences in infants and young children.* London: Pitman.

Holroyd, J. (1974). The questionnaire on resources and stress: An instrument to measure family response to a handicapped member. *Journal of Community Psychology, 2,* 92–94.

Kelly, J. F. (1982). Effects of intervention on caregiver-infant interaction when the infant is handicapped. *Journal of the Division for Early Childhood, 5,* 53–63.

Kogan, K. L. (1980). Interaction systems between preschool handicapped or developmentally delayed children and their parents. In S. Goldberg, D. Stern, T. Fields, & A. M. Sostek (Eds.), *High-risk infants and children: Adult and peer interactions.* New York: Academic Press.

Larsen, D., Attkisson, C., Hargreaves, W., & Nguyen, T. (1979). Assessment of client patient satisfaction: Development of a general scale. *Evaluation and Program Planning, 2,* 197–207.

Lynch, E. (1986). Families from different cultures. In the Family Network Series (Monograph 1): *The family of handicapped infants and young children.* University of Idaho, Moscow: Family Involvement with At-Risk and Handicapped Infants Project.

McCollum, J. (1984). Social interaction between parents and babies: Validation of an intervention procedure. *Child: Care, Health and Development, 10,* 301–315.

McCubbin, H. I., & Patterson, J. M. (1983). Family transitions: Adaptation to stress. In H. McCubbin & C. Figley (Eds.), *Stress and the family: Vol. 1. Coping with normative transitions* (pp. 5–25). New York: Brunner/Mazel.

McKeith, R. (1973). The feelings and behavior of parents of handicapped children. *Developmental Medicine and Child Neurology, 15,* 524–527.

McMahon, R. J., Forehand, R., Griest, D. L., & Wells, K. C. (1981). Who drops out of treatment during parent behavior training? *Behavioral Counseling Quarterly, 1,* 79–85.

Mott, S. E., Fewell, R. R., Lewis, M., Meisels, S. J., Shonkoff, J. P., & Simeonsson, R. J. (1986). Methods for assessing child and family outcomes in early childhood special education programs: Some views from the field. *Topics in Early Childhood Special Education, 6,* 1–15.

Murphy, M. A. (1982). The family with a handicapped child: A review of the literature. *Developmental and Behavioral Pediatrics, 3,* 73–82.

Odom, S. L., & Shuster, S. K. (1986). Naturalistic inquiry and the assessment of young handicapped children and their families. *Topics in Early Childhood Special Education, 6*(2), 68–82.

Pollner, M., & McDonald-Wikler, L. (1985). The social construction of unreality: A case study of a family's attribution of competence to a severely retarded child. *Family Process, 24,* 241–254.

Rosenberg, S., Robinson, C., & Beckman, P. (1984). Teaching skills inventory: A measure of parent performance. *Journal of the Division for Early Childhood, 8,* 107–113.

Sameroff, A. J., & Chandler, M. J. (1975). Reproductive risk and the continuum of caretaking causality. In F. D. Horowitz, M. Hetherington, S. Scarr-Salapatek, & G. Siegel (Eds.), *Review of child development research* (Vol. 4, pp. 187–244). Chicago: University of Chicago Press.

Schilling, R. F., Gilchrist, L. D., & Schinke, S. P. (1984). Coping and social support in families of developmentally disabled children. *Family Relations, 33,* 47–54.

Shearer, D. E., & Shearer, M. S. (1977). The Portage project: A model for early childhood intervention. In T. D. Tjossem (Ed.), *Intervention strategies for high risk infants and young children* (pp. 335–350). Baltimore: University Park Press.

Simeonsson, R. J., & Bailey, D. B. (1986). Siblings of handicapped children. In J. J. Gallagher & P. M. Vietze (Eds.), *Families of handicapped persons* (pp. 67–77). Baltimore: Paul H. Brookes.

Simeonsson, R. J., Cooper, D. H., & Scheiner, A. P. (1982). A review and analysis of the effectiveness of early intervention programs. *Pediatrics, 69,* 635–641.

Simeonsson, R. J., Huntington, G. S., Short, R. J., & Ware, W. B. (1982). The Carolina record of individual behavior: Characteristics of handicapped infants and children. *Topics in Early Childhood Special Education, 2*(2), 43–55.

Solomon, M. A. (1973). A developmental conceptual premise for family therapy. *Family Process, 12,* 179–188.

Spanier, G. B. (1976). Measuring dyadic adjustment: New scales for assessing the quality of marriage and similar dyads. *Journal of Marriage and the Family, 38,* 15–28.

Sprunger, L. W., Boyce, W. T., & Gaines, J. A. (1985). Family-infant congruence: Routines and rhythmicity in family adaptations to a young infant. *Child Development, 56,* 564–572.

Stoneman, Z., Brody, G. H., & Abbott, D. (1983). In-home observations of young Down syndrome children with their mothers and fathers. *American Journal of Mental Deficiency, 87,* 591–600.

Thomas, A., & Chess, S. (1977). *Temperament and development.* New York: Brunner/Mazel.

Tseng, W. S., & McDermott, J. F. (1979). Triaxial family classifications: A proposal. *Journal of the American Academy of Child Psychiatry, 18,* 22–43.

Turnbull, A. P., Summers, J. A., & Brotherson, M. J. (1984). *Working with families with disabled members: A family systems approach.* Lawrence: Kansas University Affiliated Facility.

Turnbull, A. P., & Turnbull, H. R. (1986). Stepping back from early intervention: An ethical perspective. *Journal of the Division for Early Childhood, 10,* 106–117.

Wandersman, L., Wandersman, A., & Kahn, S. (1980). Social support in the transition to parenthood. *Journal of Community Psychology, 8,* 332–342.

Weber, T., McKeever, J. E., & McDaniel, S. H. (1985). A beginner's guide to the problem-oriented first family interview. *Family Process, 24,* 357–364.

Wikler, L., Wasow, M., & Hatfield, E. (1981). Chronic sorrow revisited: Parent vs. professional depiction of the adjustment of parents of mentally retarded children. *American Journal of Orthopsychiatry, 51,* 63–70.

Winton, P. J., & Bailey, D. B. (in press). The family-focused interview: A collaborative mechanism for family assessment and goal-setting. *Journal of the Division for Early Childhood.*

Wynne, L. C., McDaniel, S. H.., & Weber, T. T. (1987). Professional politics and the concepts of family therapy, family consultation, and systems consultation. *Family Process, 26,* 153–166.

Yoder, P. J. (1987). Relationship between degree of infant handicap and clarity of infant cues. *American Journal of Mental Deficiency, 91,* 639–641.

2

Unique Characteristics of Families with Young Handicapped Children

The family is an institution that is experienced universally in one form or another, yet it is not easily defined. This problem is distilled in the title of a recent article: "What/who is the family system?" (Massey, 1986). The family possesses both private and public characteristics, each contributing to a complex and often-changing entity. The private characteristics include feelings, values, and interpersonal relationships; whereas family size, configuration, and behavior are public characteristics. Massey referred to the "inside" view of the family as the psychological/experiential dimension and the "outside" view as the sociological/observational dimension. These two views have been associated with distinct and separate therapeutic orientations. For example, the inside, or private, view has been associated with a psychodynamic orientation, while the outside, or public, view has been associated with "structural" therapies that focus on family subsystems and boundaries. Massey contends that an integrative view is needed that approaches the family as a social/psychological system.

Assessing family characteristics, like assessing child characteristics, requires an understanding of features common to family development and functioning. This chapter draws on such features and on relevant clinical,

---

This chapter was contributed by Rune J. Simeonsson, University of North Carolina at Chapel Hill.

theoretical, and empirical literature to identify characteristics typical of families in general and those unique to families with young handicapped children. Specific attention is given to three issues: (1) considerations in conceptualizing the family; (2) structural, functional, and developmental characteristics of families; and (3) implications for assessment and intervention planning for the family with a handicapped child.

Massey's review reflects the continuing search for useful theoretical frameworks to identify families with significant needs and provide services to meet those needs. The wide variety of competing conceptualizations of the family is evidenced by the diversity of contributions to current clinical and research journals. The clinician providing services undoubtedly holds an implicit, if not explicit, conceptualization of the family that influences how family needs are identified and met. The importance of such a conceptual framework is emphasized in Freeman's (1976) statement that "the framework that we bring to understanding how families behave can facilitate or retard our work. If we have too narrow a view of family functioning, the types of questions, goals and strategies we can use become more of a disservice than help to families" (p. 746). For example, viewing parents primarily as teachers or change agents and focusing narrowly on parent training activities may create more stress and pressure on some families than was present before intervention.

The rapid growth and relative newness of interest in the family in early intervention for young handicapped children represent a challenge in conceptualizing families in a way that facilitates and strengthens them. A central premise of early intervention services is assessment of the client's unique needs and resources. The expanding focus of early intervention underlines the need for frameworks that approach the *family* as the client. Assessing needs and resources of the family as a complex system clearly differs from viewing the child as the client and the sole target for intervention. This changing approach to the family corresponds with three sequential phases in the chronology of early intervention efforts (Bailey & Simeonsson, 1984).

In the first phase, assessment and intervention focused almost exclusively on the infant, with staff providing services directly to the infant. In the second phase, the focus broadened to recognize parents as teachers of their child. Early intervention in this phase was often based on a behavior modification paradigm, in which parents were trained to increase the child's skills or decrease disruptive behaviors. Various other, more general models to train parents to work with their children were also used. Although the view of parents as teachers clearly provided specific means to increase parental involvement and extend professional services, not all parents uniformly desired to be teachers (Winton & Turnbull, 1981). In the third and most recent phase in early intervention, the focus on parents has been expanded to recognize the family as a target for assessment and intervention in its own right. This focus builds on the premise that the family constitutes the ecological context in which the infant functions (Bronfenbrenner, 1979) and is also consistent with current conceptualizations of the family as a system with individual and collective needs (Campbell & Draper, 1985).

In the first two phases of intervention efforts, assessment involved an inventory of the developmental and behavioral characteristics of the handicapped child and/or documentation of the parents' teaching skills. Identification of the family as a client, however, has shifted the emphasis to family assessment as an essential activity in its own right. Family assessment does not exclude the referred child but rather is comprehensive: it views the family as a unit. This inclusive view forms the basis for the review of the family in this chapter.

CONCEPTUALIZING THE FAMILY

Identifying essential characteristics of families presumes some formal or informal conceptualizations of the "family" that may vary widely along dimensions of structure, function, and development. The *structural dimension* of families refers to the relationships among family members and the extent to which those relationships determine how the family deals with daily tasks. The *functional dimension* refers to the responsibilities or tasks assumed by family members that contribute to the adaptation of individual members and the family as a system. The *developmental dimension* focuses on the stages or phases through which the family progresses over time.

A number of formal models have been suggested for approaching assessment and intervention with families. The triaxial model of Tseng and McDermott (1979) has incorporated all three dimensions of structure, function, and development. Viewing the family from a systems perspective is common in the family therapy literature (Massey, 1986). Combrinck-Graham (1985) has proposed a combination of the family systems approach with a developmental orientation. This model identifies two major components in the family life spiral: *centrifugal forces* that contribute to the family moving apart, and *centripetal forces* that act to organize or bring the family together. These forces act on the family in different ways at different times, such that family change is seen as a "series of oscillations between centripetal organization, and centrifugal coming apart during the course of its life cycle" (p. 147). This conceptualization of the family life cycle can also be described in terms of the changing roles of family members and the family unit over time. Certain phases, such as the birth and early rearing of children, constitute functions for parents and grandparents that serve to bring the family together and focus energies and resources on support for the family. The period of adolescence constitutes a phase in which the child's increasing independence and separation, paralleled by decreasing dependence on the parents, results in forces moving the family apart. The cycle repeats itself when the adolescent becomes a young adult and forms a primary family unit, resulting in a refocusing of support and energy on the family by parent and grandparent. Thus, centripetal and centrifugal forces can be seen as factors related to support and autonomy of the family, respectively.

The family has also been viewed from a behavioral perspective, focusing on the role of contingencies in interpersonal relationships. The classic work of Patterson and Gullion (1968) on the use of behavioral principles in parent-child relationships has served as a catalyst for many models, such as that of Elder (1986), in which caring, reinforcement, time-out, and extinction are proposed as strategies for families of developmentally delayed children to use for enhancing functioning. Although in practice the behavioral approach has usually taken the form of specific applications rather than more formal models, it does reflect a conceptualization in which typical as well as atypical family behavior can be understood.

These conceptualizations of the family are selected representatives of the larger array of models that exist in the theoretical and clinical litera-ture (Guerin, 1976). Because a given model may be too limiting, aspects of various models can make unique and relevant contributions; thus a ma-jor trend in therapeutic contexts is the integration of models (Sluzki, 1983).

In searching for characteristics of families that may influence their adaptation to living with a handicapped child, it is important to recognize that the study of families is perhaps as much subjective as objective. Doherty (1986) made this point in an intriguing presentation of implica-tions of quantum physics for family research. Building on the premise that a significant subjective element exists even in the "hard" science of physics, Doherty argues for acknowledging the role of subjectivity in the softer science of family studies. A subjective view incorporates the issues of a relational perspective, process and time, and dynamic causation. A *rela-tional view* of the child and family has several implications: (1) families and those who study them share common experiences and interpretations of events, (2) historical and cultural contexts influence what is studied and what is considered significant, and (3) complementary theories may be more productive than an attempt to find some objective "truth" about families.

In regard to *process and time,* Doherty endorses the developmental and cyclical nature of the family. Change and transformation, rather than permanence, characterize families. Although some change may be cyclical, other transformations may be unique and unpredictable. In Doherty's words, transformations following a crisis may constitute a *quantum change*—that is, a dramatic and unforseen change, as may occur, for example, if an outgoing family becomes introverted after the birth of a severely impaired infant. The complex and unpredictable factors in family adaptation force a recognition that adaptation is often context-specific and highly idiosyncratic.

The third implication of physics for the study of the family is the concept of *dynamic causation*. Doherty stresses that any conceptualization of the family must allow for spontaneous change—change that may be neither readily predicted nor causally determined. This perspective of the dynamic nature of the family is consistent with the transactional model of the child's development (Sameroff, 1976), in which exchanges between the child and the environment over time account for idiosyncratic change. The development of the family, like that of the child, is characterized by self-righting and self-organizing tendencies. Farber (1959) concludes that families often make as little change as possible. Basically, it is safer and easier to maintain the status quo unless forced to adapt by a crisis or situation that becomes impossible to incorporate into ongoing family patterns and routines. One important implication is to provide intervention that involves the least amount of adaptation—that is, intervention that can most easily be incorporated into ongoing family routines and patterns.

CHARACTERISTICS OF TYPICAL FAMILIES

In light of the considerations discussed, what characteristics can be identifed as typical and essential in families? Identification of such characteristics is complicated by the variety of idealized and mythical views of families that exist. Foremost among these, perhaps, is the view of the typical family configuration as having two parents present, one of whom assumes the full-time role of care in the home. The substantial proportion of single-parent families and the continued increase in the number of working mothers, particularly mothers of preschool children, disprove that myth. The demographic realities are contributing to changing beliefs about prescribed roles for mothers and fathers in caregiving and about the relative importance of home care over day care in the socialization and upbringing of young children. Furthermore, most models in family theory and much of the available research build on a cultural perspective that is primarily middle class and Caucasian in orientation. Socioeconomic status and ethnic group membership clearly contribute to variability in how families function and to the values assigned to such functions as independence and support within the family system. Sensitivity to cultural differences should always be a primary consideration in assessment and intervention with families of young handicapped children.

Some characteristics, however, appear to be typical of most families. In keeping with earlier discussions in this chapter, such characteristics will be examined in terms of structural, functional, and developmental dimensions. Bentovim (1986) has listed six salient facets of family functioning that reflect these dimensions to varying degrees singly and in combination. The facets focusing on communication and feelings are expressive in nature; they most likely contribute to, and perhaps determine, other facets—namely, family atmosphere and cohesiveness. Variation in family functioning would thus be a reflection of the extent to which communication, emotional expression, and a sense of cohesiveness contribute to the family climate. Bentovim proposes that climate is also influenced by the structural boundaries that a family builds. Finally a family is characterized by operations: those functions carried out to adapt to predictable and unpredictable demands across the family life cycle. Table 2.1 combines the three major family dimensions of structure, function, and development with the six family aspects proposed by Bentovim and may provide a useful framework in which to examine essential characteristics of families.

Structural Characteristics

A consideration of family structure must recognize the individuality of family members. The immediate family of parents and siblings represents individuals with needs uniquely defined as functions of responsibility (e.g., caregiving), developmental status (e.g., preschool versus adolescence), or familial status (e.g., older versus younger sibling). Variations in parenting roles, both as perceived and as desired by mothers and fathers, have been explored by Gallagher, Cross, and Scharfman (1981).

A structural view of the family can be expressed in at least two forms. One structural analysis can focus on the composition of the family itself—who are the members that make up the family? Although the definition of the family has been broadened in recent years (Simeonsson & Simeonsson, 1981), reflecting sociological trends of single-parent families and high divorce rates, it is still possible to consider the composition of immediate

TABLE 2.1
Relationship of Family Dimensions and Facets of Family Functioning

	Family Dimensions		
Facets of Functioning	Structural	Functional	Developmental
Communication		X	X
Feelings	X		
Atmosphere	X		
Cohesiveness	X		
Climate	X		X
Operations		X	

and extended families. A definition of the family can, of course, encompass units with or without children. Given the focus of this text, however, the term *family* will be used to define contexts in which children are present. The immediate family can be conceptualized as a parent-child unit in which the child's nurturing needs are met by one or more parents. The structure of such a family thus consists of one or more children and a mother and/or a father, with both parent and child having unique needs and roles. Additional children in the family context have roles as recipients as well as agents in the socialization of siblings.

Consideration of extended family structure typically focuses on maternal and paternal grandparents. Grandparent involvement may range from high intensity to total noninvolvement. The degree of involvement is influenced by a variety of factors, including sense of investment and physical proximity. These two aspects may interact—proximity may contribute to higher involvement, whereas distance between extended and immediate family may contribute to reduced mutual involvement. Cousins, aunts, and uncles may also be key players in the extended family and thereby constitute important structural elements. Again, the degree of their involvement may vary as a function of both psychological and physical factors. Although the composition of immediate and extended families may often be obvious, in some instances the actual roles of family members may be less readily ascertained because of high rates of separation, divorce, and remarriage. Defining the functional family unit and significant members of that unit is important, however, in assessing family functioning and developing realistic intervention plans.

Seen from this perspective, the structure of the immediate and the extended family involves a number of individual members, each bringing individual histories and needs to family relationships. To meet the individual and collective needs of a family, it is necessary to ascertain its composition—the nature and number of its members.

A second level of the structural analysis of the family focuses on systemic properties. The conceptualization of the family as a system is a widely accepted approach in both theoretical and clinical considerations of the family, although there are a variety of systems models (Sluzki, 1983). Massey (1986) has indicated that the multiple approaches to defining family systems represent a continuum rather than a dichotomy, varying along dimensions of style, foci, and language.

Perhaps the major factor contributing to the growth of systems theory in the conceptualization of the family has been the recognition of the family in context—namely, that the dynamic relationship of the members of the family transcends the role of individuals. Viewing families from a systems perspective assumes an "interlocking of social structure and personal development. Individuals create and reinforce structure. Structure socializes and controls persons" (Massey, 1986, p. 26). The systems and subsystems of the family that make up its structure are characterized by defined boundaries that may vary significantly in their permeability from rigid and impermeable to ambiguous and highly permeable. An effectively functioning family is characterized by boundaries that define the uniqueness and autonomy of subsystems but also are sufficiently permeable to allow communication. Families that are functioning inadequately in a structural sense may be characterized by the lack of boundaries and total enmeshment of family members. Alternately, boundaries may be so rigid that there is no communication or involvement among family members (Bentovim, 1986).

The structural approach to families has been a particularly productive strategy in clinical contexts. McCubbin and McCubbin (1987) have developed the T-Double ABCX Model of Family Adjustment and Adaptation in the context of a family systems perspective. The model has been developed as part of a long-term program focusing on variables that might help to explain individual differences in how families manage demands and crises. The model addresses three levels of family functioning—the individual family member, the family unit, and the community. The model focuses on four dimensions in family adjustment, each representing distinct aspects that need to be considered in assessment and intervention. Family adaptation is thus seen in terms of demands (stressors and strains) and capabilities (resources and coping) mediated by appraisal (situational and schema) that can lead to adequate family functioning (adjustment and adaptation). From this model a number of applications have been derived, including family typologies. Typologies reflect unique aspects of the family system in terms of patterns, rules, and norms. Identification of characteristics that define a particular typology is based on the family's placement on two specific dimensions. Four family typologies have been presented as representative of how the structure of the family influences its functioning and adaptation (McCubbin & Thompson, 1987). An analysis of these four typologies on the basis of pairs of family dimensions yields 16 distinct combinations (Table 2.2). Each of the four family system types—regenerative, resilient, rhythmic, and traditionalistic—has been examined across the family life cycle. Although there was evidence of durability and stability of family traits, variability of distribution of family types was also observed as a function of family type and/or stage of family life. The utility of these four major typologies was supported by findings showing some relationship among different family types, indicating that family strengths shared some common dimensions. The relationship, however, was only low to moderate, indicating that the nature of family strengths may vary.

Adopting a systems approach to the family has been of direct value in family assessment and therapy. The major implication of a structural approach is that problems affecting a family on a system level must be understood and dealt with at a system level. Illustrative of this approach is systemic family therapy involving three specific facets: hypothesizing, circularity, and neutrality (Martin, 1985). *Hypothesizing* refers to formula-

TABLE 2.2
A Summary of McCubbin and Thompson's (1987) Family Typologies

First Dimension Second Dimension	Low Low	Low High	High Low	High High
Coherence Hardiness	Vulnerable families	Secure families	Durable families	Regenerative families
Family bonding Family flexibility	Fragile families	Bonded families	Pliant families	Resilient families
Valuing of family Time and routines	Unpatterned families	Intentional families	Structuralized families	Rhythmic families
Family traditions Family celebrations	Situational families	Traditionalistic families	Celebratory families	Ritualistic families

tions about the family that must be systemic in nature, encompassing all components of the family as a system. *Circularity* refers to the role of feedback in examining family relationships. *Neutrality* refers to focusing hypotheses about family problems, needs, and interventions on systems, not individuals. Neutrality implies that the family is approached as a unit and not by singling out individuals. In interventions for families of handicapped young children, such an approach can prevent a narrow focus on the handicapped child's needs or the family member's coping responses from dominating the intervention efforts, obscuring or excluding family needs at the system level.

Functional Characteristics

A second major approach to families examines the functions they must fulfill in the process of adaptation and adjustment. Bentovim (1986) has identified family operations as one important facet of family functioning. Such operations may be the responsibilities of individual family members or subsystems. Bentovim's operations include those of a daily nature dealing with conflict resolution, decision making, and problem solving. Turnbull, Summers, and Brotherson (1984) have listed nine types of functions specific to the family: economic, physical, rest and recuperation, socialization, self-definition, affection, guidance, education, and vocational. Some of these functions (e.g., self-definition) reflect the role of the family as a system, whereas others (e.g., guidance) may be assumed by subsystems or individual members. Individual family members also have unique functions to fulfill. Gallagher et al. (1983) have identified 20 functions or roles that either the mother, the father, or both may be responsible for within the home. Included in these functional family roles are teacher, nurse, money manager, and transportation provider. Assessment of these family roles is detailed in Chapter 7. Although the assumption of specific functions may often follow traditional guidelines for mothers and fathers, the extent to which they are distributed within a particular family may be unique to that family. Functional roles for children within a family are not as readily defined as those of parents. Clearly, any role for a child would be a function of the child's developmental stage and status as a singleton or sibling. It may, in fact, be easier to identify functional roles for siblings than for singletons, because siblings are simultaneously targets of the family socialization and agents of such socialization for other children in the family. Table 2.3 summarizes the functional roles of family members, including those of children and siblings. Although these roles have been defined according to individual family members, subsystems of the family may also carry out unique functions or functions typically assumed by individual family members. In some instances, functional roles may be shifted from one family member or subsystem to another—for example, when one or more older children assume caregiving roles for siblings that have been abdicated by a parent. Research has shown that older female siblings, particularly in families with low socioeconomic status, often have to assume a primary caregiving role for the handicapped child.

The implication for intervention is that the presence of a handicapped child may limit the family's ability to fulfill typical functions. The family may also face additional functional roles that it may find difficult to handle, such

TABLE 2.3
Representative Roles of Family Members

Member	Role
Parent	Teacher
	Disciplinarian
	Health care provider
	Provider of material needs
	Moral/ethical leader
	Home caretaker
Child	Target for family nurturance
	Member of family system
Sibling	Role model for sibling
	Parent surrogate
	Playmate and peer
Grandparent	Advisor to adult children
	Nurturer of grandchildren
	Resource for extended family

as extended or unusual caregiving demands. Early intervention programs can provide an important service by facilitating the achievement of family functions to maintain or restore family adjustment.

Developmental Characteristics

The third major way in which to view the family is within a developmental frame. As Tseng and McDermott (1979) have proposed in their triaxial model, the developmental dimension should not be considered apart from structural or functional axes. The developmental axis of the family takes into account the stages from the formation of the basic family unit through the stages of (1) childbearing, (2) childrearing, (3) the launching of adult children, and (4) older parents in later life. Superimposed on the developmental stages of the family as a unit are the developmental stages of individual family members. In this context it may be useful to consider the developmental stages of the child from a Piagetian perspective (Piaget, 1970) or developmental phases of parents within Erikson's (1963) perspective of eight life crises. The developmental models of Piaget, Erikson, Freud, and others, whether applied to individual members or to the family as a unit, represent a unidirectional and linear approach to change over time. Combrinck-Graham (1985) has proposed a developmental model of family systems that is cyclical in nature to account for nonlinear changes in individual members and family systems. This cyclical model, the family life spiral, conceptualizes the developmental tasks of a family in the context of several generations. Different developmental tasks of one generation are seen as reciprocal to the tasks of another generation; thus, "the family life spiral is a representation of the cycles of individuals in the family in relationship to the cycles of individuals in other generations" (p. 142). This conceptualization of the family accounts for developmental changes in terms of two phases, or periods, across the lives of generations. One of these periods is centripetal in nature and is characterized by forces that tend to bring the family together. Some of these forces operate within the family; others are part of the larger social context of the family. Centripetal periods across generations thus involve birth, childrearing, and grandparenthood—events that pull the family together. At other times, generational events lead to centrifugal periods characterized by forces that separate family members. Adolescence and the reevaluation of middle life represent centrifugal periods across generations. The family life spiral thus accounts for developmental change in families in a cyclical fashion, with periods of centripetal forces giving way to periods of centrifugal forces across the generations. "The family will undergo three oscillations during an individual's average expected lifetime: the birth and adolescence of the child, the birth and adolescence of the child's children, and then the birth and adolescence of the child's grandchildren" (Combrinck-Graham, 1985, p. 144).

The family-life-spiral model assumes progressive shifts from organization and connectedness to disengagement and coming apart. This cycle represents normal changes in the life of the family. These progressive shifts or oscillations provide opportunities for the family as a system to reexperience similar events across generations and similar events across levels of maturity for the individual. The expression of these generational shifts may vary as a function of cultural differences. The attitudes and values toward family togetherness and separation may differ from one culture to the next in the form and function of family roles. Moving beyond the generational aspect of immediate and extended family, the sociohistorical aspect of the family life cycle may also be considered (Turnbull et al., 1984). Sociohistorical change may be family adaptation to demands of opportunities attributable to social contexts or expectations tied to the history of families or cultures. Viewed in this context, the family normally moves through, and learns from, successive cycles of centripetal organization and centrifugal disengagement and individuation. The implications of a family-life-cycle conception for intervention with families are twofold. The first is to recognize that the family system, in a generational sense, is perpetually involved in a repetitive cycle of formation as a unit and of separation as individuals. This recognition emphasizes a cyclical rather than a linear approach, in which family adaptation can be understood in both its immediate and extended context. A second implication for intervention lies in the utility of the model to explain family dysfunction. Disruptions in the family life spiral may represent developmental misfit, a situation that "can occur in a family system that does not change with time to become either more centripetal or centrifugal. Developmental misfit can also occur in a family that seems to be evolving well but in which one individual seems markedly out of phase" (Combrinck-Graham, 1985, p. 148). Both of these situations may reflect the disruptions to adaptation that occur in families with a handicapped child. The development of the handicapped child may be in marked asynchrony with the development of the family. The additional demand characteristics of a handicapped child are likely to prolong or maintain the centripetal period of contributions to dysfunctional adaptation, within and across generations of the family system.

FAMILIES WITH YOUNG HANDICAPPED CHILDREN

The preceding review has sketched major characteristics of families along structural, functional, and developmental lines. While some reference has already been made to families with handicapped children, it may be useful to examine these characteristics more specifically as they pertain to such families.

At a structural level, how may individual family members be affected by the presence of a young handicapped child? Much of the earlier research on adaptation of family members has focused on the mother to the exclusion of other family members, but recently there has been a growing interest in the adjustment of fathers (Gallagher, Cross, & Scharfman, 1981; Gallagher et al., 1983), siblings, and members of the extended family. The evidence reveals that the experience of mothers is perhaps the most substantially affected. In a study in which parents of young, severely handicapped children under 5 years of age were interviewed on three successive occasions, mothers defined stress in terms of fatigue, a sense of isolation, and the stigma of the child's handicap (Rees, 1983). The greater stress reported by mothers may have been attributable to the fact that most fathers felt unable to share in the tasks of child care. Highlighting the role of extended family and friends, families who perceived themselves as having four or more dependable relatives and friends felt they could manage the child at home. The comparative impact of the handicapped child on other members of the family system was examined in a study by Molsa and Ikonen-Molsa (1985), who interviewed parents, siblings, and grandparents about family crises. The study, while retrospective in nature, addressed adaptation from a system-theoretic basis, in which the effects on the family as a whole were considered. Findings revealed differences among family members in terms of the predominant reaction at three time points. Adaptation accounted for more than 40% of the reactions of grandparents and siblings at the initial and transitional stage. On the other hand, denial and depression accounted for more than two-thirds of the predominant reactions of parents at these two stages. Only at the third stage was adaptation the predominant reaction of all three groups. A similar generational effect has been reported by Harris, Handelman, and Palmer (1985) on the impact of the autistic child on the family system. In a comparison of responses, grandparents were found to take a more positive view than parents of the handicapped child. The reactions of grandmothers and grandfathers were also found to be associated, indicating a common perspective of their child's and grandchild's experience.

These results illustrate that individual family members respond to the demands of a handicapped child in different ways at different times of the family life cycle. The family may also react at the system level, as illustrated in a study by Pollner and McDonald-Wikler (1985). Using a case-study format, Pollner and McDonald-Wikler described a family who constructed and maintained a common delusion of competence in their severely retarded child. This construction of unreality by the family system was evident in the interactions among family members. Although the coping patterns of most families with handicapped children are likely to be more adaptive, the findings of this study illustrate the importance of attending to family adaptation at the system level.

The functional responsibilities of families with a handicapped child are likely to be increased and attenuated. The protective, nurturing, socializing, and educational roles of parents are all functions that are directly impacted by characteristics of the handicapped child. One expression of the impact of increased or attenuated functional responsibilities is the elevation in stress levels. Research by Wilton and Renaut (1986) with mothers of preschool handicapped children revealed higher levels of reported stress on 13 of 15 scales of the Questionnaire on Resources and Stress compared to families with nonhandicapped children. These findings of elevated stress were consistent with earlier research by Friedrich and Friedrich (1981) and Beckman (1983), indicating that caring for a handicapped child impairs family functions.

The developmental courses of the handicapped child and the family are influenced in a number of ways. Given the impact of most handicaps, development of handicapped children is often delayed or arrested. Many handicapped children will master fewer of the normal developmental tasks faced in childhood. In addition, handicapped children may face other tasks not faced by their nonhandicapped peers (Simeonsson & Simeonsson, 1981). Included among these are such tasks as dealing with frequent hospitalizations, unusual and intrusive medical procedures, and the associated social consequences of separation from family; and being exposed to large numbers of unfamiliar adults in early life (Battle, 1974). The additional tasks faced by the handicapped child often translate into additional tasks for the family. Included among these are sleep interruption, provision of complicated diets or medical treatments, and the acceptance of limited or atypical responses to nurturance and stimulation (Travis, 1976; Marcus, 1977; Fraiberg, 1974). These additional tasks may be faced only once or twice, or they may be faced repeatedly in different forms. Farran, Metzger, and Sparling (1986) have emphasized that because the demands of raising a handicapped child are not constant, there will be immediate changes in the family as well as repeated crises and role changes. This position has been nicely articulated by Berry and Zimmerman (1983), who indicated that the adaptive steps of denial, anger, bargaining, depression, and acceptance of the handicap do not simply occur once. One or more of the steps may be retraced at any time as a function of a chronic condition or a spontaneous or anticipated crisis. Systematic assessment of the impact of such additional demands must be made to provide a basis for understanding individual family development.

SUMMARY

This chapter is based on the premise that families are characterized by structural, functional, and developmental features. Knowledge of these essential characteristics contributes to an understanding of the commonalities as well as the uniqueness of families. To understand and provide assistance to the family with a handicapped child, its characteristics should be assessed on an individual basis. Furthermore, because the family is a dynamic entity, it should be approached in a manner that recognizes the developmental and cyclical nature of adaptation. Although the family with a young handicapped child has much in common with any family in regard to structural, functional, and developmental characteristics, it may also face additional demands in day-to-day as well as life-cycle adaptation.

REFERENCES

Bailey, D. B., & Simeonsson, R. J. (1984). Critical issues underlying research and intervention with families of young handicapped children. *Journal of the Division for Early Childhood, 9,* 38–48.

Battle, C. V. (1974). Disruptions in the socialization of a young severely handicapped child. *Rehabilitation Literature, 35,* 130–140.

Beckman, P. J. (1983). Influence of selected child characteristics on stress in families of handicapped infants. *American Journal of Mental Deficiency, 88,* 150–156.

Bentovim, A. (1986). Family therapy when the child is the referred patient. In S. Block (Ed.), *An introduction to the psychotherapies* (pp. 198–221). Oxford: Oxford University Press.

Berry, J. O., & Zimmerman, W. W. (1983). The stage model revisited. *Rehabilitation Literature, 44*(9–10), 275–277.

Bronfenbrenner, U. (1979). *The ecology of human development: Experiments by nature and design.* Cambridge, Mass.: Harvard University Press.

Campbell, D., & Draper, R. (1985). *Applications of systematic family therapy.* London: Grune & Stratton.

Combrinck-Graham, L. (1985). A developmental model for family systems. *Family Process, 24*(2), 139–150.

Doherty, W. J. (1986). Quanta, quarks, and families: Implications of quantum physics for family research. *Family Process, 25,* 249–264.

Elder, J. H. (1986). Behavioral management training for families of emotionally handicapped and/or developmentally delayed children. *Issues in Mental Health Nursing, 8,* 37–49.

Erikson, E. H. (1963). *Childhood and society* (2nd ed.). New York: W. W. Norton.

Farber, B. (1959). Effects of a severely mentally retarded child on family integration. *Monographs of the Society for Research in Child Development, 24* (2, Serial No. 71).

Farran, D. C., Metzger, J., & Sparling, J. (1986). Immediate and continuing adaptations in parents of handicapped children. In J. Gallagher, & P. Vietze (Eds.), *Families of handicapped persons* (pp. 143–163). Baltimore: Paul H. Brookes.

Fraiberg, S. (1974). Blind infants and their mothers: An examination of the sign system. In M. Lewis & L. A. Rosenblum (Eds.), *The effect of the infant on its caregiver* (pp. 215–232). New York: John Wiley & Sons.

Freeman, D. S. (1976). The family as a system: Fact or fancy. *Comprehensive Psychiatry, 17,* 735–749.

Friedrich, W. N., & Friedrich, W. L. (1981). Psychosocial assets of parents of handicapped and nonhandicapped children. *American Journal of Mental Deficiency, 85,* 551–553.

Gallagher, J. J., Beckman, P., & Cross, A. H. (1983). Families of handicapped children: Sources of stress and its amelioration. *Exceptional Children, 50,* 10–19.

Gallagher, J. J., Cross, A., & Scharfman, W. (1981). Parental adaptation to a young handicapped child: The father's role. *Journal of the Division for Early Childhood, 3,* 3–14.

Guerin, P. J., Jr. (1976). *Family therapy: Theory and practice.* New York: Gardner Press.

Harris, S. L., Handelman, J. P., & Palmer, C. (1985). Parents and grandparents view the autistic child. *Journal of Autism and Developmental Disorders, 15*(2), 127–137.

Marcus, L. M. (1977). Patterns of coping in families of psychotic children. *American Journal of Orthopsychiatry, 47,* 388–399.

Martin, F. (1985). The development of systemic family therapy and its place in the field. In D. Campbell & R. Draper (Eds.), *Applications of systemic family therapy* (pp. 11–22). London: Grune & Stratton.

Massey, R. F. (1986). What/who is the family system? *American Journal of Family Therapy, 14*(1), 23–39.

McCubbin, H. I., & Thompson, A. I. (1987). Family typologies and family assessment. In H. I. McCubbin & A. I. Thompson (Eds.), *Family assessment inventories for research and practice.* Madison: University of Wisconsin.

McCubbin, M. A., & McCubbin, H. I. (1987). The T-Double ABCX model of family adjustment and adaptation. In H. I. McCubbin & A. I. Thompson (Eds.), *Family assessment inventories for research and practice* (pp. 3–32). Madison: University of Wisconsin.

Molsa, P. K., & Ikonen-Molsa, S. A. (1985). The mentally handicapped child and family crisis. *Journal of Mental Deficiency Research, 29,* 309–314.

Patterson, G. R., & Gullion, M. E. (1968). *Living with children: New models for parents and teachers.* Champaign, Ill.: Research Press.

Piaget, J. (1970). Piaget's theory. In P. H. Mussen (Ed.), *Carmichael's manual of child psychology* (vol. 1, pp. 702–732). New York: John Wiley & Sons.

Pollner, M., & McDonald-Wikler, L. (1985). The social construction of unreality: A case study of a family's attribution of competence to a severely retarded child. *Family Process, 24,* 241–254.

Rees, S. J. (1983). Families' perceptions of services for handicapped children. *International Journal of Rehabilitation Research, 6*(4), 475–476.

Sameroff, A. J. (1976). Early influences on development: Fact or fancy. *Merrill-Palmer Quarterly, 21,* 267–294.

Simeonsson, R. J., & Simeonsson, N. E. (1981). Parenting handicapped children: Psychological aspects. In J. L. Paul (Ed.), *Understanding and working with parents of children with special needs* (pp. 51–88). New York: Holt, Rinehart and Winston.

Sluzki, C. E. (1983). Process, structure and world views: Toward an integrated view of system models in family therapy. *Family Process, 22,* 469–476.

Travis, G. (1976). *Chronic illness: Its impact on child and family.* Stanford, Calif.: Stanford University Press.

Tseng, W. S., & McDermott, J. F. (1979). Triaxial family classifications: A proposal. *Journal of the American Academy of Child Psychiatry, 18,* 22–43.

Turnbull, A. P., Summers, J. A., & Brotherson, M. J. (1984). *Working with families with disabled members: A family systems approach.* Lawrence: Kansas University Affiliated Facility.

Wilton, K., & Renaut, J. (1986). Stress levels in families with intellectually handicapped preschool children and families with nonhandicapped preschool children. *Journal of Mental Deficiency Research, 30,* 163–169.

Winton, P. J., & Turnbull, A. P. (1981). Parent involvement as viewed by parents of preschool handicapped children. *Topics in Early Childhood Special Education, 1,* 11–19.

3

Assessing Child Characteristics That Influence Family Functioning

F amily functioning is influenced by many factors. Some, such as parental education and occupation, locus of control, or philosophical belief system, are parent focused; while others, such as age, birth order, sex, developmental status, and temperament, are child centered. Although not all these factors can be affected by intervention, all can impact on family functioning. If effective and appropriate intervention services are to be offered to families of young handicapped children, child characteristics that affect the family must be evaluated. This chapter presents a rationale for assessing such characteristics, discusses the effects of child characteristics on the family, offers some general considerations for planning assessments, describes representative instruments, and suggests ways for translating assessment findings into family-related goals.

THE RATIONALE FOR ASSESSING CHILD CHARACTERISTICS

The assessment of child characteristics needed to provide appropriate services has been mandated by law. Both Public Law 94–142 and Public Law

This chapter was contributed by Gail S. Huntington, University of North Carolina at Chapel Hill.

99–457 require comprehensive, multidisciplinary evaluation of the functioning of all handicapped infants and toddlers. The results of this evaluation are to be incorporated into the individualized family services plan (IFSP), as required by Public Law 99–457, which details explicit services to be provided to the child and family. Without an accurate and broad-based picture of the child's status, the development of the IFSP would be greatly hindered. The creation of an individualized intervention plan requires the evaluation of assessment results and their integration into individualized child, family, and program goals.

Although assessment of child status per se is important in early intervention, in the larger context as service providers plan programs to meet the needs of handicapped children, child characteristics that impinge upon family functioning must also be evaluated. The mandate to plan family goals following assessment of family strengths and needs requires interventionists to be aware of the influence of the child on those qualities.

RELEVANT CHILD CHARACTERISTICS AND THEIR EFFECTS ON FAMILIES

Traditionally, handicapped children have been assessed in terms of cognitive, motor, social, self-help, and language development. Theories of child development and recent research findings with infants and young children have suggested additional domains that may have potential for documenting the complexities of handicapped child behavior as it impacts on the family. Three of these characteristics, summarized in Table 3.1, are temperament, readability, and behavior.

Temperament

The recent interest in the concept of temperament has been an outgrowth of the work of Thomas and Chess (1977), and their colleagues, in their research with the New York Longitudinal Study. Temperament is defined by this group as individual differences in behavioral style—that is, the "how" of behavior rather than the "why" (motivation) or "what" (capabilities). Within the context of the family, the temperament attributes of the infant or child may function as markers for the demands of the child with which the family must cope and which influence the mutual adaptation of family and infant. In fact, infant temperament has been shown to affect parental behavior as early as the neonatal period (Sirignano & Lachman, 1985). In a prospective, short-term longitudinal study of first-time parents and childless couples, self-rating scales were used to obtain both global-trait and situation-specific state measures for efficacy expectations, personal control, anxiety, and depression. The parent group showed more positive change than the nonparent group on efficacy and anxiety. In addition, new parents

TABLE 3.1
Behavioral Domains Relevant to Family Functioning

Domain	Relevance to Family	Assessment Procedures
Temperament	Documents variability of child's behavioral style Possible index of child's contribution to parent-child interaction	Parent-report measures for infants and toddlers Observation of behaviors in multiple situations
Readability	Impacts parents' feelings of efficacy and competence Impacts development of child's feelings of competence	Parents' perceptions of child's responsiveness and predictability Observations of child's reaction to contingent reinforcement
Behavior	Excessive caregiving demands increase family stress Child's contribution to "goodness-of-fit"	Various assessment measures available—e.g., IBR (Bayley, 1969), CRIB (Simeonsson, 1978), child characteristics domain of PSI (Abidin, 1986)

who perceived their infants as having easier temperaments experienced more positive change, especially in personal control, than did parents whose infants were seen as more difficult. The results of a study of infant and family adjustment in the first year (Sprunger, Boyce, & Gaines, 1985) indicated that infant temperament continues to affect family functioning beyond the neonatal period. Examining the notion of infant-family congruence through the construct of rhythmicity (the degree of predictable regularity in both infant and family), Sprunger et al. found that the amount of mismatch in family-infant congruence was significantly predictive of overall family adjustment.

The role of temperament in parent-child interaction has been examined extensively in nonhandicapped groups (Lerner & Galambos, 1985; Simpson & Stevenson-Hinde, 1985; Thomas & Chess, 1977). Findings indicate that specific temperament traits can affect the attitudes and behaviors of parents in many ways, a finding that can be extended to families of handicapped children. In a group of handicapped infants and toddlers, the clinically relevant temperament clusters of difficult, easy, and slow-to-warm-up differentiated among mothers on the basis of the appropriateness and quality of mother-child interactions. Mothers whose children were rated as easy had the most optimal scores on both aspects of interaction, compared with mothers whose children were rated as belonging to either of the other two categories (Huntington, Simeonsson, Bailey, & Comfort, 1987).

Readability

A second child characteristic relevant to family functioning is readability— that is, "the extent to which an infant's behaviors are clearly defined and produce distinctive signals and cues for adults" (Goldberg, 1977, p. 177). Readability refers to the relative ease with which the parent can attach meaning to the child's behavior—can observe the child and know he or she is sleepy, is hungry, or wants to be held. Children perceived as readable are likely to enhance parental feelings of efficacy and competence, because when parents correctly estimate the meaning of the child's cues, parent-child interactions often bring about desired results. Reciprocally, readable infants experience parental behaviors that are responsive to expressed needs and develop feelings of competence in their ability to influence their surroundings. Unfortunately, handicapped children may not strengthen parental feelings of competence, because they may be less readable than their nonhandicapped peers (Bailey & Wolery, 1984; McCollum & Stayton, 1985). The work of Yoder (1987) supports this notion, as he reports observers were significantly less often able to agree on the occurrence of a communicative cue for severely handicapped infants than for less handicapped infants. However, readability exists only within the context of an interaction and may increase with familiarity. Parents may find their own child more readable than do those unfamiliar with the child's cues. In a longitudinal study of parental perceptions of the readability of their infants' cues of distress, happiness, interest in toys or social interaction, and under-standing/learning (Goldman & Johnson-Martin, 1987), mothers of handicapped and nonhandicapped infants perceived their infants to be equally readable for cues regarding distress and happiness. On the other hand, mothers of handicapped infants were less sure of their infants' cues regarding learning and interest in social interactions. Familiarity may play a part in this discrepancy, as handicapped infants may emit fewer cues of this nature, thus providing an impoverished context for learning their cues. However, two conclusions are implicit in these findings. First, despite some degree of familiarity with the cues, mothers still found handicapped infants across ages to be less readable than nonhandicapped infants for some behaviors. Second, readability does not appear to be a unitary construct, indicating that intervention to help parents more easily interpret their infant's cues might be more effective if the various types of cues were assessed individually and only those perceived to be difficult were targeted for intervention (Goldman & Johnson-Martin, 1987). The implications of readability for parental functioning and subsequent infant development are clearly important. Interventions to assist parents to recognize subtle cues and to help infants understand the relationship between their own behavior and its results may improve family satisfaction and adaptation.

Behavior

Although professionals often assume that a handicapped child will adversely affect the family, the research has not always supported this belief. Many parents report little effect on family life as a consequence of having a handicapped child (Blackard & Barsh, 1982; Wishart, Bidder & Gray, 1981). The one area that seems to be troublesome, even for families reporting little or no effect, is that of restriction of family activities, especially if the child is severely handicapped. This difference appears to be related to the availability of respite care services.

These findings, however, do not mean that families of handicapped infants and young children never experience stress related to the child. Caring for an infant or young child is time-consuming and tiring for any parent. Parents of both handicapped and nonhandicapped young children report feelings of stress, but it appears that parenting a young handicapped child may produce higher levels of stress than parenting a nonhandicapped child (Dyson & Fewell, 1986; Friedrich & Friedrich, 1981). Although most families adapt successfully to the presence of a handicapped child, high levels of parental stress can affect family functioning through decreased marital satisfaction and increased psychological dysfunction and health problems for the parents.

Many aspects of the child, including behavioral characteristics, have been implicated in the additional stress reported by parents. Beckman (1983) reported that mothers with more parental and family problems, as measured by the Questionnaire on Resources and Stress (Holroyd, 1974), had children who were socially unresponsive, displayed more repetitive behaviors, and had more caregiving needs. Overall, the child characteristic most related to stress for these mothers was the number of the child's demands for caregiving. In an examination of sources of stress in families of young handicapped and nonhandicapped children, Dyson and Fewell (1986) reported that higher stress levels of the parents of the handicapped children were related to behavioral or attitudinal deficits on the part of the child, such as lack of self-help skills or the inability to communicate with others. Increased severity of the handicap with its associated physical incapacities were found to exacerbate parental stress.

It must not be assumed, however, that handicapped children exert a homogeneous influence on family functioning. It is likely that the unique demand characteristics of specific handicaps will differentially affect family functioning. Some effects of specific handicaps on the child's behavior that might influence family functioning are displayed in Table 3.2. As a further example of this influence, Holroyd and McArthur (1976) investigated the effects of autistic and Down syndrome children on mothers and families.

TABLE 3.2
Some Effects of Specific Handicaps on Children's Interactional Skills

Handicap	Reported Findings
Mental retardation	Reduced responsivity to others Decreased vocalization Lack of smiling or delayed smiling More solitary play Fewer initiations to others More likely to resist or not respond to cuddling
Hearing impairment	Impaired communication Inconsistent responses to communicative attempts Fewer social initiations
Visual impairment	Irregular smiling Smiling in response to auditory cues only Child must "maintain contact" by tactile and auditory (rather than visual) cues
Physical and motor impairments	Limp or physically unresponsive Difficulty in relaxing Decreased ability to laugh or smile Smile may look like a grimace Impaired communication skills Impaired locomotion skills prevent child from independently seeking out parent

From D. B. Bailey and M. Wolery. *Teaching infants and preschoolers with handicaps.* Columbus, Oh.: Merrill Publishing Company, 1984. Reprinted with permission.

They found that normal personal and family functioning was more disrupted by the presence of a child with autism than by one with Down syndrome. It is assumed that this finding resulted because autistic children, while appearing to be normal, have more conspicuous and difficult behavior problems and present more caregiving demands than do children with Down syndrome.

Collectively, these findings indicate that the behavioral characteristics of handicapped children can exert a negative effect on family functioning, but do not necessarily do so. Although the presence of a handicapped child may affect the family, the responses of the family also affect the child (Crnic, Friedrich, & Greenberg, 1983). This relationship has been underlined by the findings of Nihira, Meyers, and Mink (1983) in a study of 268 families of handicapped children. Their results support the contention that family adjustments and functioning are related not only to child characteristics and behavior but also to aspects of the family. The findings reported by Nihira et al. underscore the interactive nature of the child-family system as the impact on the parents was related to the handicapped child's lack of adaptive competence, and the child's lack of competence was, in turn, related to successful parental coping. The outcomes of these interactions may be positive or negative, but they are the result of multiple dimensions of child and family influencing each other over time. Thomas and Chess (1977) have called the outcome of this process "goodness or poorness of fit." Goodness-of-fit exists when the demand characteristics of the child are compatible with the capabilities and expectations of the parents. The reverse is also true—that is, goodness-of-fit is present when the demands of family and environment are compatible with the temperament and abilities of the child. When goodness-of-fit is present, families adapt and function smoothly, and child development is not disrupted (Chess & Thomas, 1986). The usefulness of the concept has been demonstrated in clinical studies of deaf children (Chess & Fernandez, 1980), as well as research on psychosocial adaptation of adolescents (Lerner, 1983). A recent study examined the extent to which the goodness-of-fit of child, maternal, and support variables were able to document good or poor maternal adaptation in families of almost 200 handicapped children (Simeonsson, Bailey, Huntington, & Comfort, 1986). Findings indicated that an index of maternal and child characteristics, and measures of locus of control, child temperament, and social support collectively contributed to the correct identification of 77% of the mothers as having a high or low level of involvement with their child. These findings not only illustrate the applicability of the concept of goodness-of-fit, but also provide support for efforts focused on maximizing the fit of child, family, and environment variables in early intervention.

This review clearly shows that child and family functioning are inextricably intertwined. To assess family functioning in the absence of information about the child is to omit a critical part of the whole. Child characteristics influence parental and family adaptation and satisfaction just as parental and family characteristics influence the adaptation and development of the child. Assessment of child and family functioning complement each other and both must be part of a total assessment plan.

CONSIDERATIONS FOR ASSESSING CHILD CHARACTERISTICS

Although there is a need for valid assessment of behavioral characteristics of young handicapped children, a number of factors, singly or in combination, significantly limit the achievement of this aim. These factors include definitional issues, limitations of the child and the examiner, and problems of measurement (Simeonsson, Huntington, & Parse, 1980a). These issues are summarized in Table 3.3.

Clinical Judgment

Regardless of the acknowledged limitations, valid assessment of handicapped youngsters must be considered a realistic goal for those who work with exceptional populations. However, if the goal is to be realized, the means whereby the assessment process can be improved should be considered. Because the interest is on child characteristics as they influence parental and family functioning, assessment procedures must include parents' and other family members' perceptions of the child's impact on the family. Offered the opportunity, parents can be accurate reporters of their child's behavior (Chee, Kreutzeberg, & Clark, 1978). In addition, interventionists and other professionals closely involved with the child and family have the opportunity to exercise their own clinical judgment regarding the

TABLE 3.3
Assessment Limitations

Limitations	Issues
Definitional	Lack of agreement on definitions of basic terms
	Need for designations that will reflect both the presence of a handicap and the degree of impairment
Child	Impaired function in more than one area
	Performance and functioning affected by medication and state
	Presence of idiosyncratic behaviors
	Variability in rate of development across areas
Examiner	Lack of knowledge/experience with special children
	Personal biases and expectations
	Invalid assumptions concerning effects of the handicap
	Difficulty interpreting a child's responses
	Lack of special communication skills (e.g., signing)
Measurement	Standardization populations exclude handicapped
	Extreme normative values cannot be derived
	Test assumptions violated when used with handicapped
	Difficult to compare results from different tests
	Insufficient data base for the various handicapping conditions

From R. J. Simeonsson. *Psychological and developmental assessment of special children.* Boston: Allyn & Bacon, 1986. Reprinted with permission.

effect of the child's behavior on the family. There has been a disproportionate reliance on formal assessment conducted by professional examiners to the exclusion of the insights, knowledge, and judgments of parents and staff who work directly with children. Although it must be recognized that the very nature of clinical judgment makes it subject to bias, distortion, and inaccuracies, if precautions are taken, the degree of confidence in clinical judgments of parents and staff can be greatly enhanced. For example, important ways of increasing the reliability of clinical judgments may include taking care to avoid eliciting socially desirable responses, eliminating value-laden labels, presenting behaviors along a continuum rather than in a dichotomy (Wolfensberger & Kurtz, 1974), and sensitizing participants to relevant dimensions.

Multiple Sources and Methods

A second way in which assessment of child characteristics may be improved is by using multiple "windows"—that is, gathering information from several sources and through several modes. Early intervention has moved from a reliance on a single measure of child-development status to one that incorporates evaluations of many aspects of development (Fewell, 1983; Peterson & Meier, 1987). Given the complex nature of child-family reciprocity, an approach employing multiple measures and/or strategies is essential. Parents are clearly a valuable source of information about the child's effect on family adaptation and functioning. Parents and other caregivers may be uniquely sensitive to subtle characteristics of the handicapped child not measured by traditional tests and not immediately apparent to the casual observer.

Parents represent an important source of information for the evaluation of child characteristics, but they are not the only source. Other family members, particularly siblings, can furnish both corroborative and unique perspectives of the child's impact on the family. Professionals involved with the family also have significant knowledge and perceptions to add to the picture. Although their contact with child and family may be more limited than that of family members, training can sharpen their ability to detect and evaluate child characteristics of consequence to family adaptation.

Along with multiple sources of information, the assessment program should consider the use of multiple methods. Parental perceptions can be expressed verbally in more or less structured situations (e. g., conversations with the therapist or during a structured interview) and in writing through the use of standardized assessment measures. Initial assessment of temperament and behavior can be gathered through the use of paper-and-pencil instruments and validated through interviews or observations. Professional observation of family-child interaction, either in the home or in a more structured setting, offer additional opportunities both to confirm parental (and professional) perceptions and to gather new information. Observations furnish information about the behavior in everyday settings through everyday interactions. Although the presence of an observer may disrupt or bias the behavior—a caveat that also applies to the observation of behavior in a structured setting—observational procedures have considerable merit as one form of information gathering and should be included in an overall assessment program. Odom and Shuster (1986) present suggestions for reducing observer bias and increasing the validity of observer information through naturalistic inquiry by participant observers. Although this technique can be very time consuming, it is a source of rich and unique information.

The information obtained from each source can be both overlapping and unique. The inclusion of multiple sources through multiple methods should increase the likelihood of identifying the singular characteristics of each child in the context of the family and the family's adaptation to the child.

Situational Effects

A third consideration in the assessment of child characteristics is the effect of situational or setting variables on the child's behavior. Much assessment of child characteristics is completed in a "testing room" or laboratory situation. This is generally an environment that is unfamiliar to the child. When this is so, sufficient time needs to be allowed for any child to become acclimated to the surroundings. In addition, specific needs of handicapped infants and toddlers must be met if an accurate evaluation of child behavior is to be made. For example, the child with motor impairments must be positioned correctly. Furthermore, novel environments that have not been tactually explored by the visually impaired child or those that do not support the residual hearing of the hearing-impaired child may inhibit the child, providing a distorted representation of the child's modal behavior. On the other hand, it must be remembered that children may very well behave differently in different settings. Just as children have demand characteristics, so too do settings, and even very young children may adjust their behavior to meet those demands. For that reason, it is essential to have evaluations of the child's behavior in a variety of settings, including the home, with a variety of persons, including parents and family.

REPRESENTATIVE MEASURES AND PROCEDURES

Child characteristcs that influence family functioning can be assessed in a number of ways. The following is a discussion of suggested procedures and appropriate scales.

Temperament

Measuring temperament in young handicapped children provides a way to consider characteristics of the child as they influence or are perceived by the parent or caregiver. Consequently, most temperament scales are parent-report measures. Much of the current interest in temperament is associated with the work of Thomas, Chess, and Birch (1968), who have demonstrated the concurrent and predictive utility of nine categories of temperament and three personality clusters that arise from them. The nine categories are activity, rhythmicity, adaptability, approach, mood, intensity, distractibility, persistence, and threshold. Subsequent research has followed this general model, but substantial effort has gone into the development of simpler, more direct assessment procedures than the interview technique first employed by Thomas et al. Carey and McDevitt (1978) have developed an Infant Temperament Questionnaire that was standardized on 203 infants 4–8 months of age. Clinical and research instruments to measure temperament in toddlers between 12 and 36 months (Fullard, McDevitt, & Carey, 1984) and young children 3–7 years (McDevitt & Carey, 1978) have also been developed by Carey and his associates. Each questionnaire consists of a series of statements to which the respondent replies on a scale of 1–almost never to 6–almost always, rating the degree to which the statement reflects the child's behavior. For example, an item on the toddler scale reads "The child stops play and watches when someone walks by." The category scores can be grouped into personality clusters of difficult, easy, slow-to-warm-up, and intermediate. The clusters have demonstrated some utility in predicting later behavior disorders (Thomas & Chess, 1977; Terestman, 1980) and have practical utility as markers of concern in parent-child interaction.

Several other temperament scales have also been developed in response to the interest in the concept and to perceived limitations of other instruments. Garside et al. (1975) used a brief questionnaire with a random sample of nursery school children in England and found four meaningful components of temperament: (1) withdrawal; (2) high activity, intensity, and distractibility; (3) moodiness/sulkiness; and (4) irregularity. Although the names are somewhat different, the categories are very similar to those from Thomas et al. (1968). In an effort to avoid the problems of asking parents to make judgments and to make distant recollections, Rothbart (1981) developed the Infant Behavior Questionnaire, a caregiver-report instrument, with items designed to refer to specific, concrete examples of the infant's behaviors in the immediate past week. The six dimensions assessed by the IBQ are activity level, smiling and laughter, fear, distress to limitations, soothability, and duration of orienting. Rothbart (1986) reports moderate convergence between IBQ and home observations at three ages, as well as stability of temperament ratings over the three points. Other investigators (Pedersen, Anderson, & Cain, 1980), who felt that some scales were vulnerable to social desirability and acquiescence responses by parents, have developed the Perception of Baby Temperament Scale based on the nine dimensions of temperament defined by Thomas et al. (1968). An additional feature of their scale is that the items were designed to be appropriate for fathers as well as mothers, reflecting an interest in viewing child temperament in a larger context of family interactions.

As this brief review makes clear, a number of appropriate instruments exist for assessing the temperament of infants and toddlers. Although all were developed for use with nonhandicapped populations, they have also been used with handicapped children. Temperament appears to be relatively independent of age markers within the infant and toddler range (Huntington & Simeonsson, 1987). For that reason, the chronologically age-appropriate scales should be used with both nonhandicapped and handicapped children.

Readability

Parents' feelings of efficacy and competence arise from their evaluation of interactions with their child. Consequently, the parents' perceptions of the child's behavior and characteristics are probably more powerful determinants of parent-child interactions than any assessment of the infant (Goldberg, 1977). Thus, any assessment procedure must include verbal or written information of the parents' perceptions of the child's readability, predictability, and responsiveness. This is one area in which an interview will be of considerable assistance in defining the specific difficulties experienced by the family. Information from temperament and process behavior assessments can form the basis of the interview, because they capture many of the particular behaviors that constitute the concepts of predictability and responsiveness. Clarification can be facilitated through observation of the infant and of the infant with the family, both in the home and, when possible, in other settings.

Behavior

Behavioral characteristics of infants and young children that can affect parental adaptation and family functioning can be documented in a number of ways. For example, the number of additional or unusual caregiving demands can be ascertained through parental report (Beckman, 1983). A second parental source for gathering information about the child is the child characteristics domain on the Parenting Stress Index (Abidin, 1986). The measure has six subscales that examine the child's contribution to stress in the parent-child system. The scale is particularly useful for ages birth to 3, although it has been used with children up to 10 years of age. The PSI yields both a total score and domain scores, which provide more information about the specific types and sources of stress experienced by the family. A complete description of the PSI is given in Chapter 5 of this book.

In addition to parent reports, observational measures completed by the interventionist or other program staff will document behavioral characteristics of the child that are generic in nature and not tied to a particular task or test. One measure designed for this purpose is the Infant Behavior Record (Bayley, 1969), the third part of the Bayley Scales of Infant Development. The IBR offers a summary estimate of a wide variety of behaviors observed during a testing situation. It consists of 30 items, 25 of which are 5- or 9-point rating scales. However, the ratings are inconsistent in that the optimal score can vary from the midpoint to the end or somewhere in between. Also, although modal values are available across different ages, these values were based on a relatively small sample size and are difficult to interpret for comparative purposes (Simeonsson, Huntington, & Parse, 1980b; Matheny, 1980). However, the IBR does seem to tap important infant behaviors and may be useful clinically, despite any methodological limitations. The utility of the IBR to assess behavior was reinforced in a comprehensive investigation by Dolan, Matheny, and Wilson (1974) with infants from the Louisville Twin Study. The distribution of ratings for IBR scores at ages 3, 6, 9, 12, 18, 24, and 30 months was compared with that of the original standardization sample. Although small differences were found between the two samples, 80% agreement was obtained for modal ratings. Dolan et al. felt that the findings supported the IBR's sensitivity to maturational changes, sex differences, and response clusters of behavior.

The characteristics of handicapped children have prompted the development of behavior inventories designed to be uniquely sensitive to their problems. For example, the Children's Handicaps Behavior and Skills Schedule is an instrument developed by Wing and Gould (1978). The CHBS includes 42 sections that assess developmental skills and 21 sections that evaluate the abnormalities of behavior so often present in handicapped populations (for example, stereotyped activities). The abnormal behavior items are rated according to the level of severity. In an analysis of 104 children, Wing and Gould found an overall agreement above 70% between parents and professionals. Interestingly, greater agreement was found for the absence of abnormalities than for their presence, a finding that should be kept in mind when assessing handicapped children.

A second scale, designed particularly to assess the behavior of persons functioning in the sensory-motor level, is the Carolina Record of Individual Behavior (Simeonsson, Huntington, Short, & Ware, 1982). The scale is observational in nature and was developed, in part, to redress the limitations of the IBR. The CRIB, which is appropriate for handicapped infants and toddlers, consists of two parts to be completed after a period of observation or interaction with the child. The first part of the CRIB documents the child's level of arousal or state. State seems to be an appropriate area to assess in handicapped children, not only to document its influence on performance, but also because inconsistency of state organization has been found to be indicative of dysfunction (Thoman, Denenberg, Sieval, Zeidner, & Becker, 1981).

The second part of the CRIB includes three sections. Section A consists of eight developmental behaviors that are ordinal in nature, with each rated on a 9-point scale with 1 the most basic level and 9 the most developmentally advanced. The eight behaviors assessed in this section are social orientation, participation, motivation, endurance, receptive communication, expressive communication, object orientation, and consolability.

Section B also rates eight behaviors on a 9-point scale. These behaviors are normally distributed, and items are developed so that 1 and 9 reflect polar extremes (hypo- and hyper- for example) and 5 is the optimal score. The eight behaviors assessed in this section are activity, reactivity, goal directedness, response to frustration, attention span, responsiveness to caregiver, tone of body, and responsiveness to examiner. Figure 3.1 displays a sample subscale from the A and B scales.

Section C lists 23 specific behaviors, such as exploratory patterns, communicative styles, and a number of rhythmic habit patterns. These are rated on a 4-point scale indicating the frequency with which they are exhibited.

A factor analysis of the 16 subscales revealed four factors—communication (A5, A6, A7, A8, B1); interaction (A1, A2, A3, A4, B3, B8); responsivity (B1, B2, B3, B4, B5, B6, B8); and tone (B7). Reliability of the CRIB is determined on the basis of interrater agreement of + or − 1 point (Gaensbauer, 1982). The mean percentage of agreement was 81% for the 16 subscales in a recent study with 65 home-based interventionists, while Beckman, Thiele, Pokorni, and Balzer-Martin (1986) reported a mean percentage of agreement of 97% for a total of 73 observations over three occasions.

Given the salience of behavioral characteristics for parental adaptation, an important question is the stability of these characteristics in infants and young children. Beckman et al. conducted a longitudinal study of 39 high-risk infants over the first year of life. Findings with the CRIB indicated that stability was greatest when the time between observations was relatively small and that the most stability was observed on the A-scale items, which are developmentally based. As has previously been shown, even very young infants exert some influence on parental adaptation and functioning. Knowledge of which behavioral characteristics remain stable and which do not may contribute to a better understanding of the mutual child-family influences.

FIGURE 3.1
Sample Subscales from the Carolina Record of Individual Behavior

A5

Expressive Communication: Score for evidence of intentional communication; movements, babbling and/or other vocalizations should not be scored simply because they are present, but only if they show evidence of intentional communication.

1. Child gives no evidence of any communication.

2. Child communicates needs/wants by total body movements—gross movement toward or away from source of stimulation.

3. Child communicates needs/wants by partial body movement—movement of trunk, facial expressions, eye movements, etc.

4. Child indicates needs/wants by use of upper extremities—reaches out/pushes away with hands.

5. Child indicates needs/wants by fine motor movements—pointing, waving, etc.

6. Child communicates with simple vocalizations and/or gestures—hand to mouth = "eating," etc.

7. Child communicates with idiosyncratic single words or signs.

8. Child can communicate with single words or signs that are generally understood.

9. Child can communicate with phrases using words or formal signs (including such systems as Bliss Symbols) with persons in general.

B3

Goal Directedness: Persistence in goal directed effort relative to task demands.

1. No evidence of directed effort—holds or releases materials passively at examiner's instigation.

2. Evidence of only one attempt to get an object and/or achieve a goal problem.

3. Makes only a few attempts to reach goal, is easily distracted and/or gives up easily.

4. Makes several attempts but may be less than appropriate for task demands.

5. Efforts to achieve goals appropriate to task demands.

6. Makes persistent attempts to reach goal: repeats same strategy.

7. Perseverates on tasks, difficult to shift to new task.

8. Compulsive absorption, nothing distracts.

9. Refuses to leave task until completed, object has to be physically removed.

From Simeonsson (1978).

USING CHILD-ASSESSMENT DATA TO PLAN
GOALS AND SERVICES FOR FAMILIES

Assessment of child functioning helps to establish goals that reflect the program's efforts to enhance the handicapped child's developmental and behavioral achievement. A related and perhaps equally important purpose is to incorporate child characteristics that influence parental and family functioning into goals designed to improve or facilitate the family's adaptation to the handicapped child, as well as adaptation in general. Deriving goals is a collaborative process between families and professionals that requires cooperation and negotiation. As we have suggested elsewhere (Bailey et al., 1986; Winton & Bailey, in press), the focused interview offers the opportunity for parents and professionals to discuss assessment results in the context of the family's functioning. For example, parents may have rated their infant as having characteristics associated with a difficult temperament, and the interventionist reviewing the assessment information may assume that this difficulty is an important dimension to consider in writing goals. However, during the interview the interventionist may learn that the parents do not find that the child's characteristics pose a problem for them or their family. Another family whose child presents similar characteristics may, on the other hand, find them to be a major problem that influences their functioning. The process of collaborative goal setting will reveal these divergent views and ensure that the setting of goals is individualized and appropriate for the family.

During goal setting, parents and professionals have the chance to discuss the effect of the child's behavior on the family. For example, Child A and Child B may both be perceived as having difficult temperaments; however, Child A's specific disruptive behavior may be unpredictable sleep patterns, and Child B's may be finicky eating habits. Professionals can plan collaboratively with parents to help them take a direct approach in changing Child A's sleep/wake cycle from irregularity to greater predictability. In addition, professionals can help Child B's parents move more slowly in introducing new foods into the diet of a child who seems slow to adapt. The very act of making a plan that parents feel they can carry out should help to reduce their feelings of stress. Although temperament functions in large degree as a mediator of the child's responses and the environment's demands, specific aspects of temperament that affect family functioning can be the target of family goals.

An irritable infant or toddler with excessive caregiving demands can be a source of stress for parents and family. Although it may be difficult to alter stressful caregiving demands, parents can be helped to modify their own expectations or behaviors to reduce the associated stress. A creative approach to providing parents with relief from the demands of the child may be valuable. Parents who are unwilling to leave the child may need to develop a plan whereby each parent provides the other with specific free time each week. Others may need to call on extended family or explore community facilities that offer opportunities for respite care. The goal of relief from constant caregiving may be an appropriate one, but if it is to be realistic, it must be tailored to fit the beliefs of the family.

Parents are not the only family members to be affected by the handicapped child. The caregiving demands of a handicapped infant or toddler, and parental responses to those demands, may exhaust the parent's resources, leaving little time or energy for siblings. In this case, family stress may be attributed to the acting-out behavior of a sibling, when it actually should be attributed to the family demands of coping with the handicapped child. Appropriate goals for such a family would include the needs of the sibling, the handicapped child, and the larger family relationship.

SUMMARY

This chapter has focused on child characteristics that can affect family functioning. Although most families adapt quite well to the presence of a handicapped child, specific behaviors of the child can at times place excessive stress on the family. The handicapped child's temperament, readability, and behavioral differences have been suggested as areas to assess. These characteristics often mediate the child's responses to environmental demands, including family expectations and demands. Specific child characteristics that parents find stressful should be identified and efforts made to alleviate their effects. Parents and professionals can design goals in a collaborative manner to relieve the stress resulting from these behaviors.

REFERENCES

Abidin, R. R. (1986). *Parenting stress index* (2nd ed.) Charlottesville, Va.: Pediatric Pschology Press.

Bailey, D. B., Simeonsson, R. J., Winton, P. J., Huntington, G. S., Comfort, M., Isbell, P., O'Donnell, K. J., & Helm, J. M. (1986). Family-focused intervention: A functional model for planning, implementing, and evaluating individualized family services in early intervention. *Journal of the Division for Early Childhood, 10,* 156–171.

Bailey, D. B., & Wolery, M. (1984). *Teaching infants and preschoolers with handicaps.* Columbus, Oh.: Merrill Publishing Company.

Bayley, N. (1969). *Manual for Bayley Scales of Infant Development.* New York: Psychological Corporation.

Beckman, P. J. (1983). Influence of selected child characteristics on stress in families of handicapped infants. *American Journal of Mental Deficiency, 88,* 150–156.

Beckman, P. J., Thiele, J. E., Pokorni, J. L., & Balzer-Martin, L. (1986). Stability of behavioral characteristics in preterm infants. *Topics in Early Childhood Special Education, 6*(2), 57–67.

Blackard, M. K., & Barsh, E. T. (1982). Parents' and professionals' perceptions of the handicapped child's impact on the family. *TASH Journal, 7,* 62–70.

Carey, W. B., & McDevitt, S. C. (1978). Revision of the infant temperament questionnaire. *Pediatrics, 61,* 735–738.

Chee, F. K. W., Kreutzeberg, J. R., & Clark, D. (1978). Semicircular canal stimulation in cerebral palsied children. *Physical Therapy, 58,* 1071–1075.

Chess, S., & Fernandez, P. (1980). Do deaf children have a typical personality? *Journal of the American Academy of Child Psychiatry, 19,* 654–664.

Chess, S., & Thomas, A. (1986). *Temperament in clinical practice.* New York: Guilford Press.

Crnic, K. A., Friedrich, W. N., & Greenberg, M. T. (1983). Adaptation of families with mentally retarded children: A model of stress, coping, and family ecology. *American Journal of Mental Deficiency, 88,* 125–138.

Dolan, A. B., Matheny, A. P., & Wilson, R. S. (1974). Bayley's Infant Behavior Record: Age trends, sex differences, and behavioral correlates. *JSAS Catalog of Selected Documents in Psychology, 4*(9), MS No. 551.

Dyson, L., & Fewell, R. R. (1986). Stress and adaptation in parents of young handicapped and nonhandicapped children: A comparative study. *Journal of the Division for Early Childhood, 10*(1), 25–34.

Fewell, R. R. (1983). Assessing handicapped infants. In S. G. Garwood & R. R. Fewell (Eds.), *Educating handicapped infants* (pp. 257–297). Rockville, Md.: Aspen Systems Corporation.

Friedrich, W. N., & Friedrich, W. L. (1981). Psychosocial assets of parents of handicapped and nonhandicapped children. *American Journal of Mental Deficiency, 85,* 551–553.

Fullard, W., McDevitt, S. C. & Carey, W. B. (1984). Assessing temperament in one- to three-year-old children. *Journal of Pediatric Psychology, 9*(2), 205–217.

Gaensbauer, T. T. (1982). Regulation of emotional expression in infants from two contrasting caretaking environments. *American Academy of Child Psychiatry, 21*(2), 163–171.

Garside, R. F., Birch, H., Scott, D., Chambers, S., Kolvin, I., Tweddle, E. G., & Barber, L. M. (1975). Dimensions of temperament in infant school children. *Journal of Child Psychology and Psychiatry, 16,* 219–231.

Goldberg, S. (1977). Social competence in infancy: A model of parent-infant interaction. *Merrill-Palmer Quarterly, 23,* 163–177.

Goldman, B. D., & Johnson-Martin, N. (1987, April). *Understanding babies' cues: A comparison of parents of normally developing and handicapped infants.* Paper presented at the Biennial Meeting of the Society for Research on Child Development, Baltimore.

Holroyd, J. (1974). The questionnaire on resources and stress: An instrument to measure family response to a handicapped member. *Journal of Community Psychology, 2,* 92–94.

Holroyd, J., & McArthur, D. (1976). Mental retardation and stress on the parents: A contrast between Down's syndrome and childhood autism. *American Journal of Mental Deficiency, 80,* 431–436.

Huntington, G. S., & Simeonsson, R. J. (1987). Down's syndrome and toddler temperament. *Child: Care, Health and Development, 13,* 1–11.

Huntington, G. S., Simeonsson, R. J. Bailey, D. B., & Comfort, M. (1987). Handicapped child characteristics and maternal involvement. *Journal of Reproductive and Infant Psychology, 5,* 105–118.

Lerner, J. V. (1983). The role of temperament in psychosocial adaptation in early adolescents: A test of a "goodness of fit" model. *Journal of Genetic Psychology, 143,* 149–157.

Lerner, J. V., & Galambos, N. L. (1985). Maternal role satisfaction, mother-child interaction, and child temperament: A process model. *Developmental Psychology, 21,*(6), 1157–1164.

Matheny, A. P., Jr. (1980). Bayley's Infant Behavior Record: Behavioral components and twin analyses. *Child Development, 51,* 1157–1167.

McCollum, J. A., & Stayton, V. D. (1985). Infant/parent interaction: Studies and intervention guidelines based on the SIAI model. *Journal of the Division for Early Childhood, 9*(2), 125–135.

McDevitt, S. C., & Carey, W. B. (1978). The measurement of temperament in 3–7 year old children. *Journal of Child Psychology and Psychiatry, 19,* 245–253.

Nihira, K., Meyers, C. E., & Mink, I. (1983). Reciprocal relationships between home environment and development of TMR adolescents. *American Journal of Mental Deficiency, 88,* 139–149.

Odom, S. L., & Shuster, S. K. (1986). Natualistic inquiry and the assessment of young handicapped children and their families. *Topics in Early Childhood Special Education, 6,*(2), 68–82.

Pedersen, F., Anderson, B., & Cain, R. (1980). *Perception of Baby Temperament.* ASJS Documents.

Peterson, N. L., & Meier, J. H. (1987). Assessment and evaluation processes. In N. L. Peterson (Ed.), *Early intervention for handicapped and at-risk children* (pp. 275–326). Denver: Love Publishing.

Rothbart, M. K. (1981). Measurement of temperament in infancy. *Child Development, 52,* 569–578.

Rothbart, M. K. (1986). Longitudinal observation of infant temperament. *Developmental Psychology, 22*(3), 356–365.

Simeonsson, R. J. (1978). *Carolina Record of Individual Behavior.* Unpublished instrument. University of North Carolina, Chapel Hill, North Carolina.

Simeonsson, R. J. (1986). *Psychological and developmental assessment of special children.* Boston: Allyn and Bacon.

Simeonsson, R. J., Bailey, D. B., Huntington, G. S., & Comfort, M. (1986). Testing the concept of goodness of fit in early intervention. *Infant Mental Health Journal, 7,* 81–94.

Simeonsson, R. J., Huntington, G. S., & Parse, S. A. (1980a). Assessment of children with severe handicaps: Multiple problems—multivariate goals. *Journal of the Association for the Severely Handicapped, 5*(1), 55–72.

Simeonsson, R. J., Huntington, G. S., & Parse, S. A. (1980b). Expanding the developmental assessment of young handicapped children. *New Directions for Exceptional Children, 3,* 51–74.

Simeonsson, R. J., Huntington, G. S., Short, R. J., & Ware, W. B. (1982). The Carolina record of individual behavior: Characteristics of handicapped infants and children. *Topics in Early Childhood Special Education, 2*(2), 43–55.

Simpson, A. E., & Stevenson-Hinde, J. (1985). Temperamental characteristics of three- to four-year old boys and girls and child-family interactions. *Journal of Child Psychology and Psychiatry, 26*(1), 43–53.

Sirignano, S. W., & Lachman, M. E. (1985). Personality change during the transition to parenthood: The role of perceived infant temperament. *Developmental Psychology, 21*(3), 558–567.

Sprunger, L. W., Boyce, W. T., & Gaines, J. A. (1985). Family-infant congruence: Routines and rhythmicity in family adaptations to a young infant. *Child Development, 56*, 564–572.

Terestman, N. (1980). Mood quality and intensity in the nursery school children as a predictor of behavior disorder. *American Journal of Orthopsychiatry, 50*, 125–138.

Thoman, E. B., Denenberg, V. H., Sieval, J., Zeidner, L. P., & Becker, P. (1981). State organization in neonates: Developmental inconsistency indicates risk for developmental dysfunction. *Neuropediatrics, 12*, 45–54.

Thomas, A., & Chess, S. (1977). *Temperament and development.* New York: Brunner/Mazel.

Thomas, A., Chess, S., & Birch N. G. (1968). *Temperament and behavior disorders in children.* New York: New York University Press.

Wing, L., & Gould, J. (1978). Systematic recording of behaviors and skills of retarded and psychotic children. *Journal of Autism and Childhood Schizophrenia, 8*(1) 79–97.

Winton, P. J., & Bailey, D. B. (in press). The family-focused interview: A collaborative mechanism for family assessment and goal-setting. *Journal of the Division for Early Childhood.*

Wishart, M. C., Bidder, R. T., & Gray, O. P. (1981). Parents' report of family life with a developmentally delayed child. *Child: Care, Health and Development, 7*, 267–279.

Wolfensberger, W., & Kurtz, R. A. (1974). Measurement of parents' perception of their child's development. *Genetic Psychology Monographs, 83*, 3–92.

Yoder, P. J. (1987). Relationship between degree of infant handicap and clarity of infant cues. *American Journal of Mental Deficiency, 91*, 639–641.

4

Assessing Parent-Child Interaction

I nteractions between parents and their young children are the substance of routine family activities. Daily activities such as physical child care, incidental teaching, play activities, and problem solving promote the child's growth and development. The parent-child exchanges that occur during these tasks provide an index of family functioning. Furthermore, research has shown that parent-infant interaction is related to later child development and associated with other elements of the family system.

This chapter delineates the rationale and considerations for observational assessment of parent-child interaction and suggests criteria for selecting an assessment instrument. Examples of representative measures that have been useful in clinical settings are presented. Finally, guidelines are offered for translating assessments into goals and intervention strategies.

THE RATIONALE FOR ASSESSING PARENT-CHILD INTERACTION

Assessing parent-child interaction is important because it provides an indication of the way a family functions, the child's later development, and an

This chapter was contributed by Marilee Comfort, Wheelock College.

association with the other dimensions of family functioning. In addition, children with high-risk or handicapping conditions may require changes in typical parent-child interaction patterns.

An Index of Parent-Child Relationship and Family Functioning

The nature of the parent-child relationship and family functioning may be examined in many ways: by requesting an account of the daily activities the parent and child engage in together (McHale & Huston, 1984), by rating the physical or emotional environment of the home with an assessment instrument (Caldwell & Bradley, 1979; Meyers, Nihira, & Mink, 1984), or by asking for the parent's perception of the child (O'Donnell & Vaughn, 1985). Each approach offers valuable information about how parents and children relate to one another. Another method is to conduct observations of parent and child behavior.

Observational assessment of parent-child interactions offers the unique opportunity for an objective observer to describe the quantity and quality of interpersonal dynamics among family members. This method provides a different perspective than parental self-report questionnaires or interviews. Further, it is a more direct measure of the behaviors involved in the process of interaction than a rating of the family climate (Meyers, Mink, & Nihira, 1977; Olson, Portner, & Lavee, 1985) or the home environment (Caldwell & Bradley, 1979). A single observation is presumed to be a sample of the exchanges that occur most of the time within the family. Multiple observations provide a more complete picture. Further observation of the child with each of his or her caregivers provides a fuller understanding of the child's total caregiving environment.

Until recently, most research and intervention efforts were preoccupied with the interchange between mother and child. This communication was heralded as the infant's first social experience and the family's prime contribution to the development of the child (Sigel, Dreyer, & McGillicuddy-DeLisi, 1984). In effect, developmental psychologists promoted the concept of the single-parent family long before the recent rise in its incidence (Minuchin, 1985). Fathers were credited merely with indirect effects on infants, channeled through the mother's behavior (Lamb, 1981b). Studies conducted over the past 15 years, however, have demonstrated the competence of fathers in play and caregiving with children and their unique contributions to child development (Lamb, 1981a).

Although fathers have typically relinquished child care responsibilities to mothers in favor of play activities, empirical evidence demonstrates the salience of paternal involvement with children in both aspects of parenting when fathers choose to participate (Parke & Tinsley, 1981). In a study of single-parent families in which fathers were the primary caregivers, they performed the instrumental (e.g., physical care, teaching, social supervision) and expressive (e.g., nurturance, problem solving) tasks of "mothering" and reported satisfaction with their roles and relationships with their children (Risman, 1986). Other research on primary and shared caregiving by fathers confirms these results (Lamb, 1982). Thus, assessment of parent-child interaction should include the mother, father, or principal caregivers.

Later Child Development

Early social interactions between parents and child become the foundation for future relationships between child and parents (Cath, Gurwitt, & Ross, 1982; Lamb, 1981a; Maccoby & Martin, 1983), siblings (Vandell & Wilson, 1987), and peers (Waters, Wippman, & Sroufe, 1979). Such interactions affect development of cognitive abilities (Bee et al., 1982; Ramey, Farran, & Campbell, 1979), language (Bruner, 1977), social skills (Maccoby & Martin, 1983; Tronick & Gianino, 1986), and emotional stability (Cicchetti & Serafica, 1981). Research suggests that a flexible style of parental behavior that fits well with the child's behavior promotes mutually satisfying parent-child exchanges and, in turn, fosters the development of the child. More precisely, optimal parental behaviors with young children include (1) sensitivity to infant cues (Bee et al., 1982); (2) responsiveness to child distress (Crockenberg, 1981); (3) moderate levels of reciprocal interaction (Belsky, Rovine, & Taylor, 1984); (4) affectionate, cognitively stimulating behavior (Clarke-Stewart, 1973; Pettit & Bates, 1984); (5) parental enjoyment (Mahoney, Finger, & Powell, 1985); and (6) responsive turn-taking exchanges (Vandell & Wilson, 1987). Child behaviors that characterize effective parent-child interaction include readable cues (McGehee & Eckerman, 1983; Fraiberg, 1974), predictable behavior (Huntington, 1985), coping behaviors for repairing mismatches in parent-child behavior (Tronick & Gianino, 1986), and social turn taking (Vandell & Wilson, 1987). The link between parent-child interaction and the child development underscores the need to assess early social experiences within the family.

Other Elements of the Family System and Environment

From the family systems perspective (introduced in Chapter 2), the child's early life experiences with the parents are inseparable from the influences of other family subsystems (e.g., husband-wife, sibling-sibling) and the roles of family members (Belsky, 1981; Minuchin, 1985). In a literature review on early infant experiences within the family, Belsky (1981) emphasized the need to recognize the mutual influences of parenting, the marital relationship, and infant behavior and development. Subsequently, he presented a conceptual model of the determinants of parenting (Belsky, 1984) that included (1) parental characteristics (e.g., developmental history, personality); (2) child characteristics (e.g., temperament, developmental status); and (3) social context of the family (e.g., marital relationship, employment, social network).

Clearly, a full understanding of the complexities of family functioning and development requires a consideration of the interactions within and among family subsystems. These interactions, as well as the characteristics and behavior of individuals and the entire family, must then be interpreted within the context of the extended family, the social and work networks, and the community (Belsky, 1984; Bronfenbrenner, Moen, & Garbarino, 1984; Garbarino, 1982). Coupling an ecological view of family functioning with the family systems perspective, we can describe the family as having ongoing reciprocal interactions among its members and with the sociocultural, economic, and political environments in which it is embedded (Bronfenbrenner et al., 1984).

Children with High-Risk or Handicapping Conditions

The presence in the family of an infant with a high-risk or handicapping condition presents a different set of circumstances for parent-child interaction. Assessment of this interaction in families with high-risk or handicapped children is particularly essential for understanding the alterations that occur. For these parents and children, an optimal dyadic match may be difficult to achieve (Bromwich, 1976; Goldberg, 1977). Idiosyncratic cues of developmentally delayed or impaired children are typically confusing. Preterm babies, for example, have been described as "responsive but unreadable" social partners (McGehee & Eckerman, 1983), owing to their disorganized responses to external stimuli. Blind infants often substitute hand movements for eye contact (Fraiberg, 1974) or become immobile instead of turning toward the parent's voice (Als, Tronick, & Brazelton, 1980), thereby altering commonly expected interpersonal behaviors.

Explaining the difficulty that caregivers may have in interpreting child cues, Goldberg (1977) suggests that parents' feelings of competence during interactions with their infants are based on infant readability, predictability, and responsiveness. If problems occur in any one of these areas, the dyad may become trapped in a cycle of trial-and-error responses to unintelligible behavioral cues. Presented with unique child characteristics or behaviors, parents of developmentally delayed or handicapped children often develop interaction patterns that differ from those of parents of normally developing children (Ainsworth, 1979; Goldberg, 1977; Marfo, 1984). Although these behaviors differ from the norm, they are not necessarily maladaptive and should be assessed carefully to detect patterns of strengths and weaknesses.

KEY CONCEPTS FOR UNDERSTANDING PARENT-CHILD INTERACTION

An understanding of key concepts related to parent-child interaction facilitates observational scoring and interpretation of assessments. Much of the recent theoretical work on this topic is based on attachment theory (Ainsworth, 1979; Bowlby, 1982), and the family systems (Minuchin, 1985) and transactional perspectives (Sameroff, 1982) of child and family development. Over the past two decades, conceptual discourse on parent-child interaction has been advanced from the fields of developmental psychology, developmental pediatrics, and family therapy. The interested reader is referred to the available reviews, which are extensive (e.g., Bristol & Gallagher, 1986; Lamb, 1981a; Maccoby & Martin, 1983; Parke & Tinsley, 1981). A brief synopsis of key concepts follows.

Early social interactions between parent and child are characterized as *bidirectional* (Bell & Harper, 1977; Lewis & Rosenblum, 1974) and *homeostatic* (Brazelton, 1982; Tronick & Gianino, 1986). In other words, both members of the dyad are viewed as active agents who affect each other's behavior and share in the self-righting balance that is negotiated continually within the partnership. The *transactions* that occur involve mutual adaptations of caregiver and child in a context of ongoing environmental changes (Sameroff, 1982). In the *joint regulation* of parent-infant behavior, the parent initially acts as an "envelope" to facilitate organization of infant behavior and state, thereby allowing the baby to join the process (Brazelton, 1982). To promote social competence, the parent "frames" the infant's behavior, acting as if the baby is an incredibly bright, communicative being (Kaye, 1982). These early social interchanges are seen as the forerunners of language (Bruner, 1977).

As the infant becomes more competent, assuming more responsibility within social exchanges, a gradual *progression toward shared reciprocity* occurs (Ainsworth, 1979; Kaye, 1982). In regulating the reciprocity with the parent, the socially capable infant uses a set of coping strategies described by Tronick and Gianino (1986) to promote a *match* of parent and child behaviors. The *"goodness-of-fit"* (Thomas & Chess, 1977) between the child and the caregiving environment is believed to lead to optimal interchanges and development of the child (Simeonsson, Bailey, Huntington, & Comfort, 1986).

From a broader context, parent-child interaction is viewed as *embedded* in the processes of the family system (Minuchin, 1985), which, in turn, influence and are influenced by the dynamics of the *social network, community,* and *society* (Bronfenbrenner, 1979). What is learned in the early relations between parent and infant will impact on more distal infant-sibling and infant-peer relationships (Vandell & Wilson, 1987) and later peer relationships (Waters, Wippman, & Sroufe, 1979).

This synopsis of key concepts illustrates the rich foundation established by researchers from various perspectives regarding the interactive process between parent and child. Assessing families with high-risk or handicapped children is facilitated when the interventionist has a basic familiarity with how parents and children engage one another under normal circumstances.

One of the forerunners to translate theoretical concepts into parent-child assessment and developmental intervention with medically and environmentally high-risk babies was Rose Bromwich (1981). She devised a qualitative system (described in Table 4.2 on p.80) for assessing mother-infant relations that gave practitioners a sound conceptual base to guide and evaluate their work with families. During the last five years, attention to parent-child interaction has flourished in early intervention services (Kysela & Marfo, 1983). A number of assessment scales have been developed to enable systematic observation of play, teaching, and feeding behaviors, as will be illustrated later in this chapter. In addition, several early intervention programs focus exclusively on dyadic interaction in their work with families of children with developmental delays (e.g., Bromwich, 1981; Mahoney & Powell, 1986; McCollum, 1984; Sanders, 1987). The efficacy of these programs has been demonstrated in part with parent-child interaction measures.

PARAMETERS OF PARENT-CHILD INTERACTION ASSESSMENT

To ensure meaningful assessment of parent-child interaction, some decisions must precede the observational session. These decisions involve defining the parameters that best fit the purpose of assessment, and the resources and constraints of the families and the service program. The following section outlines choices regarding the situational context of parent-child observation, the level of behaviors of interest, the types of coding systems available, and the operational definitions of behaviors to be observed.

Situational Context

At least five questions must be addressed in planning the situational context of parent-child interaction assessment. First, what is the *activity* of most interest for observation? Interactions between parent and child normally occur during feeding, bathing, and play. Play interchanges often include teaching or problem-solving episodes. Any one of these activities can be a useful forum for assessing the nature of parent-child interaction. However, behaviors will differ among activities owing to the change in context (Power & Parke, 1982).

Play is the activity most frequently observed in clinical and research settings because the behaviors observed generalize to other activities, such as dressing or bathing, that may incorporate play. Feeding and bathing behaviors are more specialized, and observation of these activities is more difficult in terms of timing and materials. When observation is conducted for the purpose of individual family assessment, it is most useful to select the activity that matches the needs and interests of the family. For example, if a mother, father, and baby tremendously enjoy playing together but the parents express distress with the amount of time, diminished nutrition, and unpleasant atmosphere involved in meals, feeding would be the logical choice of activity to assess parent-child interaction. If parent-child interaction is being assessed to evaluate intervention services, the choice of activity must match program goals and objectives.

The second question is, what *setting* will be used? Parents and children may be observed in the home or in the developmental center, preschool, or clinic playroom or therapy room. Often, the choice hinges on practical factors such as availability of space, equipment, transportation, babysitting, travel costs, scheduling, or security of equipment. Human factors, however, such as family comfort and convenience, and staff time and energy, are equally important considerations in creating a valid assessment situation. The best setting is one that elicits the most typical sample of dyadic behavior that can be obtained, given the resources and constraints of the families and the program. However, one must also consider whether the behaviors of particular interest for assessment (e.g., limit-setting, gross motor exploration) can emerge within the selected setting (Power & Parke, 1982).

A third consideration is the *structure* of the observation session. "Free" play sessions are left relatively unstructured to promote a naturalistic environment for interaction. The parent is usually asked to "play with your child as you normally would when you have a few minutes to yourselves" (Mahoney et al., 1985; Farran et al., 1987). Feeding observations follow similar open-ended procedures (Barnard & Bee, 1984). On the other hand, the parent could be given a specific task to teach the child (Rosenberg, Robinson, & Beckman, 1984; Barnard & Bee, 1984) or a problem to be solved, such as unlocking a toy chest (S. J. Meisels, personal communication, November 24, 1986). Instructions sometimes include the degree or type (e.g., verbal, physical prompts) of assistance that the parent is allowed to provide in accomplishing the task.

Two other dimensions of structure for consideration are materials and length of observation. For play observations, a standard set of developmentally appropriate toys and equipment may be provided or the parent and child may be permitted to use their own *materials*. The choice of materials may influence the interaction. If, for example, the family is accustomed to a developmental specialist arriving for a home visit with a bag of toys each week, it may be quite natural for a standard set of toys to be presented for the observation session. However, if the usual practice for home visits is to use the child's own toys and household items, the introduction of unfamiliar items during the observation session could be disruptive for the child or stressful to the parent. Likewise, providing an infant seat as part of the standard equipment for interaction sessions may convey to the parent that it must be used, whether or not the infant and parent are accustomed to it. Decide what materials and equipment will best facilitate the desired observation. Then inform the parent that their use is discretionary, unless a specific task is assigned.

The *length of time* for observation typically ranges from 3 to 20 minutes, depending on the activity and the structure of the session. Many assessment scales recommend a minimal time to obtain a meaningful sample of behavior to score validly with the particular instrument. In general, 10 to 20 minutes is a long enough time span to obtain a representative sample of parent-child interaction to make frequency counts or qualitative judgments about behavior. With behavior counts, shorter periods of observation are sometimes used because of the intense nature of the coding system. Observations of a single activity for more than 20 minutes tend to tax the patience and attention span of both parent and child. If given the choice, however, it is better to err on the side of more than less observation time.

The fourth question regarding situational context is, who are the *participants* to be observed? As mentioned previously, mother and child have been the members of the family most commonly observed for parent-child interaction assessment. As fathers and other caregivers (e.g., grandmothers) are increasingly included in the intervention process (Meyer, Vadasy, Fewell, & Schell, 1982; Markowitz, 1984), they also need to be included in caregiver-child assessment. In fact, even if the intervention program does not actively involve more than one caregiver, observation of all principal caregivers offers valuable contextual information for interpreting the assessment of and planning goals regarding interactions of the child with the primary caregiver.

Most often, interactional assessments have been limited to dyadic observations because of the limitations of observational methodology and scheduling difficulties. However, the parameters may be extended in a variety of combinations to observe family groupings such as mother-father-child (Clarke-Stewart, 1978; Pedersen, 1980; Stoneman, Brody, & Abbott, 1983), mother-child-sibling, grandmother-mother-child, or mother-father-child-sibling (Lewis & Feiring, 1982). Of course, as the number of participants increases, so does the need for multiple observers, the complexity of the assessment system, the interpretation of the scores, and the complications of scheduling and videotaping. If these barriers can be overcome, assessment of the interactions of a natural family grouping certainly would yield pertinent information about the family that might offer interesting contextual background for interpretation of assessments of smaller family subsystems.

The final consideration concerning the situational context is the *format* of assessment. Will it be conducted live or from videotape? Both methods have advantages and disadvantages. Live observation and scoring require that the trained observer or observers be present (or behind an observation window) and that reliability of scoring be well established, although no special equipment or expertise is necessary to conduct the session. The observer can move readily or shift attention as necessary to keep pace with momentary changes in interactive behaviors of the parent and child. However, the presence of an observer could be distracting or intimidating to either partner of the dyad, and there is no opportunity for replays of episodes the observer might miss.

Where videotapes are used, the interactive session is preserved for subsequent viewing by observers, the family, or other staff members. The tapes can be assessed at a later, more convenient time, and visual comparisons can be made between tapes filmed at different times, such as pre- and postintervention. Drawbacks to the use of videotapes include the cost of video equipment and supplies and the need to plan for operation and maintenance of the equipment. The position or immobility of a camera sometimes precludes a clear picture of the parent's or child's behavior, whereas the presence of a camera operator for flexible filming may be intrusive for some families. To yield meaningful information for assessment, the tape must capture concurrent facial, body, and vocal expressions of the parent and child in relation to each other. There are trade-offs to be made with either format. The best choice is the one that fits most easily with family preferences, the routine of the ongoing services, and the resources of the program.

Planning the situational context for parent-child interaction assessment is a detailed task, but one that will determine to a great extent the usefulness of the resulting data. It is especially desirable to standardize the situational context when group comparisons are of interest. However, for individual family assessment and goal planning, family comfort may ultimately be the most helpful barometer in planning the parent-child interaction observation. One must establish a good rapport with the family before requesting an observation of them, to determine the best situational context for them and to gain their trust. After all, if the observation session is not representative of typical parent-child behavior, it is of little use in planning intervention.

Comparisons of parent-child interaction across various activities, settings, structural details (Power & Parke, 1982) and participants (Lamb & Elster, 1985; Stoneman, Brody, & Abbott, 1983) indicate that the situational context does indeed influence interaction patterns. For example, Stoneman, Brody, and Abbott (1983) found that during father-child observation, fathers appeared highly involved in interchange with their children when observed in depth. In contrast, when mother, father, and child were present during play, father behaved differently, seeming to be uninvolved in the interaction. Therefore, it is necessary to decide which combination of contextual factors is most meaningful for individual family assessment and program evaluation. This may entail planning a flexible context for individual family assessment and a standardized context for group comparisons and program evaluation. During the initial comprehensive family assessment, parent-child observations should be scheduled at a relaxed time, after the practitioner has established rapport with the family and when the parent and child are not exhausted from other assessments.

Level of Behaviors of Interest

After establishing the situational context for the observation of parent-child interaction, the level of specificity of behavior that will be assessed must be determined. Again, the decision depends on the purpose of assessment. Two levels of behavior can be distinguished for scoring. *Molecular behaviors* are detailed behaviors of parent and child that define the flow of interactive exchange. *Molar dimensions* represent broader units of behavior that are clusters of molecular behaviors or more abstract properties of the parent-child interchange. For example, smile, gentle touch, and positive vocalization are several molecular behaviors encompassed in the molar dimension of affectionate maternal behavior. Assessment of molecular levels of behavior are used most often when specific behaviors, such as eye contact, vocal imitation, or object play, are targeted for change (McCollum & Stayton, 1985). Molar dimensions are used to characterize the style of interaction that occurs between parent and child (Farran, Kasari, Comfort, & Jay, 1986; Mahoney et al., 1985). The level of behavior selected for assessment should match the focus of intervention. For example, a public health nurse who spends much time orienting mothers to engagement and disengagement cues of high-risk babies may prefer a checklist of molecular behaviors to assess maternal progress (Barnard & Bee, 1984). In contrast, a social worker who works globally on enhancing socioemotional aspects of maternal-infant relations may favor a set of molar dimensions to evaluate parent-infant interaction (Bromwich, 1981). In reality, the level of behaviors on assessment scales designed for clinical use may not fit neatly into the molecular and molar categories. More often, the wording of the items falls between the two extremes. Nevertheless, the choice of the level of behaviors that fits well with the family or program goals being assessed will result in a more meaningful evaluation.

Type of Assessment Scale

Three types of assessment scales are available. A *behavioral count* system involves counting the frequency of specified parent and/or child behaviors during a series of set intervals. The behaviors are usually defined at the molecular level and are recorded over intervals ranging from 1 to 40 seconds. The total frequency of each behavior is tallied to obtain a quantitative assessment of the interaction. A *rating scale* is a set of molar dimensions for which the observer makes qualitative judgments about the behavior of parent and/or child. The scoring system is arranged on a multipoint scale, often defined by behavioral anchors that provide guidance and a standard of evaluation for the observer. A *binary checklist* is a list of parent and/or child behaviors stated in measurable terms. Observers record whether each behavior occurs during the interactive session. It is similar to a behavioral count in that it assesses the occurrences of specific behaviors, yet it most often addresses larger types of behaviors, such as "parent describes perceptual qualities of the task materials to the child" (Barnard & Bee, 1984). In some respects the three types of parent-child observational tools represent a continuum, with the behavioral count at one pole, the rating scale at the opposite pole, and the binary checklist in the middle. The assessment scales presented in this chapter fit along this continuum at various points, depending on the type of scale and the level of behavior each represents.

Definitions of Observed Behaviors

Despite the increasing number of scales available to assess parent-child interaction, there is a remarkable overlap in the behaviors identified for observation. This similarity is a result of the various authors' reliance on a common strain of child development empirical literature in developing the instruments. However, the likenesses are more often in nomenclature than definition. To illustrate this point, Table 4.1 presents four examples of definitions for "responsive" behavior of parent and/or child during teaching or play episodes.

The diversity in definitions of "responsive" behavior illustrated in Table 4.1 demonstrates the need to examine assessment instruments carefully before making a selection. Molar dimensions in particular, which are multifaceted constructs, understandably have a variety of meanings to different people. In selecting an assessment tool, the practitioner should meticulously review the wording, rather than assuming that the author of the scale uses definitions identical with his or her own. In addition, such a review will reveal the clarity with which the items are written. If the author's definitions are ambiguous, it may be difficult to gain reliability on the scale.

SELECTING A PARENT-CHILD INTERACTION SCALE

The goal in selecting a parent-child interaction assessment scale is to obtain a "goodness-of-fit" between the needs of the service program and the characteristics of the instrument by considering the following factors:

1. Purpose of assessment
2. Characteristics of the families being assessed
3. Behaviors of interest
4. Resources available for training, assessment, and intervention

First, potential purposes of assessment of parent-child interaction include individual family assessment upon entry into a program, changes in family functioning during transition periods, evaluation of services, and comparison of a network of statewide intervention programs. Different ap-

TABLE 4.1
Examples of Definitions of Responsive Behavior

From Rosenberg and Robinson, 1985

1 Parent is entirely unresponsive to the child's interests and moods. Tasks are presented in an uncaring way.

to

7 Parent is entirely responsive to the child's interests and moods.

From Mahoney, 1985

1 Highly unresponsive. There is a chronic failure to react to the child's expressions. The extremely unresponsive mother seems geared almost exclusively to her own wishes, moods, and activities. Mother's interventions and initiations of interaction are prompted or shaped largely by signals within herself.

to

5 Highly responsive. This mother responds promptly and appropriately to the child's signals. Her responses are temporally contingent upon the child's signals and communications. She nearly always gives the child what he indicates that he wants, although not invariably so. When she feels that it is best not to comply with his demands, she is tactful in acknowledging his communication and in offering an acceptable alternative.

proaches to assessment may be required for various purposes. For example, to assess individual family progress, a program might use a behavioral count of individualized target behaviors. To compare a statewide set of programs, the tool of choice might be a rating scale of molar dimensions applicable to diverse intervention perspectives.

A second consideration in selecting an instrument is determining the characteristics of the families being assessed. All assessment instruments are not appropriate for all families. A scale that emphasizes parental teaching skills (e.g., Rosenberg et al., 1984), for example, would be useless in evaluating a mother who sees no value in and channels no effort into teaching her baby. Likewise, a multiple baseline behavioral count that requires videotaping or the conspicuous presence of a coder for interval coding of behaviors (e.g., McCollum, 1984) would not be the best instrument to use in assessing a father who thinks he is suspected of mistreating his handicapped child.

A third issue to consider is which interactive behaviors are of most interest for assessment and intervention. This issue goes one step beyond the questions previously discussed regarding the level of behaviors of interest

TABLE 4.1
Continued

From Farran, Kasari, Comfort, and Jay, 1986

Amount of Responsiveness

1 Adult never responds to child's initiations, verbalizations, demands, and distress.

to

5 Adult almost always responds to child's initiations, verbalizations, demands, and distress.

Quality of Responsiveness

1 Adult responds abruptly, forcefully, very intensely, harshly.

to

5 Adult responds in a gentle, sensitive, positive manner; may respond enthusiastically, with delight and spontaneity.

Appropriateness of Responsiveness

1 Seldom good synchrony of response to child's activities; adult overwhelms child with quickness of response or is too slow in response.

to

5 Adult's response to child is almost always appropriate to child's needs. Good synchrony of response; neither too quick nor too slow.

From Barnard and Bee, 1984

Parent's Response to Distress
Sum of items regarding verbalizations, positioning, handling, diverting attention.

Child's Responsiveness to Parents
Sum of items regarding gaze, eye contact, vocalizations, smile, nonverbal cues.

---

and relates to identification of particular behaviors that would prove most meaningful for planning intervention with the families being assessed. The goal is to choose an instrument that reveals information about the aspects of parent-child interaction valued by the families and the service program. This process can be facilitated by talking with families about what aspects are important, discussing a few case examples with fellow staff members, reading case studies presented in the literature (e.g., Bromwich, 1981; McCollum, 1984), and reviewing the content of available assessment scales.

TABLE 4.2
Parent-Child Interaction Assessment Instruments

Dyadic Parent-Child Interaction Coding System

(Robinson & Eyberg, 1981; Eyberg & Robinson, 1982)

Type of scale	Behavioral count
Purpose	To assess degree to which parent's or child's behavior during play is deviant and to evaluate effectiveness of treatment
Reported population	Children with behavior problems, also normal children, 2–7 years; mothers and fathers of low- and mid-class, single and 2-parent families with ± 2 children, parent age = 28–32 years
Examples of behaviors assessed	Parent's direct and indirect commands, labeled and unlabeled praise, positive and negative physical contact, descriptive statement or question; child's compliance, noncompliance, whine, yell
Administration procedures	Count frequency of behaviors continuously during two 5-minute play sessions—child-directed interaction, parent-directed interaction—in clinic playroom; dyads observed twice, one week apart
Training	Read manual; practice coding role-played videotapes; practice coding live clinic families; train to .90 reliability
Reliability	Reliability maintained by providing feedback to coders on 80% of the sessions and requiring live codings of families periodically
Validity	Correctly classified 94% of families as those with and without problems and predicted 61% of variance in child behavior problems reported at home by parents
Reference	E. A. Robinson & S. M. Eyberg. The dyadic parent-child interaction coding system: Standardization and validation. *Journal of Consulting and Clinical Psychology,* 1981, *49,* 245–250.

Finally, given the resources available for training, assessment, and intervention in a particular service program, which instrument is most feasible to use? Assessment systems vary widely in the requirements for training, equipment, and supplies. The needs for staff time, clinical experience, and ease of interpretation and translation into goals vary as well. All these requisites must be weighed in the context of financial and staff resources and the time constraints of the service program when selecting a parent-child interaction scale.

TABLE 4.2
Continued

Social Interaction Assessment/Intervention (McCollum, 1984; McCollum & Stayton, 1985)	
Type of scale	Behavioral count
Purpose	Evaluation of parent-handicapped child interaction pre-/postintervention to increase parent's ability to make independent adjustments to child's behavior during play
Reported population	Severely motor- and cognitively delayed children, 2–34 months; mothers of lower mid-income families with 1 and 2 parents, 0–3 siblings, ages = 20s–30s
Examples of behaviors assessed	Communicative social interaction; individualized target behaviors for parent and child, e.g., imitation, vocalization, turn taking
Administration procedures	Videotapes of 4-minute play episodes in home; count target behaviors in 5–10 second intervals; 10 weeks of taping baseline and two intervention phases in multiple baseline design, plus follow-up tape
Training	Not reported
Reliability	Interrater = .80; maintained by random check of 20% of tapes
Validity	Demonstrated changes in parent and child behaviors in various contexts
Reference	J. A. McCollum & V. D. Stayton. Infant/parent interaction: Studies and intervention guidelines based on the SIAI model. *Journal of the Division for Early Childhood*, 1985, *9*(2), 125–135.

Because these factors differ from one program to the next, no single assessment scale can be recommended for all practitioners. It would be ideal for individual family assessment and program evaluation if an instrument could be developed and tailored especially to the needs and resources of each program. However, given the time and expertise required for such work, that is not a plausible solution. Furthermore, comparisons among programs and populations would be facilitated greatly by widespread use of a few, rather than a multitude of, parent-child interaction assessment scales (Towle, Farran, & Comfort, in press). The varieties of available instruments with demonstrated utility and flexibility in different clinical settings make it unnecessary for each program to develop its own tool.

Eight examples of parent-child interaction observational instruments are described in Table 4.2. They were selected from a broader review of obser-

TABLE 4.2
Continued

Parent Behavior Progression

(Bromwich, 1976, 1981)

Type of scale	Binary checklist
Purpose	Assess infant-related maternal behaviors to develop short-term goals aimed at changing maternal attitudes and behavior for the purpose of enhancing maternal-infant interaction
Reported population	Parents of premature/low-birthweight infants at risk for health or developmental problems, 9–24 months; heterogeneous SES, maternal age and family structure, black, Caucasian, Chicano
Examples of behaviors assessed	Six levels ranging from maternal enjoyment of infant to mother independently providing developmentally appropriate activities; behaviors such as parent's pleasure in watching infant, physical proximity, awareness of signs of distress, comfort, provides stable caregiver, provides variety of stimulation
Administration procedures	For use by practitioners familiar with family being assessed; two forms for birth–9 months, 9–36 months; establish rapport, observe spontaneous interaction, talk informally about activities with infant; *after* session with parent check behaviors on PBP if evidence from observation or parent report
Training	Not reported
Reliability	Not reported
Validity	Utility in understanding maternal behavior and intervening with families demonstrated with case studies
Reference	R. Bromwich. *Working with parents and infants: An interactional approach.* Baltimore: University Park Press, 1981.

vational coding systems developed for research and evaluation of social interaction between parents and children with high-risk or handicapping conditions (Towle et al., in press). Each tool in the table was designed specifically for practitioners, although most are also appropriate for research use.

TABLE 4.2
Continued

Nursing Child Assessment Teaching and Feeding Scales

(Barnard & Bee, 1984; Bee et al. 1982)

Type of scale	Binary checklist
Purpose	Assessment of parent and child behaviors during teaching and feeding as screening device and pre-/postintervention
Reported population	Healthy, normally developing children, 1–36 months, preterm infants, 4–8 months; mothers of full range of educational status, 1- and 2-parent families, mostly Caucasian, also black and Hispanic (unpublished list of programs using NCAST with families of handicapped babies available from Barnard)
Examples of behaviors assessed	Parent's verbalizations, positioning, handling; child's gaze, verbal cues; factor analyzed into six subscales: parent's sensitivity to cues, response to distress, cognitive and socioemotional growth fostering; child's clarity of cues, responsiveness
Administration procedures	Check behaviors observed after 3–5 minutes of teaching; feeding observed time varies per dyad; rating time = 15 minutes per scale; 73/76–item binary checklists
Training	Nine-day sequence (total 54 hours) led by trained instructors who facilitate use of numerous training videotapes; .85 reliability required with partner on five practice scorings during live home observations; substantial costs for instructor training and videotapes
Reliability	Interrater = .70–.83; Internal consistency = .67–.86
Validity	Moderate correlations of cognitive and socioemotional growth fostering with HOME scores; predicts subsequent child IQ and language development at 12 and 24 months
Reference	H. L. Bee, K. E. Barnard, S. J. Eyres, C. A. Gray, M. A. Hammond, A. L. Spietz, C. Snyder, & B. Clark. Prediction of IQ and language skill from perinatal status, child performance, family characteristics, and mother-infant interaction. *Child Development*, 1982, *53*, 1134–1156.

Four of the eight instruments in Table 4.2 are rating scales, which is the most common type of scale available for clinical use. The populations noted in the table are those reported in published articles or books describing the

TABLE 4.2
continued

Interaction Rating Scales	
(Clark & Siefer, 1985)	
Type of scale	Rating scale
Purpose	Assess parental sensitivity to child behavior and reciprocity of interactions during free play
Reported population	Heterogeneous group of Down's syndrome, neurologically impaired, multiply handicapped, and high-risk infants and their mothers (maternal characteristics not reported)
Examples of behaviors assessed	Parent's imitating, affect; child's gaze aversion, social referencing; dyadic reciprocity; behaviors grouped as interaction style, social referencing, assessment of context
Administration procedures	Rate split-screen 8-minute videotapes of parent-child unstructured play filmed pre-, mid-, and postgroup intervention; 10-item rating scale, with five levels per item
Training	Not reported
Reliability	Scoring agreement = .91 for three raters; agreement re: clinical significance = .89
Validity	Moderately high correlations with second-by-second coding of parent-child behaviors; demonstrated changes in parent behavior; related to child's cognitive development.
Reference	G. N. Clark & R. Siefer. Assessment of parents' interactions with their developmentally delayed infants. *Infant Mental Health Journal*, 1985, *6*, 214–225.

measures. The diversity of child and parental characteristics is quite broad, ranging from healthy, normally developing infants to multiply handicapped children, and low-income single parents to middle-class two-parent families. Personal communications with several of the authors indicate that a number of the instruments have been administered with other populations as well although specific information regarding their applicability is not generally available. The representative examples of behaviors assessed are not intended to include the entire repertoire of each scale. They extend over the entire continuum from molecular behaviors (e.g., McCollum, 1984; Robinson & Eyberg, 1981) to molar dimensions (e.g., Bromwich, 1981; Farran et al., 1986). Situational contexts delineated under "Administration procedures" vary greatly. The examples include play, teaching, and feeding observations conducted in centers and at home from live sessions and video-

TABLE 4.2
Continued

Teaching Skills Inventory

(Rosenberg, Robinson, & Beckman, 1984; Rosenberg & Robinson, 1985)

Type of scale	Rating scale
Purpose	Assessment of parent's teaching skills with handicapped child pre-/postintervention
Reported population	Heterogeneous group of mentally retarded children with mixed and multiple handicaps, mild to severe disabilities, 2–36 months; mothers primarily Caucasian, mid-income, at least high school graduates
Examples of behaviors assessed	Parent's clarity of verbal instruction, task modification, effectiveness of prompts; child's interest
Administration procedures	Rate 4-minute videotapes of interaction in center pre-/post verbal feedback and instruction; 10 items, seven levels/item
Training	Four-session sequence (total = 8 hours) with practice rating videotapes between sessions
Reliability	Interrater = .64–.83 on items; internal consistency = .96
Validity	Demonstrated changes in parent behavior after intervention
Reference	S. Rosenberg, C. Robinson, & P. Beckman. Teaching skills inventory: A measure of parent performance. *Journal of the Division for Early Childhood,* 1984, *8,* 107–113.

tapes. The predominant mode reported is videotaped play sessions. However, most of the instruments (other than highly specialized scales, such as the Nursing Child Assessment Teaching and Feeding Scales) could be used in alternate situational contexts.

For most of the scales, little information was provided concerning training procedures and materials. This is an unfortunate oversight, as training issues can be a crucial element in the choice of an assessment instrument. The limited information offered for the majority of the tools regarding their reliability and validity is an indication of the early stage of development of parent-child interaction observational assessment. Because most of the scales in Table 4.2 are in the throes of development, before using them one

TABLE 4.2
Continued

Maternal Behavior Rating Scale

(Mahoney, Finger, & Powell, 1985)

Type of scale	Rating scale
Purpose	Assess quality of maternal interactive behavior during play with young mentally retarded children for use in program evaluation
Reported Population	Organically impaired, mentally retarded (primarily Down's syndrome) children, 1–3 years; mid-class mothers, 60% Caucasian, mostly married, 68% unemployed
Examples of behaviors assessed	Parent's expressiveness, warmth, sensitivity to child state, achievement orientation, social stimulation, effectiveness, directiveness; child's activity level, attention span, enjoyment, expressiveness
Administration procedures	Rate immediately after viewing 10-minute videotape of dyadic free play filmed in home with standard set of toys; two raters; ratings determined by consensus of two observers if disagreement
Training	50 hours, procedure not reported
Reliability	.76 after training, .81 during study for exact agreement on total scale; .93–1.00 per item agreement within 1 point
Validity	Accounted for 25% of variance in child developmental status on Bayley scale
Reference	G. Mahoney, I. Finger, & A. Powell. Relationship of maternal behavioral style to the development of organically impaired mentally retarded infants. *American Journal of Mental Deficiency*, 1985, *90*, 296–302.

would be well-advised to contact the authors to obtain details about revisions, insights into administration procedures, and further information about training, populations, reliability, and validity.

TRANSLATING PARENT-CHILD INTERACTION ASSESSMENTS INTO GOALS

Parent-child interaction measures are mechanisms for systematic observation, rather than diagnostic or prescriptive tools. They help the observer understand the process of interaction occurring within the dyad and iden-

TABLE 4.2
Continued

Parent/Caregiver Involvement Scale

(Farran, Kasari, Comfort & Jay, 1986; Farran et al., 1987)

Type of scale	Rating scale
Purpose	Description of parent's involvement in play interaction with handicapped, high-risk, or normally developing children
Reported population	Mentally retarded, medically or environmentally high risk, multiply handicapped children, 2–57 months; normally developing children ±3 years; mothers and fathers of heterogeneous SES, low SES, or mid SES, varied parental age and number of siblings, 1- and 2-parent families, Caucasian and black
Examples of behaviors assessed	Adult's amount, quality, appropriateness of involvement via 11 behaviors—e.g., physical, verbal, responsiveness, control; overall impression of affective climate and learning environment
Administration procedures	Rate after 20-minute live or videotaped observation of free play; rating = 20 minutes for 38 items, five levels per item
Training	Three-hour session using training videotape and workbook, best when facilitated by instructor; practice ratings on tapes thereafter to demonstrate reliability of at least .85
Reliability	.77–.87 on AQAI subscales in home, .54–.93 on AQAI subscales on tape
Validity	Moderate to high correlations with behavioral counts of parent-child behaviors; associations with parental and child characteristics (e.g., locus of control, support, temperament) similar to those presented in developmental literature
Reference	D. C. Farran, C. Kasari, P. Yoder, L. Harber, G. S. Huntington & M. Comfort-Smith. Rating mother-child interactions in handicapped and at-risk infants. In T. Tamir (Ed.), *Stimulation and intervention in infant development.* London: Freund Publishing House, 1987.

tify areas that may need intervention. A cookbook approach to parent-child assessment and goal setting, therefore, is inappropriate. That is, merely teaching the parent those behaviors for which low scores were received may produce favorable changes in scores, but may not generalize to other interactive situations. Such a limited approach of "teaching to the test" undervalues the complexity of the parent-child dyad, the family system, and the individuality of families. Instead, the practitioner must build on the *patterns* of strengths and target the *patterns* of weaknesses in parent-child interaction for intervention, while considering the effects of changes on personal attributes, the family system, and the environmental context.

Most parent-child interaction goals with families of young high-risk or handicapped children define the parent as the target of intervention, at least implicitly, because the parent is the more competent partner of the dyad. The family systems perspective assumes that a change in the parent's behavior will elicit a change in the infant's behavior and, in turn, a reorganization of the family system. In setting goals, the quality and match of parent-child behaviors need to be emphasized more than the quantity of specific behaviors. As is evident when observing a highly verbal and exuberant parent versus a quiet, reflective parent during interactive sessions with their infants, there is wide variability in the frequency of behaviors shown. These individual variations in frequency may change over time and across situations, but seem to have less effect on the long-term impact of interactions than does the nature of parent-child behaviors (Belsky, Taylor, & Rovine, 1984; Easterbrooks & Goldberg, 1984).

To set realistic goals, information gained from an observational assessment of parent-child interaction should be coupled with a discussion of the parent's perspective of his or her interactions with the child. This step facilitates understanding of the family's value system, corroborates or refutes the observational assessment, and invites the parent to collaborate in identifying high-priority needs and setting goals. If observational assessments and interviews with parents are notably divergent, multiple observations in several situational contexts, or observations and interviews with other caregivers may help to clarify the discrepancies. Throughout the assessment and goal-setting process, it must be remembered that parent-child interaction is only one of many dimensions of personal and family functioning. It is most meaningful when interpreted in the context of a comprehensive assessment of multiple family attributes, resources, needs, and behavior.

To summarize, the following are steps for translating parent-child interaction assessments into goals:

1. Observe and assess parent-child interaction with an observational scale
2. Identify strengths and weaknesses in parent-child interaction behaviors
3. Look for patterns across behaviors
4. Discuss the parent's perspective of his or her interactions with the child

5. Consider patterns of strengths and weaknesses in parent-child interaction within the family and environmental contexts
6. Observe interactions of other caregivers with the child to develop a complete picture of the total caregiving environment
7. Set realistic, measurable goals collaboratively with the family

A considerable degree of clinical judgment is needed to interpret parent-child interaction measures sensitively for intervention purposes. Scores from observational scales offer a systematic means for describing parent-child interaction. However, only careful interpretation of scores within the context of parental perspective and family and environmental factors will lead to meaningful goals for intervention.

PARENT-CHILD INTERACTION INTERVENTION STRATEGIES

After parent-child interaction goals are established, the next step is intervention. This may be carried out in health or educational settings by practitioners trained in a variety of disciplines. Although a number of intervention strategies have been described in the child development, nursing, and early intervention literature, none has been identified as the sole exemplary technique for modifying parent-child behavior. Considering the individual differences in personal characteristics and interactive behaviors of families, this is not surprising. Thus, in planning intervention procedures, the practitioner needs to be familiar with various strategies and then work with the family to select techniques that fit family strengths and needs, as well as personal values, beliefs, and cultural practices. Of course, program resources must also be considered in this decision. It is important to present a flexible, accepting attitude with the parents when describing the array of strategies. A choice of strategies and adaptation to each family's preferences, style, and situation is critical for successful intervention (Affleck, McGrade, McQueeney, & Allen, 1982; Lambie, Bond, & Weikart, 1974). The point is to empower parents to participate jointly with the interventionist in planning and implementing workable intervention procedures.

Intervention strategies used to modify parent-child interaction may be grouped into direct and indirect techniques. *Direct intervention strategies* typically involve discussing parent and child characteristics and behavior, modeling, or didactic teaching.

In health care facilities, for example, practitioners can incorporate preventive information about child development and responsive parent and infant behavior into childbirth classes (Crummette, Thompson, & Beale, 1985), neonatal assessments (Widmayer & Field, 1981), and well-child visits (Casey & Whitt, 1980). The early interventionist conducting individual sessions with parents can model an appropriate interactive sequence, observe the parents' practice, and then reinforce targeted parental behaviors (Field,

1981; Shearer, 1976). Alternatively, the interventionist may comment incidentally on parental and child behaviors during a home or center visit (Fraiberg, 1974). Natural forums for modeling and discussion of parent-child behavior occur in parent-to-parent programs (Bruder & Bricker, 1985; Reschly, 1979) and cooperative day care programs (Holman & Arcus, 1987).

More structured feedback can be offered by coaching a parent during interactions (Field, 1982; Kogan & Gordon, 1975), by discussing videotapes of the parent and child engaged in an activity together (McCollum, 1984; Rosenberg & Robinson, 1985), or by using facilitated observations of staff-child interactions.

Using a didactic style of intervention, a parent can be assigned a target behavior to practice or an observational activity to complete with the child, followed by discussion of the parent-child behaviors and emotions experienced during the task (Spietz, 1985; Sanders, 1987). For those families who benefit from formal parenting classes, information can be presented regarding the process of parent-child interaction and interpretive skills for "reading" a baby's cues as predictors of behavior (Dickie & Gerber, 1980).

These direct strategies are by no means the only techniques for improving parent-child interaction. Sometimes more circuitous routes are equally effective in mediating change. *Indirect intervention strategies* involve modifications of individual or family factors other than parent-child behavior. Such alterations are made with the assumption that alleviating needs or building resources in one element of the family system will, in turn, affect parent-child interchange. Although the effects of indirect strategies have not been evaluated to the extent that the effects of direct strategies have, there is reason to believe that such techniques are effective. Increasing empirical evidence demonstrates the associations between parent-child interaction and alterable parent and child variables, such as stress, social support, locus of control, the perception of the child, the child's state of alertness, and behavior patterns (Comfort, 1986; Crnic, Greenberg, & Slough, 1986; Crockenberg, 1981; Dunst & Trivette, 1986; Simeonsson et al., 1986; Stern & Hildebrandt, 1986).

The relationships among parent, child, and interaction variables are more meaningful when translated into the functional language of intervention strategies. Information regarding respite care and developmental day care or improved competencies of a secondary caregiver, resulting in increased involvement in child care, could diminish maternal stress and heighten satisfaction with instrumental and emotional support. For the family of a medically at-risk premature newborn, in-hospital observation and facilitated practice of handling and soothing techniques might alter the parents' perceptions of their baby and, in turn, their interactions with the baby. With parents who become entangled in the health, education, and social service systems, advocacy counseling could result in a more internal sense of control of the family's life circumstances.

These indirect intervention strategies have the potential to build resources in several aspects of the family system that could then influence parent-child interchange. No doubt there are many other direct and indirect examples of effective intervention strategies. Creative techniques are needed to meet the wide range of styles shown by families with young high-risk or handicapped children.

SUMMARY

Parent-child interaction is an important area of family assessment, particularly for families of children with high-risk or handicapping conditions. Observational assessment of interactions requires a conceptual understanding of the nature of interactions and careful planning of the parameters of the assessment process. The best parent-child interaction instrument fits the needs and resources of the families being assessed as well as the service program. Influencing selection would be the purpose of assessment, the characteristics of the families, the behaviors of interest, and the resources available for training, assessment, and intervention. Parent-child interaction assessment is most meaningful when conducted as part of a comprehensive family assessment.

To translate parent-child interaction assessments into goals, the practitioner must consider the patterns of strengths and weaknesses in parent and child behaviors, the parent's perspective of the interaction, the total caregiving environment, and the family and environmental contexts of the interaction. Intervention strategies need to be planned and implemented in collaboration with the family and adapted to individual family characteristics, beliefs, and cultural styles.

REFERENCES

Affleck, G., McGrade, B. J., McQueeney, M., & Allen, D. (1982). Promise of relationship-focused early intervention in developmental disabilities. *Journal of Special Education, 16,* 413–430.

Ainsworth, M. D. (1979). Attachment as related to mother-infant interaction. In J. S. Rosenblatt, R. A. Hinde, C. Beer, & M-C. Busnel (Eds.), *Advances in the study of behavior* (vol. 9, pp. 2–51). New York: Academic Press.

Als, H., Tronick, E., & Brazelton, T. B. (1980). Stages of early behavioral organization: The study of a sighted infant and a blind infant in interaction with their mothers. In T. Field, S. Goldberg, & A. Sostek (Eds.), *High risk infants and children: Adult and peer interactions* (pp. 181–204). New York: Academic Press.

Barnard, K. E., & Bee, H. L. (1984). The assessment of parent-infant interaction by observation of feeding and teaching. In T. B. Brazelton & B. Lester (Eds.), *New approaches to developmental screening in infants.* New York: Elsevier North Holland.

Bee, H. L., Barnard, K. E., Eyres, S. J., Gray, C. A., Hammond, M. A., Spietz, A. L., Snyder, C., & Clark, B. (1982). Prediction of IQ and language skill from perinatal status, child performance, family characteristics, and mother-infant interaction. *Child Development, 53,* 1134–1156.

Bell, R. Q., & Harper, L. V. (1977). *Child effects on adults.* Hillsdale, N.J.: Lawrence Erlbaum.

Belsky, J. (1981). Early human experience: A family perspective. *Developmental Psychology, 17,* 3–23.

Belsky, J. (1984). The determinants of parenting: A process model. *Child Development, 55,* 83–96.

Belsky, J., Rovine, M., & Taylor, D. G. (1984). The Pennsylvania infant and family development project, III: The origins of individual differences in infant-mother attachment: Maternal and infant contributions. *Child Development, 55,* 718–728.

Belsky, J., Taylor, D. G., & Rovine, M. (1984). The Pennsylvania infant and family development project, II: The development of reciprocal interaction in the mother-infant dyad. *Child Development, 55,* 706–717.

Bowlby, J. (1982). *Attachment* (2nd ed.). New York: Basic Books.

Brazelton, T. B. (1982). Joint regulation of neonate-parent behavior. In E. Z. Tronick (Ed.), *Social interchange in infancy: Affect, cognition, and communication* (pp. 7–22). Baltimore: University Park Press.

Bristol, M. M., & Gallagher, J.J. (1986). Research on fathers of young handicapped children: Evolution, review, and some future directions. In J. J. Gallagher & P. M. Vietze (Eds.), *Families of handicapped persons: Research, programs, and policy issues.* Baltimore: Paul H. Brookes.

Bromwich, R. (1976). Focus on maternal behavior in infant intervention. *American Journal of Orthopsychiatry, 46,* 439–446.

Bromwich, R. (1981). *Working with parents and infants: An interactional approach.* Baltimore: University Park Press.

Bronfenbrenner, U. (1979). *The ecology of human development: Experiments by nature and design.* Cambridge, Mass.: Harvard University Press.

Bronfenbrenner, U., Moen, P., & Garbarino, J. (1984). Child, family, and community. In R. D. Parke (Ed.), *Review of child development research; The family* (vol. 7, pp. 283–328). Chicago: University of Chicago Press.

Bruder, M. B., & Bricker, D. (1985). Parents as teachers of their children and other parents. *Journal of the Division for Early Childhood, 9,* 136–150.

Bruner, J. S. (1977). Early social interaction and language acquisition. In H. R. Schaffer (Ed.), *Studies in mother-infant interaction* (pp. 271–290). New York: Academic Press.

Caldwell, B. M., & Bradley,R. H. (1979). *Home observation for measurement of the environment.* Little Rock, Ark.: Center for Child Development and Education, University of Arkansas at Little Rock.

Casey, P. H., & Whitt, J. K. (1980). Effect of the pediatrician on the mother-infant relationship. *Pediatrics, 65,* 815–820.

Cath, S. H., Gurwitt, A. R., & Ross, J. M. (1982). *Father and child: Developmental and clinical perspectives.* Boston: Little, Brown.

Cicchetti, D., & Serafica, F. C. (1981). Interplay among behavioral systems: Illustrations from the study of attachment, affiliation, and warnings in young children with Down's syndrome. *Developmental Psychology, 17,* 36–49.

Clark, G. N., & Siefer, R. (1985). Assessment of parents' interactions with their developmentally delayed infants. *Infant Mental Health Journal, 6,* 214–225.

Clarke-Stewart, K. A. (1973). Interaction among mothers and their young children: Characteristics and consequences. *Monographs of the Society for Research in Child Development, 38,* No. 153.

Clarke-Stewart, K. A. (1978). And daddy makes three: The father's impact on mother and young child. *Child Development, 49,* 466–478.

Comfort, M. (1986). *Parental involvement in play interaction and caregiving roles in families with young high risk and handicapped children: A comparison of father and mother.* Unpublished doctoral dissertation, University of North Carolina at Chapel Hill.

Crnic, K., Greenberg, M. T., & Slough, N. M. (1986). Early stress and social support influences on mothers' and high-risk infants' functioning in late infancy. *Infant Mental Health Journal, 7,* 34–58.

Crockenberg, S. B. (1981). Infant irritability, mother responsiveness, and societal support influences on the security of infant-mother attachment. *Child Development, 52,* 857–865.

Crummette, B. D., Thompson, G. M., & Beale, A. (1985). Father-infant interaction program: Preparation for parenthood. *Infant Mental Health Journal, 6,* 89–97.

Dickie, J. R., & Gerber, S. C. (1980). Training in social competence: The effect on mothers, fathers, and infants. *Child Development, 51,* 1248–1251.

Dunst, C. J., & Trivette, C. M. (1986). Looking beyond the parent-child dyad for the determinants of maternal styles of interaction. *Infant Mental Health Journal, 7,* 69–80.

Easterbrooks, M. A., & Goldberg, W. A. (1984). Toddler development in the family: Impact of father involvement and parenting characteristics. *Child Development, 55,* 740–752.

Eyberg, S. M., & Robinson, E. A. (1982). Parent-child interaction training: Effects on family functioning. *Journal of Clinical Child Psychology, 11,* 130–137.

Farran, D. C., Kasari, C., Comfort, M., & Jay, S. (1986). Parent/caregiver involvement scale. Unpublished rating scale. Available from Dale Farran, Department of Child Development and Family Relations, University of North Carolina, Greensboro, N.C. 27412-5001.

Farran, D. C., Kasari, C., Yoder, P., Harber, L., Huntington, G. S., & Comfort, M. (1987). Rating mother-child interactions in handicapped and at-risk infants. In T. Tamir (Ed.), *Stimulation and intervention in infant development.* London: Freund Publishing House.

Field, T. (1981). Early development of the preterm offspring of teenage mothers. In K. G. Scott, T. Field, & E. G. Robertson, (Eds.), *Teenage parents and their offspring.* (pp.145–176). New York: Grune & Stratton.

Field, T. (1982). Interaction coaching for high-risk infants and their parents. In H. A. Moss, R. Hess, & C. Swift (Eds.), *Early intervention programs for infants, 1,* 5–24.

Fraiberg, S. (1974). Blind infants and their mothers: An examination of the sign system. In M. Lewis & L. A. Rosenblum (Eds.), *The effect of the infant on its caregiver* (pp. 215–232). New York: John Wiley & Sons.

Garbarino, G. (1982). *Children and families in the social environment.* New York: Aldine Publishing.

Goldberg, S. (1977). Social competence in infancy: A model of parent-infant interaction. *Merrill-Palmer Quarterly, 23,* 163–177.

Holman, N., & Arcus, M.(1987). Helping adolescent mothers and their children: An integrated multi-agency approach. *Family Relations, 36,* 119–123.

Huntington, G. S. (1985). *Maternal and infant characteristics associated with maternal involvement during mother-child interaction.* Unpublished doctoral dissertation, University of North Carolina at Chapel Hill.

Kaye, K. (1982). *The mental and social life of babies: How parents create persons.* Chicago: University of Chicago Press.

Kogan, K. L., & Gordon, B. N. (1975). A mother-instruction program: Documenting change in mother-child interactions. *Child Psychiatry and Human Development, 5,* 189–200.

Kysela, G., & Marfo, K. (1983). Mother-child interactions and early intervention programmes for handicapped infants and young children. *Educational Psychology, 3,* 201–212.

Lamb, M. E. (1981a). The development of father-infant relationships. In M. E. Lamb (Ed.), *The role of the father in child development* (pp. 459–488). New York: John Wiley & Sons.

Lamb, M. E. (1981b). Fathers and child development: An integrative overview. In M. E. Lamb (Ed.), *The role of the father in child development* (pp. 1–70). New York: John Wiley & Sons.

Lamb, M. E. (1982). *Nontraditional families: Parenting and child development.* Hillsdale, N.J.: Lawrence Erlbaum.

Lamb, M. E., & Elster, A. B. (1985). Adolescent mother-infant-father relationships. *Developmental Psychology, 21,* 768–773.

Lambie, D. Z., Bond, J. T., & Weikart, D. P. (1974). *Home teaching with mothers and infants.* Ypsilanti, Mich.: High/Scope Education Research Foundation.

Lewis, M., & Feiring, C. (1982). Some American families at dinner. In L. M. Laosa & I. E. Sigel (Eds.), *Families as learning environments for children.* New York: Plenum Press.

Lewis, M., & Rosenblum, L. (Eds. (1974). *The effect of the infant on its caregiver.* New York: John Wiley & Sons.

Maccoby, E. E., & Martin, J. A. (1983). Socialization in the context of the family: Parent-child interaction. In P. H. Mussen (Ed.), *Handbook of child psychology* (vol. 4, pp. 1–101). New York: John Wiley & Sons.

Mahoney, G. (1985). Maternal behavior rating scale. Unpublished rating scale. Available from Gerald Mahoney, Pediatric Research and Training Center, Department of Pediatrics, University of Connecticut School of Medicine, Farmington, Conn. 06032.

Mahoney, G., Finger, I., & Powell, A. (1985). Relationship of maternal behavior style to the development of organically impaired mentally retarded infants. *American Journal of Mental Deficiency, 90,* 296–302.

Mahoney, G., & Powell, A. (1986). *The transactional intervention program: A child-centered approach to developmental intervention with young handicapped children.* Farmington, Conn.: Pediatric Research and Training Center.

Marfo, K. (1984). Interactions between mothers and their mentally retarded children: Integration of research findings. *Journal of Applied Developmental Psychology, 5,* 45–69.

Markowitz, J. (1984). Participation of fathers in early childhood special education programs: An exploratory study. *Journal of the Division for Early Childhood, 8,* 119–132.

McCollum, J. (1984). Social interaction between parents and babies: Validation of an intervention procedure. *Child: Care, Health and Development, 10,* 301–315.

McCollum, J. A., & Stayton, V. D. (1985). Infant/parent interaction: Studies and intervention guidelines based on the SIAI model. *Journal of the Division for Early Childhood, 9*(2), 125–135.

McGehee, L. J., & Eckerman, C. O. (1983). The preterm infant as a social partner: Responsive but unreadable. *Infant Behavior and Development, 6,* 461–470.

McHale, S. M., & Huston, T. L. (1984). Men and women as parents: Sex role orientations, employment, and parental roles with infants. *Child Development, 55,* 1349–1361.

Meyer, D. J., Vadasy, P. F., Fewell, R. R., & Schell, G. (1982). Involving fathers of handicapped infants: Translating research into program goals. *Journal of the Division for Early Childhood, 5,* 64–72.

Meyers, C. E., Mink, I., and Nihira, K. (1977). *Home quality rating scale.* NPI-Lanterman State Hospital Research Group, Pomona, Calif.

Meyers, C. E., Nihira, K., & Mink, I. T. (1984). Predicting retarded students' short-term growth from home environment. *Applied Research in Mental Retardation, 5,* 137–146.

Minuchin, P. (1985). Families and individual development: Provocations from the field of family therapy. *Child Development, 56,* 289–302.

O'Donnell, K. J., & Vaughn, B. (1985, April). The mother's view of her child and the quality of their affective tie. Paper presented at the Biennial Meeting of the Society for Research in Child Development, Toronto, Canada.

Olson, D. H., Portner, J., & Lavee, Y. (1985). Faces III. In D. H. Olson, H. I. McCubbin, H. Barnes, A. Larsen, M. Muxen, & M. Wilson. (Eds.) *Family inventories: Inventories in a national survey of families across the family life cycle.* St. Paul, Minn.: University of Minnesota, Family Social Science.

Parke, R. D., & Tinsley, B. R. (1981). The father's role in infancy: Determinants of involvement in caregiving and play. In M. E. Lamb (Ed.), *The role of the father in child development.* New York: John Wiley & Sons.

Pedersen, F. A. (Ed.). (1980). *The father-infant relationship.* New York: Praeger Publishers.

Pettit, G. S., & Bates, J. E. (1984). Continuity of individual differences in the mother-infant relationship from six to thirteen months. *Child Development, 55,* 729–739.

Power, T. G., & Parke, R. D. (1982). Play as a context for early learning. In L. M. Laosa & I. E. Sigel (Eds.), *Families as learning environments for children.* (pp. 147–178). New York: Plenum Press.

Ramey, C. T., Farran, D. C., & Campbell, F. A. (1979). Predicting IQ from mother-infant interactions. *Child Development, 50,* 804–814.

Reschly, B. (1979). *Supporting the changing family: A guide to the parent-to-parent model.* Ypsilanti, Mich.: High/Scope Educational Research Foundation.

Risman, B. J. (1986). Can men "mother"? Life as a single father. *Family Relations, 35,* 95–102.

Robinson, E. A., & Eyberg, S. M. (1981). The dyadic parent-child interaction coding system: Standardization and validation. *Journal of Consulting and Clinical Psychology, 49,* 245–250.

Rosenberg, S. A., & Robinson, C. C. (1985). Enhancement of mothers' interactional skills in an infant education program. *Education and Training of the Mentally Retarded, 20,* 163–169.

Rosenberg, S., Robinson, C., & Beckman, P. (1984). Teaching skills inventory: A measure of parent performance. *Journal of the Division for Early Childhood, 8,* 107–113.

Sameroff, A. (1982). The environmental context of developmental disabilities. In D. D. Bricker (Ed.), *Intervention with at-risk and handicapped infants: From research to application* (pp. 141–152). Baltimore: University Park Press.

Sanders, W. (1987). Georgia connection. *NCAST Newsletter, 3,* 3–4.

Shearer, M. (1976). A home-based parent training model. In D. L. Lillie & P. L. Trohanis (Eds.), *Teaching parents to teach* (pp. 131–147). New York: Walker.

Sigel, I. E., Dreyer, A. S., & McGillicuddy-DeLisi, A. V.(1984). Psychological perspectives of the family. In R. D. Parke (Ed.), *Review of child development research* (vol. 7, pp. 42–79). Chicago: University of Chicago Press.

Simeonsson, R. J., Bailey, D. B., Huntington, G. S., & Comfort, M. (1986). Testing the concept of goodness of fit in early intervention. *Infant Mental Health Journal, 7,* 81–94.

Spietz, A. (1985). Guidelines for nursing intervention: Feeding scale. *NCAST National News, 1,*1–2, 5.

Stern, M., & Hildebrandt, K. A. (1986). Prematurity stereotyping: Effects on mother-infant interaction. *Child Development, 57,* 308–315.

Stoneman, Z., Brody, G. H., & Abbott, D. (1983). In-home observations of young Down syndrome children with their mothers and fathers. *American Journal of Mental Deficiency, 87,* 591–600.

Thomas, A., & Chess, S. (1977). *Temperament and development.* New York: Brunner/Mazel.

Towle, P. O., Farran, D. C., & Comfort, M. (in press). Parent-handicapped child interaction observational coding systems: A review. In K. Marfo (Ed.), *Parent-child interaction and developmental disabilities: Theory, research, and intervention.* New York: Praeger Publishers.

Tronick, E. Z., & Gianino, A. (1986). Interactive mismatch and repair: Challenges to the coping infant. *Zero to Three, 6*(3), 1–6.

Vandell, D. L., & Wilson, K. S. (1987). Infants' interactions with mother, sibling, and peer; Contrasts and relations between interaction systems. *Child Development, 58,* 176–186.

Waters, E., Wippman, J., & Sroufe, L. A. (1979). Attachment, positive affect and competence in the peer group: Two studies in construct validation. *Child Development, 50,* 821–829.

Widmayer, S. M., & Field, T. M. (1981). Effects of Brazelton demonstrations for mothers on the development of preterm infants. *Pediatrics, 67,* 711–714.

5

Assessing Family Stress and Needs

U ndoubtedly the most commonly described effect of having a handicapped child is the subsequent stress imposed on a family. What is
stress, how is it assessed, and what factors contribute to reducing
it? This chapter addresses two primary topics. First, stress is defined,
sources of stress are identified, and commonly used measures of stress are
described. Second, the need for a more functional conceptualization of the
nature of stress is discussed and alternative strategies for assessing family
needs are described.

STRESS AND ITS EFFECTS

Stress is a difficult term to define. Yet, historically, stress has played an
important role in the interpretation of a family's response to a handicapped
child.

What Is Stress?

Stress is a word in everyone's vocabulary. We talk about it, we say we experience it, we believe we can observe it in others, and we hear the media tell

---

This chapter was contributed by Donald B. Bailey, Jr., University of North Carolina at Chapel
Hill.

us about factors that contribute to it in our lives. But what is stress? From a conceptual perspective, stress is a hypothetical construct. It cannot be defined specifically, but it is an attribute commonly used to account for variability in behavior. Stress is assumed to be experienced by a great proportion of families with handicapped children.

Pearlin, Menaghan, Lieberman, and Mullan (1981) describe stress as a conceptually ambiguous term:

> There is probably a general agreement that stress refers to a response of the organism to conditions that, either consciously or unconsciously, are experienced as noxious. (p. 341)

Beyond that conceptualization, however, stress results in a variety of effects. Although too much stress can be debilitating, some stress is necessary for growth and change to occur. Moreover, stress is probably not a single event, but rather a process that involves many factors, including a stressor, the individual's or family's perception of the stressor, available resources, and effects (Hetherington, 1984).

Stressors.   Stress may arise from a single event, such as a job layoff or the death of a spouse. Examples of these events and strategies for assessing them are described in Chapter 6. More often, however, stress is caused by pervasive and ongoing factors that may arise from specific events but have long-term ramifications. For example, the birth of a handicapped child is a stressful event, but its effects are lifelong and pervasive. Low socioeconomic status or racial discrimination are not single events, but rather long-range problems. In general, a stressor is an event or set of events that requires some form of psychological or physical adjustment (Horowitz, 1980).

Perceptions.   Hill (1949) emphasized the importance of the individual's or family's perception of a given stressful event. Perceptions define events for those experiencing them. A person with a history of job layoffs, for example, might view a recent firing quite differently from a person who had never been through such an experience. Likewise, a parent who had a handicapped sibling might view the birth of a Down syndrome child quite differently from a parent whose siblings were nonhandicapped.

Pearlin et al. (1981) suggest that events become more stressful when they affect self-concept, including one's sense of control over life's forces and one's feelings of self-worth. If the event reduces feelings of control and self-worth, stress is accentuated.

Resources.   Hill (1949) also described the importance of resources as mediators of stress. Schilling, Gilchrist, and Schinke (1984) differentiate two broad aspects of support: *personal coping strategies,* such as problem solving, taking initiative, or self-praise; and *social supports,* including family members, friends and neighbors, and professional support services. Several studies have documented the importance of resources as mediators of stress in families with handicapped children (Beavers, Hampson, Hulgus, & Beavers, 1986; Dunst, 1985; McKinney & Peterson, 1987). Dunst, Trivette, and Cross (1986) found that both satisfaction with support and number of sources of support were related to parental well-being, attitudes toward the child, and family integrity. Although resources alone generally do not remove stress, they allow the individual or family to cope with the stressor. Strategies for assessing family resources are described in Chapter 7.

Effects. Ultimately, stressors must be evaluated in terms of their effects. An event that had no effect on an individual or family would probably not be defined as a stressor. Stress has both physical and psychological consequences for individuals and families. Rahe (1975), for example, reports that numerous studies have documented that seriously stressful events may bear a direct relationship to subsequent illness and health status after the event. Horowitz (1980) describes a model of psychological responses to serious life events in which the individual is viewed as progressing through a series of psychological states or emotional phases of dealing with stress. Some responses may be seen as inappropriate and counterproductive. For example, Pollner and McDonald-Wikler (1985) describe a dramatic case study of an entire family's denial of their child's severe handicap coupled with "shared delusions" about the child's abilities. In other cases, however, stress may lead to strengthening of self-concept or more intense family bonding.

Stress in Families with Handicapped Children

Families with handicapped children are likely to experience stress as a function of parenting (Crnic, Friedrich, & Greenberg, 1983; Gallagher, Beckman, & Cross, 1983). Although not every such family experiences high levels of stress, rearing a handicapped child clearly has the potential for creating stress. The extent to which stress is experienced varies according to a number of factors. Child factors such as temperament, caregiving demands, rhythmicity, behavioral characteristics, severity of handicap, and type of handicap constitute one source of variation in stress (Beckman, 1983; Holroyd & McArthur, 1976). A second source of variation in how stress is experienced is individual and family factors, such as personal belief systems; level of psychological functioning; age of parents; economic resources; and support from extended family, friends, neighbors, and professionals (Dunst, 1985; Hill, 1949; McKinney & Peterson, 1987). The type of treatment program may also positively or negatively affect stress. For example, parents whose children are in mainstreaming environments are faced with issues not raised in self-contained environments (Bailey & Winton, 1987). Likewise, families in home-based programs have different needs and access to different kinds of services than do families in center-based programs (Bailey & Simeonsson, in press).

Stress may also relate to attempts to locate services and frustration in dealing with schools and other human service agencies. For example, a commonly cited concern is finding appropriate babysitters or other respite care services (Blackard & Barsh, 1982). Parents often have enduring concerns about their child's future, including concerns about their child's ultimate level of functioning, what services will be available in the future, and who will take care of their child when they themselves no longer can (Turnbull & Turnbull, 1986). Also, parents with handicapped children generally experience pressure to be more actively involved in their child's education by participating in the educational planning process, conducting home teaching activities, attending parent meetings, and engaging in advocacy efforts, all of which may increase stress (Winton & Turnbull, 1981).

The effects of stress in families with handicapped children have been observed in parents' attitudes toward their children, personality and emotional difficulties, marital satisfaction, siblings, and parent-child interactions (Crnic, Friedrich, & Greenberg, 1983; Gallagher, Beckman, & Cross, 1983). These and other authors caution that professionals should not assume that every family with a handicapped child is always experiencing stress. Many families cope well despite seemingly devastating circumstances. Salisbury (1987), for example, found no differences in stress levels reported by parents of young (12 to 60 months) handicapped and nonhandicapped children, a finding contrary to that obtained in other studies. Burden (1980) found a general decrease in level of depression in mothers with handicapped infants over a two-year period. Turnbull and Turnbull (1986) cite examples of positive outcomes of stress in families with handicapped children. However, families with handicapped youngsters are clearly at greater *risk* for stress and its subsequent negative consequences. Thus, professionals must be sensitive to the presence of stress and attempt to provide services in a fashion that decreases rather than increases it.

MEASUREMENT OF STRESS

Stress is generally assessed through self-report measures completed by a family member. Three commonly used measures are described here: the Questionnaire on Resources and Stress, the Parenting Stress Index, and the Impact-on-Family Scale.

Questionnaire on Resources and Stress

The oldest and most frequently used measure of stress is the Questionnaire on Resources and Stress (Holroyd, 1974; 1986). The QRS was developed to evaluate "the psychological costs to persons living with and caring for a handicapped or chronically ill relative" (Holroyd, 1974, p. 92). It consists of 285 items (at sixth-grade reading level) organized into three domains and 15 subscales:

Personal Problems Scales

1. Poor health/mood
2. Excess time demands
3. Negative attitude
4. Overprotection/dependency
5. Lack of social support
6. Overcommitment/martyrdom
7. Pessimism

Family Problems Scales

8. Lack of family integration
9. Limits on family opportunity
10. Financial problems

Problems of Index Case Scales

11. Physical incapacitation
12. Lack of activities for index case
13. Occupational limitations
14. Social obtrusiveness
15. Difficult personality characteristics

Each item consists of a statement, such as "As the time passes I think it will take more and more to care for _____," which the respondent scores as true or false. The instrument takes approximately one hour to complete.

A total score and 15 subscale scores may be derived, and a profile is used to compare the individual or family with average scores from a normative population of 100 families who did not have a handicapped or chronically ill family member. A t score is generated for each scale, and scores above a t score of 70 are considered significant. The most recent manual for the QRS (Holroyd, 1986) provides guidelines for interpreting performance within each subscale. It further suggests that the QRS helps clinicians (1) identify family problem areas that should be addressed first, and (2) determine which families should receive priority for care when resources are limited.

The manual also summarizes research using the QRS. In general the instrument appears to be reliable and a valid measure of stress. It has been used in numerous studies of families with handicapped children. Examples of its use have been to describe differential patterns of stress for different handicaps (e.g., Holroyd & McArthur, 1976) and to examine the effects of various child and family characteristics on stress (e.g., Beckman, 1983; Holroyd, 1974).

A 66-item short form of the QRS was developed by its author. Also, a 52-item short version was empirically developed and reported by Friedrich, Greenberg, and Crnic (1983). The shorter version was found to be internally consistent and valid in comparisons with other measures of stress. Four factors were found in a factor analysis: parent and family problems, pessimism, child characteristics, and physical incapacitation. Correlation between the short and long versions of the instrument was .997, indicating that if the total score is of primary interest, the short form is more efficient and equally effective (Friedrich et al., 1983). Holroyd (1986), however, suggests that the short form be used for screening purposes only and the long form for research and clinical uses.

Parenting Stress Index

The Parenting Stress Index (Abidin, 1986) is "a screening and diagnostic assessment technique designed to yield a measure of the relative magnitude of stress in the parent-child system" (Loyd & Abidin, 1985, p. 169). The instrument consists of 101 items organized into two broad domains and 13 subscales:

Child Characteristics

1. Adaptability
2. Acceptability
3. Demandingness
4. Mood
5. Distractibility/hyperactivity
6. Reinforces parent

Parent Characteristics

7. Depression
8. Attachment
9. Restrictions of role
10. Sense of competence
11. Social isolation
12. Relationship with spouse
13. Parent health

Either parent may complete the scale, although the instrument was initially developed with the mother as the primary respondent. Each item consists of a statement, such as "Since having this child I have been unable to do new and different things," which the respondent classifies on a scale from 1 (strongly agree) to 5 (strongly disagree).

The author suggests that although the instrument can be used with children up to 10 years of age, it is most applicable for the first three years of life. Several studies have documented the scale's reliability and validity (Abidin, 1986; Loyd & Abidin, 1985). Normative data are provided and respondents' scores may be compared with scores from the norm group of families. Percentile scores may be derived for each subscale, domain, and total score, with norms organized according to child age. Although the normative sample included 534 parents, most were from central Virginia and the sample was predominantly white (92%). Thus, the extent to which the normative data are representative of the U.S. population is questionable.

The following description of the scale's use with parents has been offered:

> The PSI is most frequently used as a preliminary screening device for the early identification of parent-child systems which are under stress and therefore at risk for the development of dysfunctional parenting behaviors or behavior problems in the child involved. Extremely high or low total scores, as well as marked differences in domain scores, usually indicate that the parents involved should be offered referral for professional consultation. However, such interpretations must in each case be initially considered hypothetical, and their validity needs to be established by further inquiry with any particular client. (Loyd & Abidin, 1985, p. 175)

A specific cutoff score is provided in the manual, along with the recommendation that parents whose raw scores exceed that number should be offered referral for professional consultation.

Although the manual suggests that the total score is of greatest use, subscale and domain scores can be used to gather more specific information about the type and source of stress to further individualize interventions. For example, by comparing the child domain and parent domain scores, the professional may be able to determine whether stress is due primarily to child characteristics and behavior or to aspects of the broader family system and family relationships. The manual also provides guidelines for intervention if high stress is observed in specific subscales. For example, the following is offered if high stress scores are found in the social isolation subscale:

> Interventions need to focus on assisting the parents in mobilizing their pride in their children and in their involvement with others. Usually it is not productive to place such an individual in a group as the first intervention. A home visit or individual counseling approach is a more appropriate starting point. (Abidin, 1986, p. 46)

Abidin cautions that such conclusions should be viewed as working hypotheses for possible services rather than as necessarily prescriptive solutions for all families.

The PSI also includes an optional Life Stress Scale, which consists of 19 potentially stressful events such as going deeply into debt or experiencing the death of an immediate family member. The purpose of this part of the scale is to provide information about additional stress outside the parent-child relationship.

Impact-on-Family Scale

The Impact-on-Family Scale (Stein & Reissman, 1980) was developed specifically to assess the impact of a chronically ill child on family life. However, it can also be used with families of handicapped children. The instrument consists of 24 items organized into five empirically determined factors: financial, familial, social, personal strain, and mastery. Each item consists of a statement, such as "We have little desire to go out because of my child's illness," to which parents respond on a scale ranging from 1 (strongly agree) to 5 (strongly disagree). Stein and Reissman provide reliability data on the measure and suggest that it may be useful in describing the initial impact of a chronically ill child on the family and in evaluating the effectiveness of various interventions to reduce this impact.

Evaluation of Stress Measures

Research on stress over the past quarter century has yielded several instruments with good psychometric properties. The measures have helped researchers understand families and family functioning. However, their clinical utility, particularly in the context of early intervention, is less clear. Interpretation of the psychological meaning of responses on these measures is inappropriate for professionals who lack specific training in family therapy or clinical psychology. Ultimately, family assessment tools must provide useful information for early interventionists and must be able to be used by professionals from multiple disciplines. Several characteristics of existing stress measures limit their usefulness.

One limitation is item content. Items on the measures generally were selected to document the *impact* of a handicapped child on the family. Impact is important, but it may not reflect actual *needs*. Furthermore, some families may view many items as personal or intrusive, particularly those related to financial status, mood, intrafamily fuctioning, or personal well-being. If families view the assessment process as intrusive, they may not be willing to provide important information or they may respond in a socially desirable fashion; intervention efforts may be minimally effective if families do not perceive themselves as engaged in an open, collaborative, and trusting process. This concern may be particularly relevant when the professional and family are just getting to know each other.

A second broad limitation is item format. In particular, the Likert-type scale (agree/disagree) format is confusing to many families, limiting the validity of ratings by families who cannot determine the proper way to respond. Furthermore, what is the clinical meaning of a rating of 4—agree somewhat—on a particular item? Parents may indicate that an event has had a particularly stressful impact, but do not want or perceive the need for services related to it.

The difficulties that arise in trying to use stress or impact measures to plan services are demonstrated in the following example. Assume that in response to the item "As the time passes I think it will take more and more to care for _____," a parent responds with a 4, indicating moderate agreement with the statement. What are the clinical implications of this response? Many interpretations are possible, and further questions may be raised. For example, more and more what? Time? Money? Energy? Assuming it means more time and energy, does the parent want any help with this at present? If so, what should be done? The interventionist alternately could (1) help the parent join a parent-support group, (2) provide information about future services available to alleviate the impact, or (3) recommend therapy for depression. Without further assessment, the interventionist has little information about family perceptions of the problem, the need for services, or the preferred service alternatives.

Despite these limitations, stress measures have two useful functions in early intervention. One is *screening*. Loyd and Abidin (1985), for example, suggest that the Parenting Stress Index is particularly useful in identifying parent-child systems with tremendous needs for support or assistance. Viewing an instrument as a screening measure implies that, used alone, the information provided is insufficient for intervention purposes, requiring a more comprehensive assessment before goals and services can be specified. Thus, measures such as the QRS or the PSI could be used before more detailed interviews with families. They could also be used to identify families or family members at extreme risk for successful adaptation who may profit from counseling or therapy.

A second potential use of stress measures in early intervention is for *program evaluation*. For example, a stress measure could be administered on a pre/post basis to document changes in parents' stress while they are participating in early intervention programs. Such documentation would be a useful indicator of program effectiveness. For example, Abidin (1986) describes two unpublished studies in which a reduction in PSI scores was found as a function of either parent training or parent consultation.

We urge caution, however, in the selection of stress measures for program evaluation purposes. The presence of a handicapped child in a family has the strong potential for causing permanently elevated stress. Although early intervention programs may provide needed support to families, it may be as unrealistic to expect significant changes in parental stress as it would be to expect such changes in children's IQ. For example, Wikler, Hanusa, and Stoycheff (1986) used the QRS to evaluate the effects of respite care on stress of parents with mentally retarded, behaviorally disturbed children and found that scores increased on two subscales, decreased on two, and remained the same on the others. In addition, in our own research we found only a moderate correlation between a measure of family impact (IFS) and a more functional assessment of family needs (Bailey & Simeonsson, 1987). Stress may also be cyclical (Wikler, Wasow, & Hatfield, 1981), and some intervention programs, particularly those requiring high levels of parent participation, may actually increase stress (Winton & Turnbull, 1981). Documenting the extent to which a program facilitates family attainment of specific needs or goals may be a more useful indicator of program effectiveness.

THE FUNCTIONAL ASSESSMENT OF FAMILY NEEDS

We believe that existing stress measures generally have limited use for intervention purposes. If unlimited time and resources for both programs and families were available, the measures might indeed provide interesting information. However, the QRS and the PSI, the two most well-known and well-researched measures, require considerable time for parents to complete because of their length and format. A large number of lengthy questionnaires and forms is often a barrier to effective family assessment. The use of shorter measures with items more obviously relevant for intervention may lead to the family's increased trust in the program and willingness to provide information. In this section we describe examples of two such measures: the Family Information Preference Inventory and the Family Needs Survey.

Family Information Preference Inventory

The Family Information Preference Inventory was developed by Turnbull and Turnbull (1986) to assess the needs of families and the method by which they would prefer to have those needs met. The FIPI consists of 37 items organized into five informational areas:

1. Teaching the child at home
2. Advocacy and working with professionals
3. Planning for the future
4. Helping the whole family relax and enjoy life more
5. Finding and using more support

Each item consists of a statement of a specific possible need, such as "How to teach my family and friends to care for my child's special needs while they are babysitting or providing respite care for me." Parents are first asked to rate the extent to which they need the information indicated in the item, using a 4-point rating scale: 0 = no interest in the information; 1 = information is of low priority; 2 = information is of medium priority; or 3 = information is of high priority. Next, parents indicate one of three formats in which they would like to receive the information: a group meeting with other parents, an individual meeting, or written materials. No procedures for summarizing scores are suggested; rather, each item is interpreted according to the parent's response.

The FIPI more closely meets the intervention planning needs of professionals working with parents of handicapped children than existing stress measures. The items are based on needs commonly expressed by parents and have direct clinical relevance. Asking parents to indicate a preference for the mode of service also provides helpful information about how to plan and provide service. In addition to the specific items listed on the survey, each section provides an opportunity for parents to indicate any additional needs—an important option.

In determining the survey's use in early intervention, professionals may want to consider several factors. First, its present form includes some items inappropriate to early intervention, such as items regarding sexuality and dating, residential and vocational needs, and needs related to higher education, scholarships after high school, and guardianship in adulthood. These items can be eliminated before the measure is distributed. Second, the usefulness of the 0–3 rating scale is unclear, as the authors give no guidance for evaluating the importance of addressing ratings of 1 or 2. Finally, only three options for service provision are listed. If an option does not exist or if additional options are available, the form should be modified to reflect the actual program options. Although these limitations should be considered before this instrument is administered, the FIPI appears to be a useful tool in identifying parental perceptions of needs and priorities for services.

Family Needs Survey

As part of our own work with early interventionists, we have developed the Family Needs Survey (Bailey & Simeonsson, in press a). The instrument, displayed in Table 5.1, consists of 35 items organized into six categories. The first category assesses parents' needs for information related to their child's disability or behavior, how to teach or play with their child, or information about present or future services. The second category assesses parents' needs for support from family members, friends, other parents, or a minister. It also asks if parents want reading material or time for themselves. The third category assesses parents' needs for help in explaining about their child to siblings, grandparents, friends, neighbors, or other children. The fourth category assesses needs related to obtaining community services, such as a doctor, dentist, babysitter, day care provider, or church nursery. The fifth area assesses family needs for help in paying for basic living expenses or for special equipment or services needed by their child. Finally, the last area assesses the extent to which families need help in intrafamily functioning, such as problem solving, spouse support, task allocation, and recreational activities.

Items are worded so that a positive response indicates a desire for help. For example, one item reads "I need more information on how to play with or talk to my child." Each item is responded to in one of three ways: 1 = I definitely do not need help with this, 2 = not sure, and 3 = I definitely need help with this. Items marked 3 are identified as possible targets for intervention and become potential topics for discussion in follow-up interviews with families.

TABLE 5.1
Family Needs Survey

Listed below are some of the needs expressed by parents of special children. We are interested in what you would like help with. Please read each statement. If it is definitely not a need for you at this time, circle number 1. If you are not sure about whether you would like help in this area, circle number 2. If it is definitely a need for you and *you would like help at this time,* please circle number 3.

Need	I Definitely Do Not Need Help With This	Not Sure	I Definitely Need Help With This
A. Needs for Information			
1. I need more information about my child's condition or disability.	1	2	3
2. I need more information about how to handle my child's behavior.	1	2	3
3. I need more information about how to teach my child.	1	2	3
4. I need more information on how to play with or talk to my child.	1	2	3
5. I need more information on the services that are presently available for my child.	1	2	3
6. I need more information about the services that my child might receive in the future.	1	2	3
7. I need more information about how children grow and develop.	1	2	3
B. Needs for Support			
8. I need to have someone in my family that I can talk to more about problems.	1	2	3
9. I need to have more friends that I can talk to.	1	2	3

TABLE 5.1
Continued

Need	I Definitely Do Not Need Help With This	Not Sure	I Definitely Need Help With This
10. I need to have more opportunities to meet and talk with other parents of handicapped children.	1	2	3
11. I need to have more time just to talk with my child's teacher or therapist.	1	2	3
12. I would like to meet more regularly with a counselor (psychologist, social worker, psychiatrist) to talk about problems.	1	2	3
13. I need to talk more to a minister who could help me deal with problems.	1	2	3
14. I need reading material about other parents who have a child similar to mine.	1	2	3
15. I need to have more time for myself.	1	2	3
C. Explaining to Others			
16. I need more help in how to explain my child's condition to his/her siblings.	1	2	3
17. I need more help in explaining my child's condition to either my parents or my spouse's parents.	1	2	3
18. My spouse needs help in understanding and accepting this child's condition.	1	2	3
19. I need help in knowing how to respond when friends, neighbors, or strangers ask questions about my child's condition.	1	2	3

TABLE 5.1
Continued

Need	I Definitely Do Not Need Help With This	Not Sure	I Definitely Need Help With This
20. I need help in explaining my child's condition to other children.	1	2	3
D. Community Services			
21. I need help locating a doctor who understands me and my child's needs.	1	2	3
22. I need help locating a dentist who will see my child.	1	2	3
23. I need help locating baby-sitters or respite care providers who are willing and able to care for my child.	1	2	3
24. I need help locating a day care center or preschool for my child.	1	2	3
25. I need help in getting appropriate care for my child in our church or synagogue nursery during church services.	1	2	3
E. Financial Needs			
26. I need more help in paying for expenses such as food, housing, medical care, clothing, or transportation.	1	2	3
27. I need more help in getting special equipment for my child's needs.	1	2	3

We recommend that mothers and fathers complete the FNS separately. In a study of 38 two-parent families, we found different profiles of responses for mothers and fathers, reinforcing the need for separate forms (Bailey & Simeonsson, in press a). Differences may indicate the need either for dis-

TABLE 5.1
Continued

Need	I Definitely Do Not Need Help With This	Not Sure	I Definitely Need Help With This
28. I need more help in paying for therapy, day care, or other services my child needs.	1	2	3
29. I or my spouse need more counseling or help in getting a job.	1	2	3
30. I need more help paying for babysitting or respite care.	1	2	3
31. I need more help paying for toys that my child needs.	1	2	3
F. Family Functioning			
32. Our family needs help in discussing problems and reaching solutions.	1	2	3
33. Our family needs help in learning how to support each other during difficult times.	1	2	3
34. Our family needs help in deciding who will do household chores, child care, and other family tasks.	1	2	3
35. Our family needs help in deciding on and doing recreational activities.	1	2	3

cussion of them in meetings with both parents present or for determination of some goals and services unique to each parent.

We also examined the usefulness of an open-ended format for assessing family needs by simply giving parents a piece of paper with the request "Please list your five greatest needs as a family." Although there was considerable overlap between the needs generated in this format and the needs listed on the FNS, the open-ended format provided valuable additional information that either elaborated on FNS responses or indicated new needs not listed on the FNS. The optimal assessment process should include both. The list of needs provides a concrete standard against which all families may be assessed. It also may help families become aware of possible needs and provides a context for indicating needs that they may not have been willing to share in an open-ended format. The open-ended format is important, however, because a standard survey cannot include every possible family need. Also, this format provides information about the needs of greatest priority for families, which is impossible to obtain from the FNS if a family indicates a large number of needs.

TRANSLATING DATA ON FAMILY NEEDS INTO FAMILY GOALS

In the process of assessing family needs, professionals may be tempted to make an "objective" judgment about what a family "really" needs. For example, one professional might assume that father involvement in child care is of utmost priority for a particular family. Another might identify a parent-support group as important. In each case, the interventionist assumes that he or she has a different, less biased perspective than the parent, who is assumed to be too close to the situation to assess accurately what is best for both child and family. Such assumptions are generally inappropriate, however, for at least two reasons. First, Hill's (1949) model emphasizes the importance of personal perception of the problem. Enormous variation exists in how people perceive events. What may seem important to the interventionist may not be important at all to the family. Alternately, what may be important to the family may seem trivial to the professional. Second, from a pragmatic perspective, the interventionist should address needs that families perceive as important. In so doing, the professional begins to build a trusting and collaborative relationship, because the family members perceive the professional as responsive to their own unique situation. Focusing on family priorities for services is important in itself, and it may also have secondary benefits by enabling families ultimately to accept goals the professional deems important (Bailey, 1987).

Surveys such as the Family Information Preference Inventory or the Family Needs Survey are useful because they ask parents specifically if they need a service. The authors of both measures suggest that they be used in conjunction with an open-ended format that allows parents to indicate additional needs. In the family-focused intervention model, we suggest that the information gathered through such measures be used as a basis for a follow-up focused interview (described in Chapters 9 and 10), in which parents and professionals engage in face-to-face discussions about needs and priorities for services (Winton & Bailey, in press). This sequential process greatly increases the likelihood of developing an individualized family services plan that parents enthusiastically embrace and continue to use.

To demonstrate the application of data gathered in such surveys, three case studies are described that represent actual families who participated in a study of family goal planning in home-based infant intervention programs (Bailey et al., 1988). The instrument used was the Family Needs Survey, which was part of a larger family-assessment battery. In addition to the FNS, each family was given a sheet of paper with the following directions written at the top: "Please list the greatest problems (up to five) facing your family right now." The names are fictional.

Family A

Melissa Jones is an 8-month-old white child who was born prematurely. As a result, she displays mild cognitive delays and moderate motor delays. Her father is a salesman and her mother, who was a teacher, has decided to stay home and work as a housewife and mother. Both parents have college degrees, and they live in a relatively large city. The mother is 29 and the father 30 years of age. Melissa is their first child.

The profile of mother's and father's responses to items on the Family Needs Survey is displayed in Figure 5.1. Most needs identified were in the

FIGURE 5.1
Family Needs Survey Profile, Family A

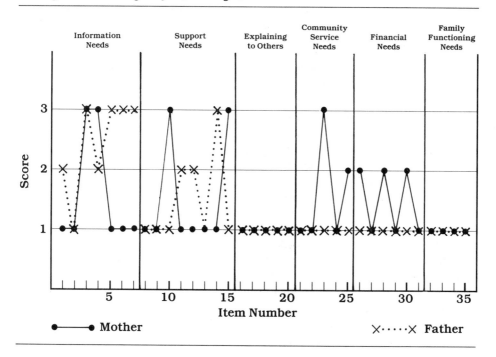

areas of information and support. Ms. Jones indicated a definite desire for help (as indicated by a response of 3) on four items in those two domains: learning how to teach her child, learning how to play or talk with her child, having opportunities to meet and talk with other parents of handicapped children, and having more time for herself. She also indicated a definite need for help in locating babysitters or respite care providers who were willing and able to care for Melissa. Mr. Jones indicated a definite desire for help on five items, only one of which was the same as Ms. Jones. His needs were learning how to teach Melissa, getting information on services presently available for her, getting information about services she might receive in the future, getting information about how children grow and develop, and reading material about other parents who have a similar child.

In response to the open-ended question, Ms. Jones listed three greatest needs facing her family right now:

1. Supporting our financial needs with one income instead of two
2. Fear that our daughter will not develop normally
3. Finding time for rest or other activities we would like to do

Mr. Jones also listed three needs:

1. Trying to get our time management problem worked out. Betty is new at full-time homemaking and I have just started traveling about two days a week
2. Whether insurance will cover all our medical bills
3. Hoping Melissa will fully develop. Not necessarily on time, but hopefully with no lifelong handicaps

In a follow-up focused interview with the family, the professional explored these and other issues. As a result of the discussion, two family goals were identified. The first related to use of respite services. The family indicated that they only left Melissa with extended-family members or friends, because they did not feel comfortable using a regular babysitter. The interventionist agreed to provide information about available resources for respite. The parents agreed to learn the channels and procedures necessary for achieving those services. At the end of six months, parents had followed through on this activity and had used the resource at least once when family and friends were not available. The second goal related to Mr. Jones's interactions with Melissa. Based on his responses on the FNS, the professional hypothesized that he would like to be involved in teaching some skills to Melissa. In the interview, Mr. Jones clarified his response to indicate that he would like to include more goal-directed activities during playtime with Melissa. The interventionist agreed to provide suggestions for activities. After six months, the professional reported that Mr. Jones did indeed use goal-directed activities in his playtime with Melissa, but that he still required specific guidance in what to do.

Family B

Jed Pickett was also born prematurely. However, his handicap is more substantial. At 16 months of age he scores in the moderate retardation range. He has cerebral palsy, a clubfoot, and serious vision problems. His father (age 32) has a high school education and is a factory worker. His mother (age 21) also has a high school education and is a housewife. They are white and live in a small town.

The profile of FNS responses for both parents is displayed in Figure 5.2. Ms. Pickett indicated eight needs spanning all six domains of the survey: learning how to teach Jed; learning how children grow and develop; reading material about other parents with a child such as Jed; having more time to herself; knowing how to respond when friends, neighbors, or strangers ask questions about Jed's condition; locating babysitters (she added a note on the survey indicating that this was a daytime problem only); paying for clothing, medical care, and transportation; and deciding on and doing recreational activities. Mr. Pickett indicated a definite need for help on eight items, three of which were identical to those identified by Ms. Pickett: getting information about Jed's disability; learning how to teach Jed; getting information about services presently available; getting information about

FIGURE 5.2
Family Needs Survey Profile, Family B

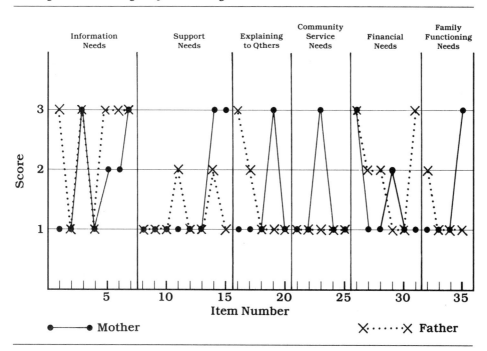

services that might be available in the future; learning how children grow and develop; explaining Jed's condition to siblings; paying for clothing, medical care, and transportation; and paying for toys.

In response to the open-ended question, Ms. Pickett indicated four greatest needs facing her family:

1. Money
2. Jed's foot and eye
3. Frank's temper (sibling)
4. Clothes for me

Mr. Pickett also listed four needs:

1. Money
2. Jed's foot
3. Jed's eye
4. Get cloth and over thing for my family (sic)

After conducting a focused interview with the family, the professional agreed to help the family apply for Crippled Children's Services and Social Security support. She also agreed to help them get a free evaluation for Jed at the regional developmental evaluation center. Three additional family goals were set. First, the interventionist agreed to provide information about a local respite program; Ms. Pickett agreed to contact the program and use the service. However, after six months, the interventionist reported that she had not done so. Second, in the interview, the mother reiterated a need for daytime respite, and the interventionist expressed a need for Jed to have some peer-socialization activities. To achieve these aims and introduce the parents to a parent-support group, the interventionist suggested they visit and use a local cooperative preschool program. At the end of six months the mother had visited the program and talked with at least one other mother about the program, but was not yet using it. Finally, in the interview the parents requested additional resource information. The interventionist agreed to provide that information and the parents agreed to read it and discuss it with the professional. A six-month follow-up indicated that this objective had been achieved.

Family C

Marcus Bynum is 17 months old and has multiple disabilities. In addition to moderate mental retardation, he has a heart defect, hydrocephaly, and hypotonia. His mother is 28 years old, an unemployed single parent with a tenth-grade education. She is black and lives in an inner-city housing project.

The profile of Ms. Bynum's responses on the Family Needs Survey is displayed in Figure 5.3. She indicated a definite need for help on 13 items: handling Marcus's behavior; learning how to teach Marcus; getting infor-

FIGURE 5.3
Family Needs Survey Profile, Family C

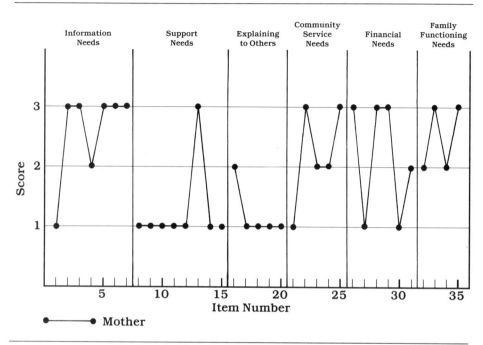

mation about services presently available; getting information about future services; learning how children grow and develop; talking more with a minister (although she wrote a note on the survey saying she already was doing this); locating a dentist who would see Marcus; getting appropriate care in her church nursery; paying for basic living expenses; paying for therapy, day care, and other services; receiving counseling in getting a job; increasing family support; and planning and doing recreational activities. In response to the open-ended question she wrote only one word: *finances*.

Obviously, this family poses multiple, complicated problems for any professional. The solution to these needs will be long-term and require the coordinated efforts of many disciplines. After an interview, four family goals were established. The first related to financial needs, which Ms. Bynum was at first reluctant to discuss. The goal was for her to discuss specific needs with the interventionist and explore recommended sources for aid. By the end of six months, she had explored different options but had not yet applied for assistance. A second goal was for Ms. Bynum to take the initiative to request specific kinds of information needed. After six months she had not only attained this goal but had joined a parent group and was discussing these issues with other parents. A third goal was for Ms. Bynum to increase her participation in the home visit, think of new activities for Marcus, and do them herself. Initially, she just observed during the entire home visit. At the end of six months, she had increased her participation to about 50% of the home visit but was not yet engaging in novel activities. Finally, a goal was set for Ms. Bynum to apply for a job and for day care for Marcus. At the end of six months she had discussed various options with the interventionist but had not yet submitted an application.

SUMMARY

This chapter addresses issues and procedures related to assessing family needs and stress. Families often experience exacerbated stress associated with the care of a handicapped child. Many measures of stress have been developed. Although they appear to be reliable and valid, their usefulness in early intervention is limited because they do not readily lend themselves to the specification of family goals.

Two instruments for assessing family needs in a functional fashion were presented, with examples of translating family-needs data into family goals. The importance of determining family perceptions of needs was emphasized, as was the usefulness of both structured and open-ended response formats. Case studies with the Family Needs Survey demonstrate the usefulness of such information but also show the complex nature of family-needs assessment and the importance of open discussion of needs before goals are established or services are provided.

REFERENCES

Abidin, R. R. (1986). *Parenting stress index* (2nd ed.). Charlottesville, Va.: Pediatric Psychology Press.

Bailey, D. B. (1987). Collaborative goal-setting with families: Resolving differences in values and priorities for services. *Topics in Early Childhood Special Education, 7*(2), 59–71.

Bailey, D. B., & Simeonsson, R. J. (in press a). Home-based early intervention. In S. L. Odom & M. B. Karnes (Eds.), *Early intervention for infants and children with handicaps: An empirical base.* Baltimore: Paul H. Brookes.

Bailey, D. B., & Simeonsson, R. J. (in press b). Assessing the needs of families with handicapped infants. *Journal of Special Education.*

Bailey, D. B., Simeonsson, R. J., Isbell, P., Huntington, G. S., Winton, P. J., Comfort, M., & Helm, J. (1988). Inservice training in family assessment and goal-setting for early interventionists: Outcomes and issues. *Journal of the Division of Early Childhood, 12,* 126–136.

Bailey, D. B., & Winton, P. J. (1987). Stability and change in parents' expectations about mainstreaming. *Topics in Early Childhood Special Education, 7*(1), 73–88.

Beavers, J., Hampson, R. B., Hulgus, Y. F., & Beavers, W. R. (1986). Coping in families with a retarded child. *Family Process, 25,* 365–378.

Beckman, P. J. (1983). Influence of selected child characteristics on stress in families of handicapped infants. *American Journal of Mental Deficiency, 88,* 150–156.

Blackard, M. K., & Barsh, E. T. (1982). Parents' and professionals' perceptions of the handicapped child's impact on the family. *TASH Journal, 7,* 62–70.

Burden, R. L. (1980). Measuring the effects of stress on the mother of handicapped infants: Must depression always follow? *Child: Care, Health, and Development, 6,* 111–125.

Crnic, K. A., Friedrich, W. N., & Greenberg, M. T. (1983). Adaptation of families with mentally retarded children: A model of stress, coping, and family ecology. *American Journal of Mental Deficiency, 88,* 125–138.

Dunst, C. J. (1985). Rethinking early intervention. *Analysis and Intervention in Developmental Disabilities, 5,* 165–201.

Dunst, C. J., Trivette, C. M., & Cross, A. H. (1986). Mediating influences of social support. *American Journal of Mental Deficiency, 90,* 403–417.

Friedrich, W. N., Greenberg, M. T., & Crnic, K. (1983). A short-form of the questionnaire on resources and stress. *American Journal of Mental Deficiency, 88,* 41–48.

Gallagher, J. J., Beckman, P., & Cross, A. H. (1983). Families of handicapped children: Sources of stress and its amelioration. *Exceptional Children, 50,* 10–19.

Hetherington, E. M. (1984). Stress and coping in children and families. In A. Doyle, D. Gold, & D. S. Moskovitz (Eds.), *Children in families under stress.* (pp. 7–33). *New Directions for Child Development,* no. 24. San Francisco: Jossey-Bass.

Hill, R. (1949). *Families under stress.* New York: Harper & Row.

Holroyd, J. (1974). The questionnaire on resources and stress: An instrument to measure family response to a handicapped member. *Journal of Community Psychology, 2,* 92–94.

Holroyd, J. (1986). *Questionnaire on resources and stress for families with a chronically ill or handicapped member: Manual.* Brandon, Vt.: Clinical Psychology Publishing.

Holroyd, J., & McArthur, D. (1976). Mental retardation and stress on the parents: A contrast between Down's syndrome and childhood autism. *American Journal of Mental Deficiency, 80,* 431–436.

Horowitz, M. D. (1980). Psychological response to serious life events. In V. Hamilton & D. M. Warburton (Eds.), *Human stress and cognition* (pp. 235–263). New York: John Wiley & Sons.

Loyd, B. H., & Abidin, R. R. (1985). Revision of the parenting stress index. *Journal of Pediatric Psychology, 10,* 169–177.

McKinney, B., & Peterson, R. A. (1987). Predictors of stress in parents of developmentally disabled children. *Journal of Pediatric Psychology, 13,* 133–150.

Pearlin, L. I., Menaghan, E. G., Lieberman, M. A., & Mullan, J. T. (1981). The stress process. *Journal of Health and Social Behavior, 22,* 337–356.

Pollner, M., & McDonald-Wikler, L. (1985). The social construction of unreality: A case study of a family's attribution of competence to a severely retarded child. *Family Process, 24,* 241–254.

Rahe, R. H. (1975). Epidemiological studies of life change and illness. *International Journal of Psychiatry in Medicine, 6,* 133–146.

Salisbury, C. L. (1987). Stressors of parents with young handicapped and non-handicapped children. *Journal of the Division for Early Childhood, 11,* 154–160.

Schilling, R. F., Gilchrist, L. D., & Schinke, S. P. (1984). Coping and social support in families of developmentally disabled children. *Family Relations, 33,* 47–54.

Stein, R. E. K., & Reissman, C. K. (1980). The development of an impact-on-family scale: Preliminary findings. *Medical Care, 18,* 465–472.

Turnbull, A. P., & Turnbull, H. R. (1986). *Families, professionals, and exceptionality: A special partnership.* Columbus, Oh.: Merrill Publishing Company.

Wikler, L. M., Hanusa, D., & Stoycheff, J. (1986). Home based respite care, the child with developmental disabilities, and family stress: Some theoretical and prognostic aspects of process evaluation. In C. Salisbury & J. Intagliata (Eds.), *Respite care: Support for persons with developmental disabilities and their families.* Baltimore: Paul H. Brookes.

Wikler, L., Wasow, M., & Hatfield, E. (1981). Chronic sorrow revisited: Parent vs. professional depiction of the adjustment of parents of mentally retarded children. *American Journal of Orthopsychiatry, 51,* 63–70.

Winton, P. J., & Bailey, D. B. (in press). The family-focused interview: A collaborative mechanism for family assessment and goal-setting. *Journal of the Division for Early Childhood.*

Winton, P. J., & Turnbull, A. P. (1981). Parent involvement as viewed by parents of preschool handicapped children. *Topics in Early Childhood Special Education, 1,* 11–19.

6

Assessing Critical Events

As a group, parents with handicapped children experience greater levels of stress than do families with nonhandicapped children (Gallagher, Beckman, & Cross, 1983; Kazak, 1986). The burden of caring for a handicapped child is generally viewed as a persistent, lifelong problem (Korn, Chess, & Fernandez, 1978). However, some studies have failed to find differences in stress between parents of handicapped and nonhandicapped children at particular ages or stages of development (e.g., Salisbury, 1987). It is quite likely that family stress is a factor that fluctuates over time. Generally fluctuations center around specific, critical life events that may cause elevated concern and stress. This chapter focuses on the rationale, procedures, and clinical use of assessing important critical events as a part of a family assessment plan.

THE RATIONALE FOR ASSESSING CRITICAL EVENTS

The assessment of critical events is important for at least three reasons. First, certain life events can prove disruptive or stressful for almost all families. Second, families with handicapped children often experience addi-

This chapter was contributed by Donald B. Bailey, Jr., University of North Carolina at Chapel Hill.

tional stressful events over and above those experienced by nonhandi-capped families. Finally, preparation for and support during critical events are important mechanisms for coping.

Stressful Events as Universal

Unfortunately, many life events are stressful to both individuals and fami-lies. Stressful events can be conceptualized as either normative or nonnor-mative (McCubbin et al., 1980).

Normative Events. Several authors have used normative or developmental models to describe particularly stressful events that occur in the process of forming and raising a family (Solomon, 1973; Tseng & McDermott, 1979). For example, Solomon (1973) proposed a sequence of major tasks or events faced by most families, including marrying, giving birth, early child rearing, allowing independence to adolescent children, and dealing with the con-tracting of families as children leave the home. McCubbin et al. (1980) extended the latter phases to include the "empty-nest" syndrome, retire-ment, widowhood, and relocation and institutionalization as functions of aging. Stress is assumed to occur across each of these events, because the events disrupt usual behavior patterns, force changes in roles and respon-sibilities, or involve the loss of *something* (e.g., curtailment of independence after marriage), the loss of a *person* (e.g., a child moving away), or an *emo-tional* loss (e.g., sadness related to children growing up or the loss of a sense of meaning in life upon retirement from a job).

Nonnormative Events. Other events may occur at any point in individual or family development, and may even recur over time. Some of the most visible, common, and stressful events include loss of job through firing or layoff; divorce; death of a spouse, parent, friend, or child; moving; serious illness; job transitions; and financial crises (Abidin, 1986; McCubbin & Figley, 1983; Holmes & Rahe, 1967; McCubbin & Patterson, 1987b). Al-though these events differ from normative events in that their occurrence is less predictable, the pattern of disruption is similar.

Effects of Stressful Life Events. The life events described are assumed to cause stress because they either create loss or force change. In many cases, the event violates expectations (e.g., job loss when employee expects to con-tinue working) and can lead to reduced feelings of self-worth and control or mastery of the environment (Pearlin, Menaghan, Lieberman, & Mullan, 1981). Horowitz (1980) proposes a pattern of common stages or responses that follow serious life events, with sequential phases of outcry, denial, intrusion, working through, and completion. Although these life events are stressful for nearly everyone who experiences them, their effects are medi-ated by how the individual or family perceives the event and the resources available for support (Hill, 1949).

Stressful Events Associated with Handicapped Children

A number of theorists have extended the developmental perspective of life events to families with handicapped youngsters. MacKeith (1973), for example, suggested that such families experience four major crisis periods. The first crisis is the point at which the family becomes aware that a child is handicapped. This may occur at birth, in early childhood when major developmental milestones are delayed or not achieved, or in school when academic problems become evident. The second major crisis is the point at which parents must decide about their child's educational placement. This may occur in early childhood when parents decide between a normal or a specialized preschool, or in public school when parents weigh the availability, costs, and benefits of various placement options. The third major crisis occurs when the handicapped child leaves school and parents are confronted with issues related to employment and independent living. The final crisis occurs as parents age and realize that soon they will no longer be able to monitor the care of their handicapped son or daughter.

Bray, Coleman, and Bracken (1981) surveyed 169 parents of handicapped offspring ranging in age from 1 to 31 years, asking the parents to describe in an open-ended format the critical events or stresses they experienced in parenting their handicapped child. Issues relating to educational placement and service were identified most frequently as critical events, followed by impact of the initial diagnosis. Other concerns included impact on one or more family members, medical management, incomplete or inaccurate diagnostic information, and prognosis for the future.

Wikler (1981) described 10 critical periods or events likely to be stressful for families of handicapped children. Five of these relate to discrepancies in expectations for the child's development: the age at which the child should have begun walking (12–15 months), the age at which the child should have begun talking (24–30 months), the beginning of public school, the onset of puberty, and the child's twenty-first birthday. Wikler suggests that the major precipitator of these crises is the gap between what is expected and what occurs. These events are highly visible attainments anticipated by all parents. When these critical periods occur, they are overt reminders of delay (e.g., puberty in an adolescent functioning at a 6-year-old level).

The other five events proposed by Wikler are nondevelopmental, may occur at any time, and may recur. They are initial and subsequent diagnoses; the matching or exceeding of the abilities of a handicapped child by a younger child; discussions about or placement of a child outside the home; exacerbated behavior, seizure, or health problems; and issues related to guardianship and care. According to Wikler,

> this second group of crises involves transitions away from the traditional carrying out of parental responsibilities, shifts away from the family and towards professionals in the assignment of decision-making. The process of negotiating with the social service delivery system and the stigma of that process contributes to the

stress of the transitional crises. The parents are reminded at each point that had their child been normal, this process would not have been necessary. This, in turn, will re-evoke the disappointment about their situation. (p. 285)

Wikler, Wasow, and Hatfield (1981) asked parents of handicapped children to rate how they felt at each of the 10 hypothesized crisis points. They also asked them to draw a free-form graph showing how their feelings (ranging from "awful" to "just great") varied over time. The vast majority of parents drew graphs depicting a series of ups and downs, as opposed to a generally stable pattern of effects. Parents rated each of the 10 crises points as stressful. Social workers who were asked to rate how they thought their clients would feel at the 10 crisis points were more likely to overestimate how stressful early experiences were and to underestimate the effects of later stressful experiences. However, the social workers drew similar graphs, reflecting a recognition of variability in parents' needs and stress over time.

Preparation for and Support during Stressful Events

Recognizing the impact of certain life events on families has important clinical implications for early interventionists. McCubbin and Figley (1983) argue that two factors play key roles in individual and family reactions to stressful events: perceptions of the event and available support. An unexpected and seemingly insurmountable event is likely to be more stressful than one for which some preparation has been made and for which families perceive adequate services and also support for coping and decision making.

Wikler et al. (1981) argue for a life-span continuum of services for families that is especially sensitive to predictable crises of families with retarded or otherwise handicapped children. They emphasize the importance of *informational needs* and *professional support* during such events. Wikler (1981) states that parental awareness and anticipation of potential crises is an important factor in dealing with events, and suggests the formation of parent groups to prepare and support parents during vulnerable periods. Finally, "parents would find themselves being less critical about their responses to the difficulties of having a mentally retarded child if they were aware of the normality of these disappointments over time" (p. 287).

PROCEDURAL CONSIDERATIONS IN ASSESSING LIFE EVENTS

The assessment of critical events is not necessarily a straightforward process. Two broad topics are discussed in this section: examples of critical events, and general guidelines and considerations in assessing those events.

Examples of Critical Events

Most theorists have discussed critical events from a life-span perspective. Early interventionists and preschool special educators must deal with those events that typically occur before age 6. Drawing and expanding on the work of others, six examples of critical events are important in the early childhood years: diagnosis, attainment of developmental milestones, obtaining and participating in initial services, transitions, medical crises, and normal life events.

Diagnosis.   Initial diagnosis of a handicap is probably the most visible and widely discussed critical event, and one that usually occurs at birth or during the infant and preschool period. It has been argued that families go through a predictable sequence of stages in reacting to the birth or subsequent diagnosis of a child with a handicap. For example, Drotar, Baskiewicz, Irwin, Kennell, and Klaus (1975) suggested five stages: shock, denial, sadness/anger/anxiety, adaptation, and reorganization. The first stage is characterized by the shock or surprise associated with diagnosis, particularly if the news is completely unexpected. The second phase is characterized by a period of denial and disbelief and may be accompanied by repeated appointments with other professionals to discuss the diagnosis, hoping a mistake was made. This period may also include an intensive search for cures or treatment. The third stage is an emotional period, often marked by depression or sadness, in which the certainty of the handicap is realized. The fourth phase involves a gradual reduction of anxiety and the beginning of acceptance of the handicap. The final phase is characterized by a reorganization and redefinition of the family to accommodate the handicapped family member and involves long-term acceptance of the situation.

The stages described are representative of those suggested by other theorists (Blacher, 1984) and are also comparable to reactions displayed to other serious life events (e.g., Horowitz, 1980). However, several cautionary notes are important. Not every family experiences these stages, and when they do occur, the stages are not experienced in the same manner or intensity. Little research has documented the universality of these stages, and thus their usefulness should be critically examined. In a study of 77 parents with severely handicapped young children, Eden-Piercy, Blacher, and Eyman (1986) found that a five-factor model of parental reactions did not adequately fit the data. Three groups of reactions were found: shock-guilt-despair, refusal-denial, and adjustment-recovery-acceptance. Futhermore, interventionists should be aware that diagnosis may not be a one-time event and may recur throughout the early childhood period. For example, a family may learn at birth that their child has Down syndrome. At 15 months they may receive an additional diagnosis of hearing impairment. At 36 months they may be told their child is severely retarded. Each of these events represents a new diagnosis and may evoke a cycle of reactions similar to those observed upon initial diagnosis.

Developmental Milestones.   A second example of critical events likely to be problematic in the early childhood years is the failure of the infant or preschooler to attain significant developmental milestones. Although overall lack of development is always problematic, certain milestones are critical, because they are "symbolic markers of important periods of growth toward independence" (Wikler, 1981, p. 285). Wikler identified two such milestones in the early childhood period: walking and talking. However, others are likely to be important, including smiling, rolling over, crawling, eating, and becoming toilet trained. Each event is a symbolic and functional step toward independence. In addition, each is talked about among families, with all families frequently asking questions such as "Is your child walking yet?" These are emotionally laden attainments for families; however, the meaning and importance of each may vary across families according to individual expectations or values. Thus, every milestone should not be assumed to be a crisis for every family. However, interventionists should be aware that although the "discrepancy factor" between handicapped and nonhandicapped youngsters always exists, some events highlight the discrepancy and cause stress among family members.

A related issue occurs when a younger, nonhandicapped child begins to demonstrate skills that the handicapped child cannot yet perform. This event becomes a reminder of the discrepancy between the children's development and can be a critical event.

Obtaining Services.   A third type of event likely to be stressful involves efforts to obtain services for the child. Obtaining initial services has often been discussed as stressful (e.g., Bernheimer, Young, & Winton, 1983), for several reasons. Parents may still be struggling with the fact that their child needs special services. They may not know where to go for services and may feel they lack the skills to evaluate and decide among competing services. They are asked to participate in interdisciplinary team meetings and contribute to the decision-making process, and often may feel they do not have sufficient knowledge to make important decisions (Goldstein & Turnbull, 1982).

Interventionists should recognize that the issues described do not pertain to obtaining initial services alone. Parents are frequently confronted with these same issues each time new decisions need to be made or resources sought for appropriate services.

Transitions.   Transitions are difficult for all of us. Changing jobs, getting married, or moving to a new city are examples of stressful changes. For parents of handicapped youngsters, transitions are unsettling because of the uncertainty that surrounds them—how their child will react, whether the quality of services will be adequate, or how the routine will be changed by the transition. Transition issues are faced by all families with handicapped youngsters from the early years through adulthood (Ianacone & Stodden, 1987). The two most common transitions during early childhood are the transition from infant (usually home-based) to preschool (usually center-based) programs and the transition from preschool to elementary school programs. These events represent important opportunities for professionals to assess child and family needs and to provide support and assistance (Fowler, 1982). Transitions are likely to be more successful and satisfying for parents if they are well planned, include multiple opportunities for discussion, involve parents in decision making, and include adequate preparation for both children and families (Johnson, Chandler, Kerns, & Fowler, 1986).

Medical Crises. A recent study found that illnessess represented the greatest source of stress across all families with infants and young children (McKim, 1987). Parents of handicapped children are more likely to be confronted with serious medical issues, such as corrective surgery, the onset of seizures, low birthweight, or medical emergencies. Obviously, these events are highly stressful. Some are unanticipated and must be dealt with spontaneously. Others (e.g., corrective surgery) are planned, and in such cases professionals can perform an important preparatory and information-sharing role.

Normal Life Events. Finally, interventionists should be aware that families with handicapped children are not exempt from normal life events such as death, divorce, financial crises, or job layoffs. Awareness of such events helps place intervention efforts in perspective and alerts professionals to times when they should provide a supportive role rather than asking too much.

Guidelines in Assessing Critical Events

Five general guidelines should be followed in regard to the assessment of critical events. First, anticipatory assessment is important. Much information gathered on family needs, such as in the measures described in Chapter 5, is based on parental perceptions of need after an event or problem has occurred. Although many events cannot be anticipated, others can. Anticipatory assessment provides a specific context within which professionals can be supportive. Furthermore, it allows families to prepare for certain events to lessen their stressfulness.

Second, both interventionist and parental perspectives on events must be emphasized. Professionals have the advantage of working with many parents of handicapped children. Thus, they can draw on an experiential basis in anticipating potentially stressful events. However, each parent views events from a different perspective. Therefore, the professional must exercise caution in assuming a problem where one does not exist and must ascertain the extent to which a given family perceives the event as problematic. Third, the interventionist should exercise caution to prevent the assessment from actually creating a problem. By highlighting certain events, professionals may inappropriately increase parents' awareness and attach significance to an event that originally had not seemed particularly important.

Fourth, the very nature of critical events is such that they may occur at any time and some may recur. This fact supports the importance of frequent monitoring of family status over time. Finally, all forms of data collection may be used to gather critical event data. For example, parents or professionals may respond to standardized checklists or surveys indicating the presence or absence of specific events. Such measures may be useful in documenting whether certain events have occurred recently or are about to occur. Interviews may then determine whether the event concerns the family or individual family members. Subsequent direct observation may guide the professional in deciding how best to provide support. For example, in preparing for an upcoming transition to a preschool or kindergarten program, the professional could visit and observe the new program with the parents to determine the specific skills the child might need for the placement to be successful.

REPRESENTATIVE PROCEDURES FOR ASSESSING CRITICAL EVENTS

Several measures have been developed for assessing life events. Most have focused on normal life events and not those events particularly associated with having a handicapped child.

Assessing Normal Life Events

The assessment of normal life events assumed to be stressful for families is typically done by having family members (usually parents) respond to checklists or surveys on which they indicate whether specific events have occurred. Three such measures are described here: the Recent Life Changes Questionnaire, the Life Experiences Survey, and the Family Inventory of Life Events and Changes.

The Recent Life Changes Questionnaire. The RLCQ (Rahe, 1975) is a revised version of an instrument originally referred to as the Schedule of Recent Events (Hawkins, Davies, & Holmes, 1957). One of the oldest and most widely used instruments to measure life changes, it consists of 55 statements regarding life changes in health, work, home/family, personal/ social, and financial areas. Respondents read each statement; if the event has occurred within the past two years, the respondent marks one of four columns indicating the length of time since the event occurred: 0–6, 7–12, 13–18, or 19–24 months. Results may be interpreted in two ways. First, responses can be compared with those obtained from a normative population of healthy individuals who were asked to estimate the average degree of adjustment required by each event (Holmes & Rahe, 1967). However, because individual reactions are likely to vary considerably, Rahe (1975) suggests that respondents go back through their questionnaire and follow these instructions.

> Persons adapt to their recent life changes in different ways. Some people find the adjustment to a residential move, for example, to be enormous, while others find very little life adjustment necessary. You are now requested to "score" each of the recent life changes that you marked with an "X" as to the amount of adjustment you needed to handle the event.
>
> Your scores can range from 1 to 100 "points." If, for example, you experienced a recent residential move but felt it required very little life adjustment, you would choose a low number and place it in the blank to the right of the question's boxes. On the other hand, if you recently changed residence and felt it required a near maximal life adjustment, you would place a high number, toward 100, in the blank to the right of that question's boxes. For intermediate life adjustment scores you would choose intermediate numbers between 1 and 100.
>
> Please go back through your questionnaire and for each recent life change you indicated with an "X," choose your personal life change adjustment score (between 1 and 100) which reflects what you saw to be the amount of life adjustment necessary to cope with or handle the event. Use both your estimates of the intensity of the life change and its duration to arrive at your scores. (p. 137)

This procedure allows respondents to describe the impact of a given event as they perceive it.

Numerous studies have documented the usefulness of the RLCQ as an indicator of life stress. The most predictable and consistent finding across these studies is that life event scores are significant predictors of rates of illness up to one year following the event, documenting the important impact of these events on families and individuals (Rahe, 1978).

The Life Experiences Survey.   The RLCQ yields an index combining both undesirable and desirable events. Sarason, Johnson, and Siegel (1978) proposed the Life Experiences Survey as an alternative instrument to assess the impact of life changes. The LES contains 57 items representing events frequently experienced in life and potentially stressful. As with the RLCQ, respondents go through a two-step process in completing the questionnaire; however, the responses are different. First, the respondent is directed to check those events experienced within the past year and to indicate whether the event happened within the last six months. Then the respondent indicates the nature and extent of the impact on his or her life on a 7-point scale ranging from −3 (extremely negative impact) to +3 (extremely positive impact). A rating of 0 indicates no impact. Data presented by the authors indicate acceptable levels of test/retest reliability for the measure. Validity studies indicate that the instrument relates to anxiety, personal maladjustment, and depression. In addition, persons with high levels of negative change tend to score in the "external" direction on locus-of-control scales. The authors also report that the LES correlated significantly higher with dependent measures than did the Schedule of Recent Events.

The Family Inventory of Life Events and Changes.   The Family Inventory of Life Events and Changes (McCubbin & Patterson, 1987b), was designed to assess the "pile-up," or accumulation, of life events experienced by a family. The most recent version of the FILE consists of 71 items grouped into nine scales:

1. Intrafamily strains conflict (e.g., a family member depends on alcohol or drugs)
2. Marital strains (e.g., spouse had an affair)
3. Pregnancy or childbearing strain (e.g., abortion or unwanted pregnancy)
4. Financial and business strains
5. Work-family transitions and strains (e.g., a family member quit or lost a job)
6. Illness and family care strains
7. Losses (e.g., death of close relative)
8. Transitions "in and out" (e.g., child begins college)
9. Family legal violation

Respondents simply check "yes" or "no" for each event to indicate whether the change happened in their family during the last 12 months. As with the other measures described, this is not an anticipatory measure but an after-the-fact documentation of events. It differs from the RLCQ and the LES in that it is a family-focused inventory that documents events experienced by *any* family member.

Reliability studies have indicated the scale to be internally consistent for total scores (.81), with lesser reliability for subscale scores. The authors therefore recommend using only the total score rather than subscale scores. Validity of the measure is supported by findings indicating that it discriminates between high-conflict and low-conflict families. Also, higher scores or stressful life events are associated with poorer family cohesion, independence, and organization (McCubbin & Patterson, 1987b).

For clinical purposes, the authors recommend that fathers and mothers complete the form separately, with both scores subsequently used to determine *family* stress. Five scoring procedures are provided, varying according to who completes the instrument and whether a weighting procedure is followed. Normative data for scale interpretation are provided. Families may then be classified as having high-, moderate-, or low-stress scores. In using the information with families, McCubbin and Patterson (1987b) suggest the following:

> Interpretation of these scores to families must be treated with care and sensitivity to their feelings and concerns. It is not generally helpful to alarm a family as to the stressfulness of their circumstances on the basis of scores either below or above the normal range. Rather, the emphasis of interpreting scores would be better

focused upon: (1) the family's vulnerability to future stressful life events or strains; (2) the family's use of important psychological, interpersonal and tangible resources and strengths that may be exhausted in the near future; (3) specific stressors and specific abilities in managing these demands (that is, what are they doing to help themselves); (4) the family's feelings about their circumstances and difficulties; and (5) the family's problem-solving ability to resolve or eliminate some of the more manageable demands. (p. 93)

In addition to the basic FILE measure, modifications of the instrument are available for use with adolescents (McCubbin & Patterson, 1987a) and young adults (Grochowski & McCubbin, 1987).

Assessing Events Specific to Families with Handicapped Children

Although the life-event inventories just described include questions related to problems of individual family members, none was designed to assess the specific events often experienced by parents with young handicapped children. To our knowledge, no such measure has been published, perhaps because family experiences are unique. Also, it is quite possible that a formal assessment tool is not needed initially to identify critical events. Informal assessments may be sufficient if used systematically and regularly.

Drawing on the work of Bray, Coleman, and Bracken (1981), Wikler (1981), MacKeith (1973), and others, we developed an informal assessment tool while operationalizing the family-focused intervention model (Bailey et al., 1986). Displayed in Table 6.1, the Critical Events Checklist contains eight questions regarding events commonly observed during the early childhood period—four developmental and four nondevelopmental. We recommend that some version of the checklist be used at regular intervals to alert the interventionist to recent or upcoming events potentially stressful for families. The checklist is completed by the professional and essentially serves a screening function. If any item is scored "yes," the interventionist uses that information for more extended discussions with family members. If the topic is important, the interventionist either gathers additional assessment information or works collaboratively with families to set goals and provide or stimulate support services.

TRANSLATING DATA ON CRITICAL EVENTS INTO GOALS AND SERVICES

The purpose of family assessment is to identify family needs and priorities for services. Identifying critical events such as those described is an important step in this process. A critical events checklist used alone, however, probably yields insufficient information for the provision of individualized service. This information can only be obtained by determining parents' perceptions of the events, usually through face-to-face discussions as de-

TABLE 6.1
Critical Events Checklist

Nondevelopmental Events		
1. Has family learned of diagnosis within the last six months?	Yes	No
2. Does handicapped child have a younger sibling who is at the point where s/he is matching or *beginning* to exceed the handicapped child's abilities?	Yes	No
3. Is the family anticipating a program transition (e.g., child will enter a developmental center) within the next six months?	Yes	No
4. Is the child expecting a medical operation within the next six months?	Yes	No
Developmental Events		
1. Has the child just reached or is s/he about to reach the age at which most children walk and is not walking?	Yes	No
2. Has the child just reached or is about to reach the age at which most children begin to feed themselves independently, and is not self-feeding?	Yes	No
3. Has the child just reached or is about to reach the age at which most children talk and is not talking?	Yes	No
4. Has the child just reached or is about to reach the age at which most children are toilet-trained (bladder control) and is not toilet-trained?	Yes	No

From D. B. Bailey, R. J. Simeonsson, P. J. Winton, G. S. Huntington, M. Comfort, P. Isbell, K. J. O'Donnell, & J. M. Helm. Family-focused intervention: A functional model for planning, implementing, and evaluating individualized family services in early intervention. *Journal of the Division for Early Childhood*, 1986, *10*, 156–171. Reprinted with permission.

scribed in Chapters 9 and 10. Once family perceptions have been identified, the interventionist can decide whether more information is needed through other assessments. If sufficient information is available, needed services, if any, could be identified.

Two events illustrate the clincial application of assessing critical events: diagnosis and transition.

Diagnosis

Family issues surrounding the diagnosis of a handicap demonstrate the importance of professional planning and support. The professional literature is full of parents' reports of dissatisfaction with how diagnostic information is presented or shared (Turnbull & Turnbull, 1985). Professionals need to recognize how emotionally laden diagnosis is for families—both initial diagnosis and subsequent diagnoses. Common complaints include insensitive communication of information and lack of sufficient time or information regarding the diagnosis. Cunningham, Morgan, and McGucken (1984) reviewed various studies of providing diagnostic information to parents. Based on that review, they developed and field tested a nine-component model of best practices to convey diagnostic information:

1. Parents are told by both a pediatrician and a home health visitor specialist
2. Parents are told as soon as possible
3. Parents are told together rather than separately
4. The infant is present
5. The meeting is held in a private place, free from disturbances, and with no other staff or students present
6. Information is presented directly and parents are given as much time as they wish to ask questions
7. Parents are given the phone number of the specialist health visitor and informed that he or she will see them as soon as and whenever they wish
8. A private place for parents to talk alone and without interruption is provided after the interview
9. A follow-up interview with both the pediatrician and the health visitor is scheduled for the next day

Field-test data clearly indicated that his process was much more satisfactory to parents than more traditional procedures. Generally, these practices do not require individualized family assessment; rather, they should be in place and provided for all families. Individualization occurs as diagnostic information is conveyed and as the professionals respond to individual concerns and reactions.

Blacher (1984) suggests that even though research has not empirically verified a sequence of stages for parental adjustment to the birth of a handicapped child, "informal but objective assessment of parental stage of adjustment could not only better sensitize professionals to the crises and feelings currently being experienced by parents, but could also influence the subsequent decisions and recommendations made" (p. 66). She suggests a four-step process. First, the professional hypothesizes the parents' stages of adjustment. Second, the professional examines the unique family situation to determine other factors contributing to family stress and to assess available resources. Third, the professional identifies the decisions to be made regarding placement, treatment, or other aspects of child and family functioning. Finally, the professional considers all this information to determine which decisions should be made and which should be postponed, as well as which option best fits the family's current understanding of the world and events affecting the family. Blacher offers the following illustration of this process:

> Consider the parent of an infant with severe handicaps (neurological impairment, gross motor delay, and suspected sensory impairment) who is clearly in shock and denying the severity of the child's impairment (Stage One). Some important individual family factors to take into account include: the presence of both parents, i.e., an intact family, two older nonhandicapped siblings, ages 8 and 11, and a strong desire of parents to raise this child just as they raised the other two. Furthermore, although the parents are having difficulty dealing with the degree of their infant's impairment, they do acknowledge an apparent physical abnormality and possible developmental delay. Recommendations might thus be to keep the child at home and begin a stimulation program with the help of a visiting home teacher. As parental denial fades in the recognition of their child's severe handicap and disappointment sets in, they may be encouraged to join a behavioral parent training program which would give them a more active role in their child's education and development, and possibly promote a more speedy adaptation to the situation. (1984, pp. 66–67)

In a later publication testing the validity of various models of family adjustment, Eden-Piercy et al. (1986) describe a 37-item questionnaire designed to assess family adjustment. As described earlier, this study found three primary categories of adjustment: shock-guilt-despair (e.g., "I feel that having a handicapped child like this is the biggest tragedy of my life"); refusal-denial (e.g., "I believe my child will one day become normal"); adjustment-recovery-acceptance (e.g., "I know my child will never be fully cured"). The authors suggest that such a questionnaire could be useful for professionals seeking to better understand parents' feelings and in stimulating discussion in parent groups.

We must caution, however, that information regarding parental adjustment is better used as a tool for interpreting parental behaviors, attitudes, and priorities. Such information helps professionals provide services in a way that is acceptable to families, given their present life view. However, the different phases of adjustment raise other issues that professionals must also address. For example, the father who denies his child's disability may resist specialized services. The parents still searching for a cure may invest large sums of money getting different diagnoses or trying various nontraditional therapies. The grieving mother may be too upset to focus on home-based training activities. Should professionals engage in practices specifically designed to move parents out of a particular stage or to accelerate parents' progress through various stages of adjustment? This question raises issues of values, professional ethics, professional boundaries, and efficacy, with no clear-cut answers. Several considerations are offered, however, as early intervention teams attempt to address such problems.

First, special educators and other therapists working with young handicapped children and their families must continue to differentiate between services they are qualified to provide and those they are not. As issues become more family oriented and more psychologically complex, they fall more into the realm of counseling. Thus, teams should, to the maximum extent possible, include social workers or trained counselors to provide more "therapeutically" oriented services.

Second, to our knowledge, no data exist regarding whether parents should experience each stage and work it out themselves, or whether active efforts to accelerate progression toward acceptance are effective and important. For some families, acceptance may end up as resignation and withdrawal from treatment rather than as progress toward investigating various treatment options. Thus, we suggest that in the absence of specialized professional support, early interventionists provide a supportive, noncritical professional environment in which parents have the resources they need to work through issues *themselves.* This recommendation does not preclude the referral of some families for more in-depth counseling. However, recognizing the commonality of various parental reactions should help professionals realize that such behaviors and reactions are not necessarily pathological or deviant but, in fact, are normal and expected.

Matheny and Vernick (1969) summarized the issues regarding support of parents during periods of adjustment as follows:

> One gains the impression from some of the articles reviewed that when the child is brought to a diagnostic clinic, it is the role of the staff to help provide amelioration of these reactions through short-term, psychotherapeutic approaches. It is not enough for the staff to show, through sympathetic regard, that they are aware of the parents' feelings; they are enjoined to explore actively those feelings. On theoretical grounds alone, emotional morbidity is not only assumed to exist in these parents, but it is often explored and sometimes treated.
>
> To take another point of view, the crisis of having an exceptional child is one which parents can and do work through without professional help. It is our contention that a learning process involving an emotional reorganization has already been embarked upon by the parents from the instant they become aware or are told that their child is different. What the parents require most from diagnostic or informative counseling is specific, clearly transmitted, honest information about the child, implications for the future, and knowledge of what concrete steps they can take to deal with the problems. Although this approach does not exclude the counselor's concern or sympathy, it avoids the pervasive exploration of suspected emotional disorders and places the greatest emphasis on helping essentially mature and rational people to learn more about their child. (pp. 953–954)

They conclude that a major priority for professionals working with families of handicapped children should be learning how to communicate effectively with parents.

Transitions

Program transitions consititute another type of critical event during which professionals can provide support for families. Examples of major transitions during the early childhood years are (1) initial program entry, (2) movement from a home-based to a center-based program, and (3) movement from preschool to kindergarten. Other transitions may include within-program changes from one class or teacher to another, changes in schedules or routines, or a move to a new city. Worthington (1987) suggests that the amount of stress and concern caused by a transition is directly related to the extent to which the transition disrupts existing schedules or routines and the number of new decisions to be made, particularly if they involve initial disagreement between parents. Knowing that a transition is imminent means that several decisions must be made. Is a transition appropriate or necessary? What placement options are available and what factors should be considered in deciding on a placement? What instructional activities or environmental modifications will maximize the likelihood of a successful transition experience? The process of answering these questions usually involves a combination of activities, including gathering additional information, visiting and evaluating placement options, and engaging in open discussions with family members.

Fowler (1980) stresses the importance of planning as a part of transition and suggests eight components necessary for successful transition from preschool to kindergarten: a transition coordinator, visits to public schools, observations in kindergarten classrooms, preschool-staff meetings, parent meetings, placement staffings, flexible and gradual transitions, and ongoing support services. Noonan and Kilgo (1987) emphasize the importance of parental involvement, interagency cooperation, and evaluation of transition efforts, and suggest that a formal individualized transition plan be developed to ensure that relevant skills are taught and necessary transition services are provided.

Vincent et al. (1980) argue that one factor important to successful transitions is the identification of "survival skills" needed in the environment to which a child is moving. Identification of key competencies has at least two implications for decision making for professionals and families. First, it provides important information about the appropriateness of the placement. If an environment is too restrictive, is not structured enough, or demands skills the child does not possess, it may be inappropriate . Second, identification of key skills provides curriculum guidance for professionals, who can focus on teaching skills likely to improve the success of transitions. Some school systems have developed inventories or checklists indicating important kindergarten survival skills (see Polloway [1987] for a review and examples of these inventories). Vincent et al. (1980) suggest four assessment strategies for determining survival skills when such checklists are unavailable:

1. The child can be placed in the new environment for a short *trial placement.* This allows parents and teachers from both programs (current and future) to observe the child to determine how well he or she functions in that environment and to identify discrepancies between current and required skills.

2. *Follow-up studies* of children who have already moved from one program to another can be conducted. Teachers in the new program could be asked to rate the degree to which the transitions were successful and identify gaps or skill deficits important for future preparatory work.
3. Teachers in the next possible placement site can be asked to generate a *list of skills* needed in their programs.
4. Through direct observation, professionals who visit programs can identify skills actually demanded of children.

In addition to assessing required child skills the parents' role in future placement sites should be investigated. If, for example, parents are expected to attend and participate in an interdisciplinary team meeting, some preparation for that experience may be important (Goldstein & Turnbull, 1982).

Finally, parents' perceptions of the upcoming transition should be assessed through open discussion. Parents often have mixed feelings about transition. For example, one mother may look forward to the respite provided by a center-based program while feeling sad that her child is no longer an infant. Another mother may want a mainstreamed program for normalization while feeling concern that her child will not receive enough specialized help. Rather than trying to convince parents of the appropriateness of a potential placement, professionals should work together with parents to explore advantages and disadvantages and to determine how, when, and where to move. Guidelines to help parents make informed decisions about transitions into preschool center-based programs are described in Winton, Turnbull, and Blacher (1984).

SUMMARY

Although having a handicapped child can be a source of continued stress for families, certain events have a high probability of creating concerns. These events provide the context for important professional support. They include normal life events experienced by most families as well as events specific to parenting a handicapped child. Five unique events include diagnoses, nonattainment of developmental milestones, obtaining services, transitions, and medical crises.

The professional's role in assessing critical events is at least twofold: (1) anticipating and planning for upcoming events such as transition or surgery and (2) reacting appropriately and supportively during and after the occurrence of unplanned events (e.g., unanticipated seizures). Although numerous life-event inventories have been published, these measures are generally not useful in identifying unique events occurring in families with handicapped children. A more informal yet systematic approach is probably best, in which the professional identifies potentially stressful events, gathers relevant follow-up information, determines parents' perceptions and resources related to the events, and discusses the events with family members to determine if and how the professional can be supportive.

REFERENCES

Abidin, R. R. (1986). *Parenting stress index* (2nd ed.) Charlottesville, Va.: Pediatric Psychology Press.

Bailey, D. B., Simeonsson, R. J., Winton, P. J., Huntington, G. S., Comfort, M., Isbell, P., O'Donnell, K. J., & Helm, J. M. (1986). Family-focused intervention: A functional model for planning, implementing, and evaluating individualized family services in early intervention. *Journal of the Division for Early Childhood, 10,* 156–171.

Bernheimer, L. P., Young, M. S., & Winton, P. J. (1983). Stress over time: Parents with young handicapped children. *Developmental and Behavioral Pediatrics, 4,* 177–181.

Blacher, J. (1984). Sequential stages of parental adjustment to the birth of a child with handicaps: Fact or artifact? *Mental Retardation, 22,*(2), 55–68.

Bray, N. M., Coleman, J. M., & Bracken, M. B. (1981). Critical events in parenting handicapped children. *Journal of the Division for Early Childhood, 3,* 26–33.

Cunningham, C. C., Morgan, P. A., & McGucken, R. B. (1984). Down's syndrome: Is dissatisfaction with disclosure of diagnosis inevitable. *Developmental Medicine and Child Neurology, 26,* 33–39.

Drotar, D., Baskiewicz, A., Irwin, N., Kennell, J., & Klaus, M. (1975). The adaptation of parents to the birth of an infant with a congenital malformation: A hypothetical model. *Pediatrics, 56,* 710–717.

Eden-Piercy, G. V. S., Blacher, J. B., & Eyman, R. K. (1986). Exploring parents' reactions to their young child with severe handicaps. *Mental Retardation, 24,* 285–291.

Fowler, S. A. (1980). Transition to public school. In K. E. Allen (Ed.), *Mainstreaming in early childhood education.* (pp. 242–254). Albany, N.Y.: Delmar.

Fowler, S. A. (1982). Transition from preschool to kindergarten for children with special needs. In K. E. Allen & E. M. Goetz (Eds.), *Early childhood education: Special problems, special solutions* (pp. 309–334). Baltimore: Aspen.

Gallagher, J. J., Beckman, P., & Cross, A. H. (1983). Families of handicapped children: Sources of stress and its amelioration. *Exceptional Children, 50,* 10–19.

Goldstein, S., & Turnbull, A. P. (1982). Strategies to increase parent participation in IEP conferences. *Exceptional Children, 48,* 360–361.

Grochowski, J., & McCubbin, H. I. (1987). Young adult family inventory of life events and changes. In H. M. McCubbin & A. I. Thompson (Eds.), *Family assessment inventories for research and practice* (pp. 111–122). Madison: University of Wisconsin-Madison.

Hawkins, N. G., Davies, R., & Holmes, T. H. (1957). Evidence of psychosocial factors in the development of pulmonary tuberculosis. *American Review of Tuberculosis and Pulmonary Disorders, 75,* 768–780.

Hill, R. (1949). *Families under stress.* New York: Harper & Row.

Holmes, T. H., & Rahe, R. H. (1967). The social readjustment rating scale. *Journal of Psychosomatic Research, 11,* 213–218.

Horowitz, M. D. (1980). Psychological response to serious life events. In V. Hamilton & D. M. Warburton (Eds.), *Human stress and cognition* (pp. 235–263). New York: John Wiley & Sons.

Ianacone, R. N., & Stodden, R. A. (Eds.) (1987). *Transition issues and directions.* Reston, Va.: Council for Exceptional Children.

Johnson, T. E., Chandler, L. K., Kerns, G. M., & Fowler, S. A. (1986). What are parents saying about family involvement in school transitions? A retrospective transition interview. *Journal of the Division for Early Childhood, 11,* 10–17.

Kazak, A. E. (1986). Families with physically handicapped children: Social ecology and family systems. *Family Process, 25,* 265–281.

Korn, S., Chess, S., & Fernandez, P. (1978). The impact of children's physical handicaps on marital quality and family interaction. In R. M. Cerner & G. B. Spanier (Eds.), *Child influences on marital and family interaction* (pp. 299–326). New York: Academic Press.

MacKeith, R. (1973). The feelings and behavior of parents of handicapped children. *Developmental Medicine and Child Neurology, 15,* 524–527.

Matheny, A. P., & Vernick, J. (1969). Parents of the mentally retarded child: Emotionally overwhelmed or informationally deprived? *Journal of Pediatrics, 74,* 953–959.

McCubbin, H. I. & Figley, C. R. (Eds.) (1983). *Stress and the family. Vol. I: Coping with normative transition.* New York: Brunner/Mazel.

McCubbin, H. I., Joy, C. B., Cauble, A. E., Comeau, J. K., Patterson, J. M., & Needle, R. H. (1980). Family stress and coping: A decade review. *Journal of Marriage and the Family, 42,* 855–871.

McCubbin, H. I., & Patterson, J. M. (1987a). Adolescent-family inventory of life events and changes. In H. M. McCubbin & A. I. Thompson (Eds.). *Family assessment inventories for research and practice* (pp. 99–110). Madison: University of Wisconsin-Madison.

McCubbin, H. I., & Patterson, J. M. (1987b). *Family inventory of life events and changes.* In H. M. McCubbin & A. I. Thompson (Eds.), *Family assessment inventories for research and practice* (pp. 79–98). Madison: University of Wisconsin-Madison.

McKim, M. K. (1987). Transition to what? New parents' problems in the first year. *Family Relations, 36,* 22–25.

Noonan, M. J., & Kilgo, J. L. (1987). Transition services for early age individuals with severe mental retardation. In R. N. Ianacone & R. A. Stodden (Eds.), *Transition issues and directions* (pp. 25–37). Reston, Va.: Council for Exceptional Children.

Pearlin, L. I., Menaghan, E. G., Lieberman, M. A., & Mullan, J. T. (1981). The stress process. *Journal of Health and Social Behavior, 22,* 337–356.

Polloway, E. A. (1987). Transition services for early age individuals with mild mental retardation. In R. N. Ianacone & R. A. Stodden (Eds.), *Transition issues and directions* (pp. 11–24). Reston, Va.: Council for Exceptional Children.

Rahe, R. H. (1975). Epidemiological studies of life change and illness. *International Journal of Psychiatry in Medicine, 6,* 133–146.

Rahe, R. H. (1978). Life change measurement clarification. *Psychosomatic Medicine, 40,* 95–98.

Salisbury, C. L. (1987). Stressors of parents with young handicapped and non-handicapped children. *Journal of the Division for Early Childhood, 11,* 154–160.

Sarason, I. G., Johnson, J. H., & Siegel, J. M. (1978). Assessing the impact of life changes: Development of the life experiences survey. *Journal of Consulting and Clinical Psychology, 46,* 932–946.

Solomon, M. A. (1973). A developmental conceptual premise for family therapy. *Family Process, 12,* 179–188.

Tseng, W. S., & McDermott, J. F. (1979). Triaxial family classifications: A proposal. *Journal of the American Academy of Child Psychiatry, 18,* 22–43.

Turnbull, A. P., & Turnbull, H. R. (1985). *Parents speak out* (2nd ed.). Columbus, Oh.: Merrill Publishing Company.

Vincent, L. J., Salisbury, C., Walter, G., Brown, P., Gruenewald, & Powers, M. (1980). Program evaluation and curriculum development in early childhood/ special education. In W. Sailor, B. Wilcox, & L. Brown (Eds.), *Methods of instruction for severely handicapped students* (pp. 303–328). Baltimore: Paul H. Brookes.

Wikler, L. (1981). Chronic stresses of families of mentally retarded children. *Family Relations, 30,* 281–288.

Wikler, L., Wasow, M., & Hatfield, E. (1981). Chronic sorrow revisited: Parent vs. professional depiction of the adjustment of parents of mentally retarded children. *American Journal of Orthopsychiatry, 51,* 63–70.

Winton, P. J., Turnbull, A., & Blacher, J. (1984). *Selecting a preschool: A guide for families of handicapped children.* Austin, Tex.: Pro-Ed.

Worthington, E. L. (1987). Treatment of families during life transitions: Matching treatment to family response. *Family Process, 26,* 295–308.

7

Assessing Family Roles and Supports

The way a family functions and deals with day-to-day responsibilities is an expression of the roles, beliefs, and values of its members. What are the important roles and beliefs influencing family functioning, and how should these characteristics be assessed? This chapter will consider the importance of assessing how families function both as a system and at the level of individual members. The role of support in family functioning will be examined in terms of personal dimensions and external dimensions. Representative measures and procedures will be reviewed and suggestions made for translating assessment into intervention.

THE RATIONALE FOR ASSESSING FAMILY ROLES AND SUPPORTS

Why assess family roles and supports? The rationale is implicit in the overall objective of this book—namely, to derive an informational base on which to plan individualized family interventions. The identification of intervention goals and their confirmation through collaborative goal setting (Bailey, 1987), described in Chapter 1, must be based on objective findings rather

This chapter was contributed by Rune J. Simeonsson, University of North Carolina at Chapel Hill.

than intuition. Brock (1986) has emphasized the importance of incorporating systematic assessment in work with families as it pertains to the related field of family therapy. "Family therapists have tended to shy away from the use of assessment tools and away from the process of diagnosis. No longer, however, is good family therapy the mere application of hunch and guesswork. We have an obligation to go through the demanding process of training ourselves in the systematic observation and diagnosis of cases before developing treatment plans" (p. 273). Brock's statement is equally, if not more, applicable to the enterprise of early intervention, in which an integrated intervention plan is developed for the family and the handicapped child. The assessment required for the development of such a plan may involve a consideration of the structural, functional, and developmental domains of the family singly or in combination. Assessment of families and their handicapped children should facilitate decision making with regard to desired intervention goals and the means to achieve such goals. The relationship of assessment to intervention can be identified in terms of three broad purposes.

One purpose is to use assessment information to provide *anticipatory guidance* for families. To provide such guidance, the developmental status of child and family must be understood. Anticipatory guidance involves providing information and services based on an understanding of these developmental needs to assist the family in coping with emerging demands. An assessment of a family, for example, may reveal an unrealistic expectation that their motor-impaired infant will master walking skills around the time most infants do. Such information can then be used to help parents revise their expectations in keeping with the developmental achievements of their infants. The Critical Events Checklist described in Chapter 6 may be particularly appropriate to derive information for anticipatory guidance.

A second purpose of assessment is to prevent *iatrogenic disability* in the family by ensuring that planned interventions facilitate, rather than hamper, the family's adaptation. The medical term *iatrogenic disease* refers to instances in which treatment results in the exacerbation rather than the amelioration of a disease condition. In work with families, plans developed by interventionists may be neither valued nor facilitating for some families. Assessment results, for example, may be used as a basis for recommending that parents become more active in formal support groups with other parents of handicapped children. The time parents spend on such activity, however, may reduce their involvement with their other children. In working with families, we need to recognize that generalizations about family functioning are often subjective, inferential, and situation-specific. As such they may do harm rather than good. This point is emphasized by Doherty's (1986) contention that "because our data base is so heavily an inferential, value-laden, human construction about shifting human conditions, we are likely to achieve no theories of human behavior that are not subject to plausible, competing interpretations of the same supporting data" (p. 260).

To minimize the development of interventions with iatrogenic potential, the interventionist should understand the family's perspective and involve the family in the negotiation of values and goals (Aponte, 1985).

A third purpose of assessment is to develop interventions that promote the *goodness-of-fit* between the abilities of the family and the demands it faces. The goodness-of-fit concept has been advocated by Chess (1986) as a conceptual model to account for positive adaptation, whereas poorness-of-fit, reflecting a lack of consonance between abilities and demands, accounts for less favorable outcomes. Chess points out that goodness-of-fit does not imply stress-free development or adaptation. On the contrary, some stress is necessary and inevitable in adaptation and development. Poorness-of-fit is defined as specific interactions in which the degree of dissonance is extreme, resulting in unfavorable outcomes. While the goodness-of-fit concept has been discussed primarily in terms of the development of the individual (Chess, 1986), the model seems appropriate when considering the match of abilities and demands in family adaptation. The nature of a good or poor fit in the family's adaptation to a handicapped infant is illustrated in Figure 7.1. The utility of the model has been examined in research on child and family variables influencing family functioning. Support for the model was illustrated in the finding of a relationship between maternal involvement and the temperament characteristic of rhythmicity in nonhandicapped infants (Sprunger, Boyce, & Gaines, 1985). The model has also been used to examine abilities and demands in maternal involvement with handicapped infants (Simeonsson, Bailey, Huntington, and Comfort, 1986) with the results interpreted in support of the fit of infant and family characteristics. At a clinical level, the goodness-of-fit concept implies that intervention plans are developed on the basis of unique infant and family characteristics. Although the demand characteristics of two 8-month-old Down syndrome infants may be similar, for example, the abilities and resources of their families may differ, indicating the need for very different intervention plans to optimize the "fit."

In meeting these broad purposes, several specific objectives of assessment can be identified. With regard to analyzing the family at the structural level, the roles of individual family members can be documented. Such documentation may be relevant to intervention planning in terms of knowing not only the distribution of roles in the family and the extent to which roles have been affected by the handicapped child, but also whether changes in family roles are desired. Documenting the role of the family as a unit may also provide important information for intervention planning. Family typologies (regenerative, resilient, rhythmic, traditionalistic), discussed in Chapter 2, represent one way in which the family can be assessed. McCubbin and Thompson (1987) propose that placing families within a typology may be valuable for making "predictions about a family unit, its capabilities, responses and outcomes in the face of stressful life events and/or crisis situations" (p. 35).

FIGURE 7.1
A Figural Representation of the Goodness of Fit Concept

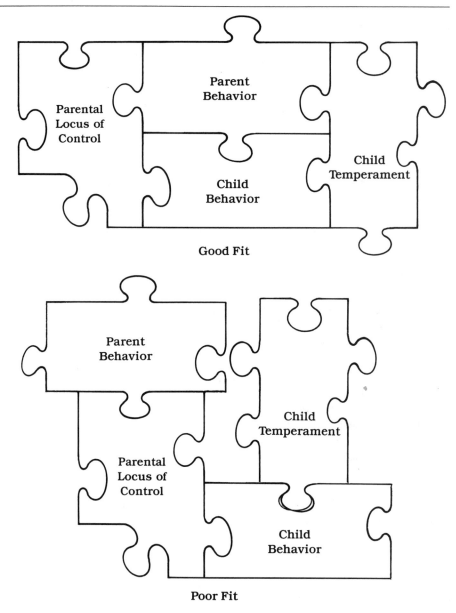

The role of support in families has been a topic of increasing interest, particularly because it has been seen as a factor moderating stress. Cooke and Lawton (1984) reported that informal support by relatives and friends of families of severely handicapped children was relatively infrequent and indistinguishable from the level provided to families of less severely handicapped children. A study by Petersen (1984) examined the importance of support relative to the stress of raising a handicapped child. Mothers with high stressors but high support were found to have fewer outcome problems than mothers with lower support. The implication of these studies is that support constitutes an important dimension to assess and target for intervention. However, that support can be defined in several ways. For the purpose of this chapter, external support is defined as support to the family provided by sources outside the family, whether physical or emotional in nature. Internal or personal support is defined as the psychological resources of a family embodied in behaviors, values, beliefs, and convictions that motivate and assure family members. Both internal and external support may facilitate the family's adaptation and are therefore important areas for assessment before the development of an individualized intervention.

PROCEDURAL CONSIDERATIONS

Before reviewing representative measures of family roles and supports, it makes sense to discuss several procedural considerations. In light of the interest in documenting social support, how should such support be measured? In a recent review of 17 social-support instruments, Orth-Gomer and Unden (1987) reported two distinct groups of instruments. One group described quantitative aspects of social networks and social interaction, whereas a second group was qualitative in nature, describing the functions and adequacy of support. The purpose of assessing support, therefore, must be considered in selecting appropriate assessment tools.

Another procedural consideration pertains to the problem of securing data that will capture information about the family as a unit. Many instruments used with families measure the perspective or response of individual members. Fisher, Kokes, Ransom, Phillips, and Rudd (1985) propose that such data can only be considered family data if they are combined or contrasted in some way, yielding data describing some relational characteristic of the family unit. To this end, they propose a variety of approaches to create relational data, including summing of scores, deriving difference scores, using methods involving combined scaling, and using multivariate procedures. Relational data thus represent information about the family in contrast to "individual level" data, which represent information by or about a single family member.

The choice of methodology is a third procedural consideration in family assessment. To some extent, this issue may depend on the variable of interest and/or the conceptual framework adopted in family assessment. If the variable of interest is the structure of relationships among family members, questionnaires are often the assessment method of choice. The role of support in the life of individual family members or of the family unit is also often assessed through questionnaires, although clinical interviews can be used productively in this regard. While constituting a widely used and rich methodology, clinical interviews often yield idiosyncratic and subjective information. These limitations can be minimized by varying the structure of the interview. Burke and DeMers (1979) have proposed that interviews be varied along three dimensions (questions, responses, and content), yielding information ranging from objective structured data to subjective unstructured data. Each dimension, in turn, is divided into three levels (degree of standardization, degree of flexibility, and breadth for questions, responses, and content). A total of 27 interview formats are thus possible, each with distinct advantages and limitations. The purpose of assessment should determine the form of the clinical interview in early intervention. More structured interview formats are recommended if comparison of information across families is desired. If the primary purpose is to explore a particular family's unique functioning, then a less structured interview format may be appropriate.

Observational methodology may be particularly useful in assessing family structure and roles. Observations, like interviews, often yield a rich array of information. Observations are time-consuming, however, and findings may be generalized only in a limited way, because they are typically specific to a certain setting. Although the choice of assessment methodology can often be determined by practical concerns of time and cost rather than by conceptual preference, we recommend that whenever possible a combination of two or more approaches be used to assess a particular domain of family functioning. Assessment of family structure, for example, could be done by interview, observation, and self-report, each yielding complementary and unique information. A multimethod approach could thus serve to identify potentially important similarities or discrepancies in information.

REPRESENTATIVE MEASURES AND PROCEDURES

In presenting representative measures within each domain, it is necessary to point out that there is substantial overlap in content across domains of roles and support. We have selected measures that seem useful in defining roles of individual family members, but they may also be useful to assess roles of the family as a unit. Furthermore, in reviewing measures of support, such measures could be equally useful in assessing resources or strategies for coping with stress as discussed in Chapter 5.

Roles of Individual Family Members

The roles of individual family members can be assessed in a variety of ways, ranging from the documentation of the immediate and extended family's composition through the use of a genogram (Hartman, 1978) to the specification of family roles in terms of responsibilities (Gallagher, Beckman, & Cross, 1983). The genogram is essentially a variation of a genealogical chart with the addition of social data; conventional symbols represent the gender and relationships of members in a family tree. Hartman (1978) has described it as a paper-and-pencil simulation of "three, four or more generations of a family which records genealogical relationships, major family events, occupational losses, family migrations and dispersal identifications and role assignments and information about alignments and communication patterns" (p. 472). A simplified genogram is shown in Figure 7.2 to illustrate the composition and relationships of an extended family. A com-

FIGURE 7.2
Sample Genogram

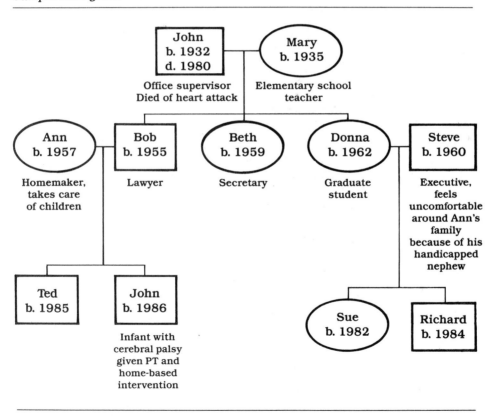

pleted genogram can organize complex data about extended families in a straightforward, visual portrayal. As such, it may be helpful in clarifying the roles of individual members of the family of the handicapped child.

A more restricted conceptualization of the roles of family members is illustrated in Breslau's (1983) research on the assessment of time use of mothers of handicapped children. An interview form was used to secure information about the amount of time mothers devoted to household work and to providing transportation and therapy for their disabled child. Although time use in this study was restricted to a few roles, the approach may lend itself to a variety of applications.

Gallagher et al. (1984) have developed the Family Roles Scale, a more detailed approach to the assessment of family roles. This scale consists of 14 general family roles and 6 child-care roles that parents may assume. The scale requires the respondent to indicate who currently performs the role, who ideally should perform that role, and the degree of satisfaction with role divisions. Representative findings for the distribution of these roles for mothers and fathers of handicapped and nonhandicapped children are presented in Figure 7.3. Assessing family roles in this fashion may facilitate the development of intervention plans in two ways: by shedding light on the burden of care shouldered by family members and by documenting the extent of consensus among family members regarding the division of general and child-specific responsibilities.

The roles of siblings in families with handicapped children is an area of increasing assessment interest. Reviews of research on these siblings indicate that adaptation may be a function of characteristics of both the handicapped child and the nonhandicapped sibling (Simeonsson & McHale, 1981). Siblings also have important and productive roles in the development of the handicapped child through teaching and modeling (Simeonsson & Bailey, 1986). Although the roles and relationships of siblings can be assessed through observation, structured interview techniques have more commonly been used. Grossman (1972) used an interview that encompassed five major domains (characteristics of the handicapped child, sibling relationships, family, friends, and curiosity). Using 37 questions, this structured interview allows comparisons of children within and across families. Results can also be compared with published research findings. The adaptation of siblings of handicapped children has not always been smooth or favorable, and there is therefore a need to assess siblings' roles to promote their functioning as family members.

Role of the Family as a Unit

The family as a unit can be assessed in a variety of ways. As with the assessment of the individual member, the domains assessed may overlap, covering such family characteristics as relationships, coping strategies, and

FIGURE 7.3

Relative Task Participation in Families with and without Handicapped Children

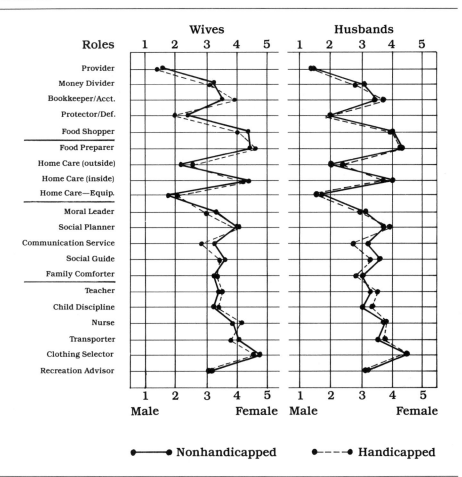

From J. J. Gallagher, W. Scharfman, & M. Bristol. The division of responsibilities in families with preschool handicapped and nonhandicapped children. *Journal of the Division for Early Childhood,* 1984, *8,* 3–12. Reprinted with permission.

the nature of resources and supports. The measures described in this section have been included because they define family functioning at a structural or system level.

Most measures of family functioning involve a questionnaire in which family members respond to an array of items. However, there are some exceptions to this strategy. One interesting approach has been described by Gehring and Wyler (1986) in the form of a three-dimensional task. Based on an assumption of structural relationships in the family, the Family-Systems-Test (FAST) assesses those relationships by quantifying hierarchies and distances among family members. The task involves a board divided into 9 × 9 squares on which figures (members) and cubes (power) can be placed to represent family relationships in terms of direction and distance. The measure is repeated several times to assess actual, ideal, and conflict representations. The representations are complemented by the analyses of semistructured interviews. To this point, the FAST has been used primarily as a clinical tool, but it represents a novel method of assessing family functioning and illustrates the importance of recognizing the dynamic aspect of family relationships in terms of actual and ideal dimensions.

A second alternative to the use of questionnaires is a rating scale based on observations of family functioning. The Beavers-Timberlawn Family Evaluation Scale (Lewis, Beavers, Gossett, & Austin-Phillips, 1976) encompasses 14 areas, with 13 areas rated on a 5-point scale and the global health/pathology index set on a 10-point scale. The 14 areas include such family characteristics as coalition, power, responsibility, permeability, and empathy. A clinician uses a videotape of a family discussion to rate family functioning in each area. Brock (1986) has reviewed the Beavers-Timberlawn Scale and endorses its value as a clinical tool, because it places the focus on changing family structure and process.

The questionnaire format encompasses many measures built on a variety of conceptual frames of the family as a unit. Several of these questionnaires have focused on family strengths. Abbott and Meredith (1986) described three such measures in a comparative study of parents with mentally retarded children and parents with nonretarded children. The Family Strengths Scale (Olson, Portner, & Bell, 1982) is a 12-item questionnaire assessing dimensions of family pride, trust, loyalty, and competence in resolving family problems. Responses are scored on a range from strongly agree to strongly disagree. The Dyadic Adjustment Scale (Spanier, 1976) is a 32-item questionnaire designed to measure marital strength. A number of specific aspects of marital interaction are assessed: cohesion, affection, satisfaction, and consensus. A third measure of family strength is the Family Adjustment Survey (Abbott & Meredith, 1986), designed specifically for the study to evaluate five major areas of family functioning. This measure uses five open-ended questions dealing with family coping, unique problems and strengths, and the nature and source of support. Abbott and Meredith found few differences between the parents of mentally retarded children and those with nonretarded children. The only two differences were found on the Family Strengths Scale, indicating that parents of mentally retarded children were less critical of family members and had a lower frequency of persistent family problems than parents of nonretarded children. The study also resulted in the identification of strengths unique to families of mentally retarded children. These strengths included the support of a spouse, parent-group participation, and religious beliefs. The assessment of family strengths through these kinds of measures may be particularly appropriate as documentation for the development of individualized family intervention plans.

A number of well-known family measures seek to assess the structural characteristics of families in one way or another. These measures, developed by different authors, are the Family APGAR, the Family Assessment Device, the Family Assessment Measure, and the Family Adaptability and Cohesion Evaluation Scales.

The FAPGAR, similar in format to the APGAR index for newborns, was developed by Smilkstein (1978) as a simple screening device of the functional state of the family. The questions are designed to elicit the family member's satisfaction with five basic areas of family function: (1) adaptation, (2) partnership, (3) growth, (4) affection, and (5) resolve. It should be emphasized that the FAPGAR is a screening instrument and should be used to complement more comprehensive measures.

The Family Assessment Device is a self-report questionnaire, also developed as a screening instrument by Epstein, Baldwin, and Bishop (1983). The 53 items on the scale cover the six areas of problem solving, communication, roles, affective responsiveness, affective involvement, behavioral control, and an index of general functioning.

The Family Assessment Measure (Skinner, Steinhauser, & Santa-Barbara, 1983) represents an operational definition of the Process Model of Family Functioning developed at McMaster University. FAM consists of 154 items distributed across (1) a general scale, (2) a dyadic relationship scale, and (3) a self-rating scale. The FAM is largely a clinical tool and can be used to assess major family strengths and weaknesses.

There are three versions of the Family Adaptability and Cohesion Evaluation Scales (FACES, I, II, and III). These versions, developed sequentially, were all derived on the basis of the Circumplex Model of family behavior. Each of the FACES instruments assesses families on the bipolar dimensions of cohesion and adaptability. FACES III (Olson, Portner, & Lavee, 1985) can yield data reflecting discrepancies between perceived and ideal family characteristics. FACES III and its earlier versions can be useful means of assessing how the family currently perceives itself. A recent review of the literature (Olson, 1986) revealed that the instrument had adequate psychometric properties supporting its use as an assessment tool in family intervention.

All the measures described were developed on the basis of various conceptual frames. In some cases a particular frame is used to derive a set of measures. One commonly used framework of family adjustment and adaptation is the T-Double ABCX Model (McCubbin & McCubbin, 1987). The T-Double ABCX is a dynamic model of family functioning with several components: (1) how a family manages stressors, (2) its capability to meet demands, (3) its appraisal of the situation, and (4) its achievement of adaptation. Four self-report measures have focused on the assessment of two of these components—namely, the pile-up of strains and stressors, and the capabilities of the family in appraisals and coping. Even though some of their content overlaps with the assessment of support, these four questionnaires are presented here, because they are designed in the context of the same conceptual framework of family adjustment. The measures, designed to assess the stressors and strains faced by a family, and three capabilities (in the form of resources, coping and appraisal) are summarized in Table 7.1 (pp. 152–153). The Family Inventory of Life Events (McCubbin, Patterson, & Wilson, 1981) was described in Chapter 6, but it is also included here, since it is a part of the set of measures. The 71-item FILE questionnaire is completed by the adult family members and yields an index of the composite demands currently faced by the family. This composite index includes markers of situational as well as developmental changes at various stages of the family's life cycle. The nine subscales and the overall index as shown in Table 7.1 reveal the comprehensive coverage of the FILE.

Assessment of the resources of the family is accomplished with the Family Inventory of Resources for Management (McCubbin, Comeau, & Harkins, 1981). The FIRM views the family as a system able to draw on resources to meet the demands assessed by the FILE. Four subscales include 98 items asking the respondent to describe the family. The four subscales of family strengths are: esteem and communication, mastery and health, support of extended family, and financial well-being. The FIRM was originally developed to assess families with handicapped children and may help to identify family resources and strengths.

Family coping capability is assessed through the Coping Health Inventory for Parents (McCubbin, McCubbin, Nevin, & Cauble, 1979). The CHIP, like the FIRM, was designed for families with special-needs children and focuses on how the family perceives its management of the child's needs. The CHIP consists of 45 items covered by three subscales assessing family coping. The coping behavior of the family is conceptualized in a hierarchical manner, proceeding from maintenance of family integration to maintenance of social support to understanding of the medical situation. The usefulness of the CHIP may lie in its ability to document a family's existing coping strategies that can be strengthened through planned interventions.

A second measure of family coping was developed for assessment of families in general—that is, for families whose children did not have identified medical conditions. The Family Crisis Oriented Personal Evaluation Scales (McCubbin, Olson, & Larsen, 1981), as shown in Table 7.1, consists of five subscales. The FCOPES was conceptualized within a family systems framework to assess both internal family interactions and those external to the family's boundaries. The 30-item inventory identifies problem-solving behaviors for acquiring social support, reframing, seeking spiritual support, family mobilization, and passive appraisal.

A review of the four measures developed within the T-Double ABCX Model reveals substantial overlap, not only in terms of such concepts as family roles in coping, problem solving, and forms of support, as addressed in Chapter 2, but also in the reciprocal concepts of demands and stress, as discussed in Chapter 5. Thus, the selection of assessment tools should be guided by the conceptual approach taken by an intervention program and the specific purpose of the assessment. The degree of overlap among measures of this kind has been examined experimentally by Bloom (1985) in a comparative study of four self-report measures of family functioning. In addition to the FACES and FAM described earlier in this chapter, families were also asked to complete the Family Concept Q-Sort (VanDerVeen, 1965) and the Family Environment Scale (Moos & Moos, 1981) described in Chapter 8 under assessment of environments. A 75-item scale, covering 15 dimensions of family functioning, was extracted from the combination of these measures. These dimensions represented three general facets of family functioning: relationships, personal growth, and values and system maintenance. Bloom's (1985) findings suggest that existing measures of the family share common characteristics and that selection of a particular measure should be based on a careful consideration of particular assessment objectives.

Although a variety of tools measure roles of the family as a system, there may remain areas for which few specific instruments exist, particularly with regard to assessing families with handicapped children, because their experiences may be quite different from those faced by families in general. In the absence of formally designed tools, it may be necessary at times to rely on clinical judgment to assess family functioning. To this end, Bagarozzi (1986) has identified 15 structural and 25 process issues that can be used to evaluate the extent of dysfunction or maladaption in the family. Important representative structural aspects include the degree to which the family system is open to outside input, the extent to which family members use positive and negative feedback, and the nature and extent of boundaries within the family subsystems. Representative process issues include the extent of appropriate role enactment of parents and children, the nature of socialization and acculturation patterns, and the degree to which problem-solving skills are facilitated or impaired in the family. A review of such issues and consideration of still other issues more specific to the unique adaptational demands faced by families of handicapped children may be significant in developing intervention plans that recognize the individuality of families.

In closing this section on assessing the roles of family members and the family as a system, it is important to emphasize that the measures employed determine the nature of the information that can be obtained. Joanning and Kuehl (1986) caution that no instrument measures family phenomena the way they really are. Assessment results are, rather, a reflection

TABLE 7.1
Summary of Self-Report Measures Based on T-Double ABCX Model

Measure	Number of Items	Subscales	Format	Reliability	Validity
Family Inventory of Life Events and Changes (FILE) (McCubbin, Patterson & Wilson, 1981)	71	I. Intra-family strains II. Marital strains III. Pregnancy and childbearing strains IV. Finance and business strains V. Work–family transitions and strains VI. Illness and family care strains VII. Family losses VIII. Family transitions in and out IX. Family legal strains X. Total family pile-up	Yes/no—Did the change happen in your family during the last 12 months?	Test/retest: .64 to .84 for the various subscales Overall Test/Retest: .80 Internal consistency: total index = .81	FILE with measure of family cohesion: −.24 With measure of independence of family members: −.16 With measure of family organization: −.14 With measure of family conflict: .23
Family Inventory of Resources for Management (FIRM) (McCubbin, Comeau & Harkins, 1981)	69	Family strengths I: Esteem and communication Family strengths II: Mastery and health Extended family support Financial well-being	0–3 scale—How well the items describe the family	Internal consistency: total = .89 Family strengths I = .85 Family strengths II = .85 Extended family support = .62 Financial well-being = .85 Test/retest: not available	FIRM with measure of family cohesion: .46 With measure of expressiveness: .27 With measure of family conflict: −.30 With measure of family organization: .25

Instrument	Items	Coping Subscales	Scale	Reliability	Validity
Coping Health Inventory for Parents (CHIP) (McCubbin, McCubbin, Nevin, & Cauble, 1979)	45	Coping I: Maintaining family integration, cooperation, and an optimistic definition of the situation Coping II: Maintaining social support, self-esteem, and psychological stability Coping III: Understanding the medical situation through communication with other parents and consultation with medical staff	0–3 scale—How helpful items were in managing home-illness situation	Internal consistency: Coping I = .79 Coping II = .79 Coping III = .71 Test/retest: not available	CHIP with independent assessments of family functioning and changes in the health status of children with cystic fibrosis *Mother:* Coping I/family cohesiveness: .21 Coping II/family expressiveness: .19 Coping III/family cohesiveness: .19 *Father:* Coping I/family organization: .32 Coping II/family organization: .22 Coping III/family control: .19 Coping I/family cohesiveness: .36 Coping I/family conflict: −.21 Also validated on health status indices
Family Crisis Oriented Personal Evaluation Scales (FCOPES) (McCubbin, Olson, & Larsen 1981)	30	Coping I: Acquiring social support Coping II: Reframing Coping III: Seeking spiritual support Coping IV: Mobilizing family to acquire and accept help Coping V: Passive appraisal	1–5 Likert scale in which respondents agree or disagree with statements regarding family coping strategies	Internal consistency: Overall = .86–.87, low of .62 for passive appraisal to a high of .84 for acquiring social support Test/Retest: Overall: .81, low of .61 for reframing to a high of .95 for seeking spiritual support	Not available

Data summarized from McCubbin & Thompson (1987).

of the way in which such phenomena are represented by predetermined items and the context in which assessment takes place. In other words, assessment results are not equivalent to the phenomena but simply one of perhaps many representations of those phenomena.

INTERNAL AND EXTERNAL SUPPORT

As mentioned earlier in this chapter, level of support can be a stress-moderating factor in families with handicapped children. Such support can be classified as internal/personal or external.

Internal/Personal Support

Internal support includes those characteristics of the family that are personal and subjective. Included among internal supports are the values, beliefs, and attitudes held by the family collectively or by individual family members. In dealing with stress or demands, what sources of support does a family draw on? Although a great deal of interest has focused on environmental and social supports, individuals and families also rely on important personal resources. These could include objective cognitive processes such as problem solving and related coping strategies, as exemplified by the Coping Health Inventory for Parents discussed earlier as part of the T-Double ABCX Model of family adaptation. In this section, emphasis is placed on more subjective and personal qualities such as flexibility, persistence, and a sense of control. The number of formal measures of these areas is limited. Many characteristics can be identified as family or individual strengths; such strengths may be highly idiosyncratic and include concepts such as self-esteem and self-evaluation. Although measures of self-concept are available for individual assessment, comparable measures of a family's self-esteem and self-evaluation have not been formalized as such. In the areas of values and beliefs, the role of religion or other moral and philosophical standards has been increasingly recognized as an important domain, although assessment is typically at a general rather than a specific level. Griffith (1986) has argued persuasively for a sensitive and systematic recognition of a family's conception of God in clinical interventions with families. In this context, the religious beliefs of a family constitute an important factor in assessing its strengths (Abbott & Meredith, 1986), coping strategies, and potential response to planned interventions. Failure to document and consider such values and beliefs may preclude or seriously limit the effectiveness of intervention.

Although a number of the measures of family strengths described in the previous section could be considered measures of internal support, a few tools more specific to this domain of assessment can be identified. The Family Coping Inventory (McCubbin et al., 1979) is a 28-item questionnaire that was used in a study of parents of young infants. The study yielded three factors, two of which may represent internal support. These two pertain to (1) maintaining family integrity, and (2) being religious, thankful, and content. The third factor is more oriented to external support and reflects a coping pattern of seeking social support. These factors would also seem likely if the instrument were used with families of handicapped children.

A second type of tool that may be useful in assessing internal support measures locus of control. The locus-of-control construct has been examined extensively, both in terms of developmental and clinical correlates. In its typical form, locus of control refers to the attribution of achievement motivation—that is, beliefs pertaining to the sources of reinforcement. Weiner (1985) has proposed that several properties of causal perceptions relate to achievement. These properties are locus, stability, and controllability, and may also include globality and intentionality. Locus of control has been found to be developmental in nature, with greater internality—that is, attribution of personal causation—found with increasing age. Although a number of locus-of-control measures exist, the one we have found useful with parents of handicapped children is the Nowicki and Duke (1974) Locus of Control Scale for Adults. This scale consists of 40 true/false items. The items are generic rather than specific and deal with issues such as the causes of physical and social events (e.g., I can keep myself from catching a cold; in school there was really not much I could do about my grades). The distinction between an internal and external locus of control is based on the proportion of items (greater than 70%) answered in an internal direction.

We have examined the utility of assessing locus of control in a research study with families of handicapped children in a statewide, home-based early intervention program. Results indicated that mothers who scored as internalizers and those who scored as externalizers occurred in approximately equal numbers. A review of the demographic characteristics of these two groups revealed that mothers defined as internalizers were somewhat older, had husbands who were older, and had more favorable socioeconomic statuses than mothers defined as externalizers. Although there was no difference between the two groups in the proportion who were married, more of the mothers with an employed spouse showed an internal locus of control. The associations found between locus of control and the SES of mothers in this research are consistent with those of the larger literature on variables related to causal perceptions of control. Locus of control, as assessed in the families we studied, substantially predicted maternal caregiver involvement. A multivariate analysis revealed that locus of control was the strongest predictor of a composite index of the quality and appropriateness of maternal caregiver behavior (Simeonsson et al., 1986).

The value of documenting locus of control in assessment and intervention can be clarified by providing a case illustration. In Table 7.2, the responses of a mother scoring in the internal direction on the Adult Locus of

TABLE 7.2

Responses of Two Mothers on Representative Locus of Control Items from Nowicki and Duke (1974) Scale

	Internal Direction	External Direction
Demographics		
Maternal age	24	26
Marital status	Married	Married
SES	Middle	Middle
Number of children	2	3
Age of index child	17 months	19 months
Developmental quotient of index child	55	58
Locus of Control Scale Items		
Better to be smart than lucky?	Yes	No
Hard to change friends' opinions?	No	Yes
Good things happen because of hard work?	Yes	No
When good things happen they happen because of hard work?	Yes	No
Someone doesn't like you, little you can do about it?	No	Yes
Some people just born lucky?	No	Yes
Lot of choice in deciding who your friends are?	Yes	No

Control Scale (Nowicki & Duke, 1974) are compared with those of a mother scoring in an external direction. Although both mothers share many demographic characteristics, they differ markedly in their perception of the causes for events in their lives. The mother who scored in the external direction is by definition more likely to attribute occurrences to luck, fate, and chance, whereas the mother with an internal score is more likely to perceive a personal role in causing events. There are several practical implications of assessing locus of control in families. At one level, documentation of locus of control will help interventionists understand a parent's sense of control over events in general. At this level, locus of control must be taken into account as a factor mediating a parent's response to intervention. Parents with an internal locus of control will generally approach a proposed intervention for their child with a different sense of personal capability to effect change than parents with an external locus of control. Thus, although the goal of intervention may be the same, the method may vary as a function of the parents' locus of control. At a second level, it may be useful to target a parent's sense of control as an intervention activity in its own right. The birth and rearing of a handicapped child may contribute to a sense of external rather than internal locus of control, in that feelings of loss and inadequacy (McKeith, 1973) are equated with a personal inability to effect change or control events. Designing interventions that help families to access information, secure resources, or change behavior in their child may promote or restore a more internal locus of control. Continued research on locus of control and related constructs such as learned helplessness (Seligman, 1979) with families of handicapped children may further reveal the usefulness of assessing such characteristics to enhance the development of individualized interventions.

External Support

The assessment of sources of support that are objective rather than subjective has been an area of significant interest for use with families of handicapped children. The ways in which social support available to a family can be assessed range from graphic representation to detailed formal measures. One straightforward method to assess external support is through the visual portrayal of an ecomap. Drawing on a systems approach to the family, Hartman (1978) proposes that the ecomap serve as an assessment, planning, and intervention tool in work with families. The ecomap is a paper-and-pencil simulation that portrays "the family in their situation; it pictures the important nurturant or conflict-laden connections between the family and the world. It demonstrates the flow of resources, or the lacks and deprivations" (p. 467). The procedure is similar to the construction of the genogram described earlier and involves the representation of the immediate family as a large circle at the center of a paper. Lines are drawn from this circle to members of the extended family and to friends, with gender represented by circles or squares. Lines are also drawn to other sources of support such as institutions (church, school) or agencies (health, social welfare). The direction and strength of flow of resources or investment can be represented by heavy or light arrows, as illustrated by Skyer (1982) in the assessment of a hearing-impaired child. The ecomap can organize complex information in a simple manner and, because of its visual benefit, can serve as the basis for interviewing or can complement other data-gathering techniques.

A second approach to the assessment of external support is the use of various interview techniques. The Support System Scale (Hirsch, 1980) is a semistructured interview in which respondents are asked to list all the people who have been important to them during a specified time. After the list is compiled, follow-up questions address the manner in which each person listed has been helpful. Depending on the degree of completeness of that description, five additional questions are asked to seek elaboration of tangible, emotional, and cognitive support; social reinforcement; and socializing. The usefulness of this approach was demonstrated in a study of coping and social supports among adolescent mothers (Panzarine, 1986).

An assessment approach that incorporates both the elements of the listing process and a form of visual portrayal has been described by Kazak and Marvin (1984) in a study of social networks of families with handicapped children. Using a network interview, each parent was asked to list up to 10 family members and up to 10 friends who were valued as important and with whom the parent had had recent contact. A social-network-density grid was then developed by placing the network lists of each parent on both horizontal and vertical axes to determine the degree to which all possible pairs of network members knew each other. A simplified illustration of this approach is presented in Figure 7.4. A boundary-density index can also be obtained by calculating the number of network members identified by both husband and wife. Kazak and Marvin found that the social support networks of families with handicapped children were significantly smaller than those of comparison families. This seemed to apply specifically to friends rather than family networks. Furthermore, the networks of families with handicapped children were also denser, in that members tended to know each other. There was also greater boundary density, defined by the fact that the networks of fathers and mothers of handicapped children showed greater overlap than the parental networks of comparison families. The simplicity and visual impact of this approach make it useful in assessment and intervention planning.

The more typical approach to assessing social support uses a structured questionnaire. A number of these have been used in studies of families with handicapped children, and the features of four are summarized in Table 7.3 (pp. 160–161). A measure of family support described by German and Maisto (1982) assessed the perceived emotional support of extended family members, friends, and the church. Additional questions focused on the physical distance and the frequency of contact with the identified support sources. In their study of factors associated with differential placement of handicapped children, German and Maisto found that grandparents constituted a particularly important source of support. Another measure, the Inventory of Parents' Experience, was described by Kirkham, Schilling, Norelius, and Schinke (1986) in a study of coping styles and social supports for mothers of handicapped children. The inventory consists of 54 items covering various aspects of social support. Questions about the nature of support were followed by questions about satisfaction with that particular support. The inventory was found to document positive changes for mothers involved in a pilot intervention program.

The Family Resource Scale (Dunst & Leet, 1987) covers areas of support available to an individual or to families. Conceptualized from a needs-hierarchy basis, the 30 items range from basic nutritional resources to interpersonal growth opportunities. Parents are asked to indicate the adequacy of each identified resource. Research with families of handicapped preschool children provided psychometric support for the instrument and revealed seven distinct factors, including one pertaining to personal growth

FIGURE 7.4
Social Network Density Grid for Mother of Handicapped Child

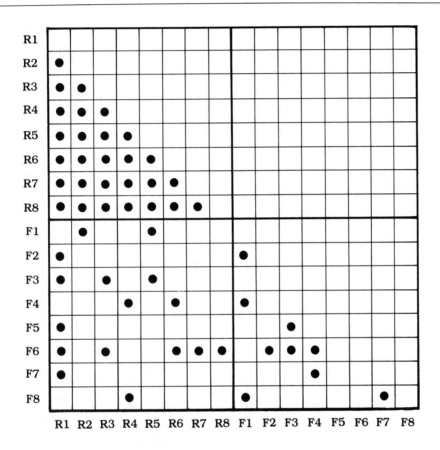

R = Relative   F = Friends

Adapted from A. E. Kazak & R. S. Marvin. Differences, difficulties and adaptation: Stress and social networks in families with a handicapped child. *Family Relations*, 1984, *33*, 67–77. As the figure shows, the mother's social network is dense for relatives and variable for friends, with some overlap between relatives and friends.

and support and another encompassing intrafamily support. Dunst and Leet propose that the Family Resource Scale can be useful in assessment and intervention because it can define the adequacy of resources available to a family. Such information is important in individualizing intervention to ensure that it is consistent with a family's current needs. The scale may also have more specific use as an intervention tool because it can "help identify parent and family needs, and provide a basis for deciding upon the

TABLE 7.3
Assessment of External Support

Measure	Number of Items	Subscales	Format	Reliability	Validity
German & Maisto (1982)	Not available	Measures included: Parent marital status Presence of additional retarded child Grandparent status Grandparent emotional support Care provided by grandparents Distance of grandparents (miles) Parent sibling emotional support Care provided by parent siblings Emotional support provided by extended family Emotional support provided by friends Church attendance Emotional support derived from church	Dichotomous (yes–no) questions and 5-point scale with high values used to indicate larger amounts of perceived care or support	Not available	Not available

Instrument	No. of Items	Content	Format	Reliability	Validity
Inventory of Parents' Experience (Kirkham, Schilling, Norelius, & Schinke, 1986)	54	Covers the respondent's social life and social supports in relation to the parenting role and general life situation	Not found	Not found	Not found
Family Resource Scale (Dunst & Leet, 1987)	30	Food and shelter Financial resources Time for family Extrafamily support Child care Specialized child resources Luxuries	5-point scale ranging from not at all adequate to almost always adequate, items ordered from most to least basic	Internal consistency: Overall = .92 average with total score = .97 Split-half = .95 Test/retest = .52	With measure of personal well-being: Total = .57 Subscale range = .22–.75 With measure of commitment to intervention: Total = .63 Subscale range = .37–.54
Maternal Social Support Index (Pascoe, Loda, Jeffries, Earp, 1981)	7	Who does various family chores (10 questions) Visits with relatives (2 questions) People that can be counted on Persons in neighborhood who would care for children Mate's expression of feeling Regular talks with persons other than husband (3 questions) Membership in organizations	Questions used in an interview; answers may be frequently, yes/no, or happy/unhappy, not sure	Not available	Not available

appropriate targets for intervention. . . . In as much as targets would be selected by the family, the probability of the intervention efforts being successful should be enhanced" (p. 123).

The Maternal Social Support Index (Pascoe, Loda, Jeffries, & Earp, 1981) consists of seven major items designed to assess internal and external support perceived by the mother. The sources of support range from immediate family members, relatives, and friends to institutions or organizations. Findings by Pascoe et al. with families of infants discharged from a neonatal intensive care unit and from our research on families with handicapped infants support the usefulness of this approach to assess social support. A disadvantage of this measure is that it is by design limited to use with mothers. The selection of measures of support, as in the case of the other measures reviewed in this chapter, should be based on a careful analysis of the intended purpose of assessment.

ASSESSMENT AND INTERVENTION

The translation of assessment findings into individualized intervention plans is a complex and inexact activity. As we propose in Chapter 11, the derivation of specific goals and intervention activities should always reflect a negotiated and collaborative process between the family and intervention professionals. In addition to the initial identification of family needs that can be defined as intervention goals, the interventionist should identify family strengths and other factors that may mediate the success of intervention. Several guidelines should govern assessment and identification of family roles and supports.

An overall guideline is that the selection of assessment tools be based on a careful consideration of the level of sophistication needed to administer and interpret the measures. Some measures are uncomplicated and can be used in a straightforward manner. Others are tied to specific conceptual frames and may require training to be used properly. The judgment about which measures are appropriate rests with the staff of the intervention program.

Second, an objective orientation should be maintained. Subjectivity may easily bias the best efforts. Much of the early literature on the family's adaptation to handicapped children presented a picture of pathology. More recent findings show that families of the handicapped are not necessarily "handicapped" themselves. In planning for family intervention, then, normality rather than pathological functioning should be assumed. The need for objectivity is also implicit in Massey's (1986) reminder that the study of families is inherently subjective because family life is an experience common to all in a historical and cultural sense.

A third guideline in translating assessment findings into intervention plans is that a parsimonious approach is required. Even when fairly simple tools are used, the findings can be interpreted in complex formulations of family characteristics. This may be particularly true for research measures based on dynamic constructs of adaptation or functioning. In the development of intervention plans, we recommend that interventionists seek simpler rather than more complex conclusions and interpretations from assessment findings. This recommendation does not discourage comprehensive assessment and planning, but rather encourages the search for simple over complex explanations of child and family needs.

A fourth consideration is the development of interventions consistent with an overall conceptual framework linking assessment and intervention. The rationale for this consideration was developed in Chapters 1 and 2 and endorses the importance of conceptual frameworks to provide scope and direction to intervention efforts. The derivation of intervention plans designed to facilitate a family's transition through a critical developmental event should thus be based on findings that reflect development status. Similarly, interventions designed to strengthen or change the family at a structural level should be derived from an appropriate structural analysis. Such matching of assessment and intervention within a conceptual frame should promote successful intervention.

SUMMARY

This chapter has focused on the assessment of the family with particular reference to its structure and sources of support. Such assessment can provide the basis for identifying intervention targets and can document characteristics that may mediate the family's responsiveness to and participation in intervention activities. Identification of family relationships, the role of extended family, and the support provided by friends and institutions may constitute strengths or resources for some families. In other families, the same documentation may reveal needs or idiosyncratic characteristics that are likely to influence the implementation or ultimate success of planned interventions. Assessing the family at the individual and system level and determining the range and strength of perceived support maximizes successful outcomes by individualizing interventions.

REFERENCES

Abbott, D. A., & Meredith, W. H. (1986). Strengths of parents with retarded children. *Family Relations, 35,* 371–375.

Aponte, H. J. (1985). The negotiation of values in therapy. *Family Process, 24,* 323–338.

Bagarozzi, D. A. (1986). Some issues to consider in the assessment of marital/family functioning. *American Journal of Family Therapy, 14,* 84–86.

Bailey, D. B. (1987). Collaborative goal-setting with families: Resolving differences in values and priorities for services. *Topics in Early Childhood Special Education, 7 (2),* 59–71.

Bloom, B. L. (1985). A factor analysis of self-report measures of family functioning. *Family Process, 24,* 225–239.

Breslau, N. (1983). Care of disabled children and women's time use. *Medical Care, 21,* 620–629.

Brock, G. W. (1986). Review of the Beavers-Timberlawn family evaluation scale. In D. A. Bagarozzi (Ed.), Family measurement techniques, *American Journal of Family Therapy, 14*(3), 271–273.

Burke, J. P., & DeMers, S. T. (1979). A paradigm for evaluating assessment interviewing techniques. *Psychology in the Schools, 16,* 51–60.

Chess, S. (1986). Early childhood development and its implications for analytic theory and practice. *American Journal of Psychoanalysis, 46,* 122–148.

Cooke, K., & Lawton, D. (1984). Informal support for the carers of disabled children. *Child: Care, Health and Development, 10,* 67–79.

Doherty, W. J. (1986). Quanta, quarks, and families: Implications of quantum physics for family research. *Family Process, 25,* 249–264.

Dunst, C. J., & Leet, H. E. (1987). Measuring the adequacy of resources in households with young children. *Child: Care, Health and Development, 13,* 111–125.

Epstein, N. B., Baldwin, L. M., & Bishop, D. S. (1983). The McMaster family assessment device. *Journal of Marital and Family Therapy, 9,* 171–180.

Fisher, L., Kokes, R. F., Ransom, D. C., Phillips, S. L., & Rudd, P. (1985). Alternative strategies for creating "relational" family data. *Family Process, 24,* 213–224.

Gallagher, J. J., Beckman, P., & Cross, A. H. (1983). Families of handicapped children: Sources of stress and its amelioration. *Exceptional Children, 50,* 10–19.

Gallagher, J. J., Scharfman, W., & Bristol, M. (1984). The division of responsibilities in families with preschool handicapped and nonhandicapped children. *Journal of the Division for Early Childhood, 8,* 3–12.

Gehring, T. M., & Wyler, I. L. (1986). Family-System-Test (FAST): A three dimensional approach to investigate family relationships. *Child Psychiatry and Human Development, 16,* 235–248.

German, M. L., & Maisto, A. A. (1982). The relationship of a perceived family support system to the institutional placement of mentally retarded children. *Education and Training of the Mentally Retarded, 17,* 17–23.

Griffith, J. L. (1986). Employing the God-family relationship in therapy with religious families. *Family Process, 25,* 609–618.

Grossman, F. K. (1972). *Brothers and sisters of retarded children.* Syracuse, N.Y.: Syracuse University Press.

Hartman, A. (1978). Diagramming assessment of family relationships. *Social Casework, 59,* 465–476.

Hirsch, B. (1980). Natural support systems and coping with major life changes. *American Journal of Community Psychology, 8,* 159–172.

Joanning, H., & Kuehl, B. P. (1986). A review of FACES III. In D. A. Bagarozzi (Ed.), Family measurement techniques, *American Journal of Family Therapy, 14,* 163–165.

Kazak, A. E., & Marvin, R. S. (1984). Differences, difficulties and adaptation: Stress and social networks in families with a handicapped child. *Family Relations, 33,* 67–77.

Kirkham, M. A., Schilling II, R. F., Norelius, K., & Schinke, S. P. (1986). Developing coping styles and social support networks: An intervention outcome study with mothers of handicapped children. *Child: Care, Health and Development, 12,* 313–323.

Lewis, J., Beavers, W. R., Gossett, J., & Austin-Phillips, V. (1976). Family system rating scales. In J. Lewis et al., *No single thread: Psychological health in family systems.* New York: Brunner/Mazel.

Massey, R. F. (1986). What/who is the family system? *American Journal of Family Therapy, 14*(1), 23–39.

McCubbin, H. I., Comeau, J., & Harkins, J. (1981). Family inventory of resources for management. In H. I. McCubbin & J. Patterson, *Family stress, resources and coping: Tools for research education and clinical intervention.* St. Paul, Minn.: Family Stress Project, University of Minnesota.

McCubbin, H. I., & McCubbin, M. A. (1987). Family system assessment in health care. In H. I. McCubbin & A. I. Thompson (Eds.), *Family assessment inventories for research and practice.* Madison: University of Wisconsin.

McCubbin, H. I., McCubbin, M., Nevin, R., & Cauble, E. (1979). *Coping-help inventory for parents.* Unpublished rating scales, School of Family and Social Sciences, University of Minnesota, St. Paul.

McCubbin, H. I., Olson, D., & Larsen, A. (1981). Family crisis oriented personal scales. In H. I. McCubbin & J. Patterson, *Family stress, resources and coping: Tools for research, education and clinical intervention.* St. Paul, Minn.: Family Stress Project, University of Minnesota.

McCubbin, H. I., Patterson, J., & Wilson, L. (1981). Family inventory of life events and changes. In H. I. McCubbin & J. Patterson, *Family stress, resources and coping: Tools for research education and clinical intervention.* St. Paul, Minnesota: Family Stress Project, University of Minnesota.

McCubbin, H. I., & Thompson, A. I. (1987). Family typologies and family assessment. In H. I. McCubbin & A. I. Thompson (Eds.), *Family assessment inventories for research and practice.* Madison: University of Wisconsin.

McKeith, R. (1973). The feelings and behavior of parents of handicapped children. *Developmental Medicine and Child Neurology, 15,* 524–527.

Moos, R. H., & Moos, B. M. (1981). *Family environment scale manual.* Palo Alto, Calif.: Consulting Psychologists Press.

Nowicki, S., & Duke, M. P. (1974). A locus of control scale for college as well as noncollege adults. *Journal of Personality Assessment, 38,* 136–137.

Olson, D. H. (1986). Circumplex model VII: Validation studies and FACES III. *Family Process, 25,* 337–351.

Olson, D. H., Portner, J., & Bell, R. (1982). *Family adaptation and cohesion evaluation scales.* Unpublished rating scales, School of Family and Social Sciences, University of Minnesota, St. Paul.

Olson, D. H., Portner, J., & Lavee, Y. (1985). Faces III. In D. H. Olson, H. I. McCubbin, H. Barnes, A. Larsen, M. Muxen, & M. Wilson (Eds.), *Family inventories: Inventories in a national survey of families across the family life cycle.* St. Paul, Minn.: University of Minnesota, Family Social Science.

Orth-Gomer, K., & Unden, A. L. (1987). The measurement of social support in population survey. *Social Science Medicine, 24,* 83–94.

Panzarine, S. (1986). Stressors, coping, and social supports of adolescent mothers. *Journal of Adolescent Health Care, 7,* 153–161.

Pascoe, J. M., Loda, F. A., Jeffries, V., & Earp, J. A. (1981). The association between mothers' social support and provision of stimulation to their children. *Developmental and Behavioral Pediatrics, 2,* 15–19.

Petersen, P. (1984). Effects of moderator variables in reducing stress outcome in mothers of children with handicaps. *Journal of Psychosomatic Research, 28,* 337–344.

Seligman, M. (1979). *Strategies for helping parents of exceptional children.* New York: Free Press.

Simeonsson, R. J., & Bailey, D. B. (1986). Siblings of handicapped children. In J. J. Gallagher & P. M. Vietze (Eds.), *Families of handicapped persons.* Baltimore: Paul H. Brookes.

Simeonsson, R. J., Bailey, D. B., Huntington, G. S., Comfort, M. (1986). Testing the concept of goodness of fit in early intervention. *Infant Mental Health Journal, 7,* 81–94.

Simeonsson, R. J., & McHale, S. M. (1981). Review: Research on handicapped children: Sibling relationships. *Child: Care, Health, and Development, 7,* 153–171.

Skinner, H. A., Steinhauser, P. D., & Santa-Barbara, J. (1983). The family assessment measure. *Canadian Journal of Community Mental Health, 2,* 91–105.

Skyer, S. C. (1982). Psycho-social aspects of deafness course as a counseling tool for the hearing impaired. *American Annals of the Deaf, 127,* 349–355.

Smilkstein, G. (1978). The family APGAR: A proposal for a family functioning test. *Journal of Family Practice, 6,* 1231–1239.

Spanier, G. B. (1976). Measuring dyadic adjustment: New scales for assessing the quality of marriage and similar dyads. *Journal of Marriage and the Family, 38,* 15–28.

Sprunger, L. W., Boyce, W. T., & Gaines, J. A. (1985). Family-infant congruence: Routines and rhythmicity in family adaptations to a young infant. *Child Development, 56,* 564–572.

VanDerVeen, F. (1965). The parents' concept of the family unit and child adjustment. *Journal of Counseling Psychology, 12,* 196–200.

Weiner, B. (1985). An attributional theory of achievement, motivation, and emotion. *Psychological Review, 92,* (4), 548–573.

8

Assessing Family Environments

Assessment in clinical services for children and families predominantly focuses on documentation of psychological or behavioral characteristics of the individual or the family system. This focus rests on the assumption that direct assessment of the child or family is the most productive step in designing interventions. The more indirect step of documenting the context of child and family functioning has had limited use. However, a growing recognition that behavior of individuals and family systems is inseparable from the physical and psychological features of the environment has been fostered by contributions from the fields of the functional analysis of behavior, ethology, and ecological psychology. The increased appreciation of the role of the environment in the child's development and behavior is in keeping with the importance of environmental factors in family functioning promoted in Bronfenbrenner's (1979) social/ecological model. The purpose of this chapter is to describe the objectives for assessing family environments and to review representative strategies and measures to perform such assessment.

This chapter was contributed by Rune J. Simeonsson, University of North Carolina at Chapel Hill.

THE RATIONALE FOR ASSESSING FAMILY ENVIRONMENTS

A number of reasons support the importance of assessing child and family environments. Most significantly, such assessment provides a way to identify the contextual and functional influences of environment on behavior. Kazak (1986) has emphasized the value of studying the relationship of persons within the setting or contexts in which they function. Drawing on Bronfenbrenner's (1979) social/ecological model, Kazak proposes two of the four levels as particularly relevant to understanding families of handicapped children. The *microsystem*, constituting the first socioecological level, involves the study of the family as a system composed of subsystems, including the handicapped child, the parental roles, the marital relationship, and the sibling effects. The second socioecological level, the *exosystem*, focuses on the family's social support network.

Assessment of family environments also yields information different from that obtained in other family assessments. These unique findings complement findings on such family characteristics as needs, resources, and relationships, described in other chapters of this book.

In addition, assessment of family environments formalizes a comprehensive approach to family assessment. Without an assessment of the environment, environmental influences may be overlooked or their significance may be assumed without a firm basis in reality. A related reason for environmental assessment is that it brings into focus the potential for environmental interventions. Recent research has documented the role of environment in the development of handicapped children. Best and Roberts (1976), for example, have shown associations between sensorimotor functioning of deaf infants and the home environment as structured by the mother. The prevailing approach of assessing psychological characteristics of children and families has been paralleled by intervention strategies focused on changing behaviors, perceptions, and feelings. Systematic modification of environment as an intervention strategy has been relatively unexplored, particularly in child and family interventions. This is surprising because alteration of the environment may constitute an alternative, possibly preferable, intervention to meet the needs of families with handicapped children. Modification of the environment may in fact be the strategy of choice in many interventions because (1) it is generally less intrusive than management or therapy, (2) it may be efficient in terms of cost and effort, and (3) it has visible, real components rather than inferred, subjective elements. For these reasons, environmental modifications may be more easily implemented.

Finally, the home environment may need to be asssessed to determine whether it is a "high-risk" environment for the infant or preschooler. Public Law 99-457 gives states the option to include with handicapped infants also those children at high risk environmentally in the infant population served. States that choose to do this need some basis for identifying high-risk environments.

In light of the value of an environmental perspective in early intervention, what assessment objectives can be derived? One objective is to document environmental characteristics. In certain instances, assessing and describing the environment may be of interest in their own right, in much the same way that individuals or events might be analyzed. A second more likely objective of assessment would be to identify the environmental correlates of behavior. This can be done in several ways: (1) by inferring relationships between observed behavior and environmental features, (2) by using assessment measures based on a particular theoretical model of the environment's role in influencing behavior, or (3) by carrying out a functional analysis of behavior that identifies environmental contingencies. A third assessment objective is to use findings to specify environmental interventions. Clearly, these assessment objectives are related, and in many instances the assessment of a given family may address all three.

PROCEDURAL CONSIDERATIONS

Two major considerations pertaining to environmental assessment are how to ensure ecological validity and how to decide the parameters of the family environment.

Ecological Validity

Brooks and Baumeister (1977) have advocated ecological validity in mental retardation research, a position that argues for contextual relevance in investigating the functioning of handicapped individuals.

In assessment practice, concern for ecological validity should translate into the use of measures and strategies that have greater, rather than less, immediate relevance to the behavior or setting being observed. The more ecologically valid an assessment is, the more immediate and obvious to intervention priorities are its findings. Efforts should be made to use measures for assessment of family environments with high relevance and applicability to identified needs of children and families. In practical terms, for example, an intervention concern may focus on the lack of appropriate parent-child interaction in a particular family. Although assessment of parent-child interaction patterns may be useful in planning a program to modify that interaction, it may be equally useful to assess the physical and psychological environments in the home to identify environmental alternatives that could promote better interaction. In many instances, both forms of assessment may be necessary to yield complementary findings, whereas in other instances one assessment approach may be more appropriate than the other.

Ecological validity of assessment can be enhanced by an awareness of the content and format of assessment tools and the selection of measures appropriate to referral concerns. Ecological validity of assessment also implies sensitivity to cultural, socioeconomic, and ethnic dimensions of environments. In earlier chapters we have discussed the general issue of personal values and subjectivity in assessing and working with families (Doherty, 1986). Environments are likely to vary from one family to the next, not only across social and cultural levels but also within ethnic, social, or economic groups. Recognizing the diversity of environments may be particularly important in work with minority families whose environments may differ markedly in form and structure. Ensuring the ecological validity of assessment should thus encompass sensitivity to value judgments and bias in the selection of measures and the interpretation of findings. Kazdin and Matson (1981) have proposed the concept of *social validation* as a way of promoting sensitivity to ecological validity in assessment and enhancing the relevance and social acceptability of intervention efforts. The selection and use of assessment tools may be made more ecologically valid by considering two methods: social comparison and subjective evaluation. *Social comparison*, for example, defines an appropriate or desirable environment by documenting environments that are characterized as adaptive and functional. This can be accomplished by identifying desired environments, making a detailed inventory of their characteristics, and using that inventory as a standard for comparison. In the case of early intervention, the concept of a stimulating or enriching environment for a handicapped infant could be assessed accordingly. *Subjective evaluation* determines what should be defined as appropriate in assessment and intervention by securing the opinions of persons knowledgeable in the area of concern. In early intervention contexts, this method could involve determining quality caregiving behavior by the consensus judgments of experts. Clearly, these methods of social validation are not mutually exclusive and can be used as guides to ensure the validity of priorities in intervention planning as well.

What Constitutes the Environment?

A second major procedural consideration in environmental assessment pertains to the definition of the environment. Any environment has both physical and nonphysical properties. Much research and practice with children and families has focused on the nonphysical or psychological properties of environments. But physical and psychological properties are interdependent and contribute jointly to environmental factors that influence behavior. Measures to assess environments should be selected with respect to the kinds of environmental characteristics to be assessed. In most instances, psychological characteristics are likely to be of primary interest. Sometimes, however, there may be reasons for documenting the physical environment in terms of props, such as furniture, and dimensions, such as size and configuration. Assessment, for example, may involve comparisons of spacing patterns in mentally retarded and nonretarded children (Burgess, 1981). Applications in the assessment of the psychological environment have been varied and can perhaps best be defined as assessments of behavior settings as "a specific set of time, place and object props, and an attached standing pattern of behavior. Both clusters are necessary and they are interdependent" (Scott, 1980). Broader and more conceptual approaches to assessment of environments are represented by an emphasis on the biosociocultural context (Gehring, 1985) of child and family functioning. Although such conceptualizations are clearly more comprehensive, they are also more difficult to translate into efficient assessment strategies. The review of procedures and measures in this chapter will thus focus on documentation of the physical and psychological environments in more delimited ways.

REPRESENTATIVE PROCEDURES AND MEASURES

Family environments can be assessed in a variety of ways. The selection of a particular procedure or measure will depend on the specific purpose of assessment and the extent to which concerns about ecological validity can be met with a given measure or procedure. In reviewing the ways in which family environments can be assessed, it is helpful to examine three broad approaches to assessment: (1) graphic representation, (2) systematic observation, and (3) the use of formal measures. These approaches can be used singly or in combination, depending on the purpose of assessment and the level of complexity desired. All three approaches are applicable to the assessment of child, parent-child, and family characteristics; in the case of formal measures, separate reviews will be made of measures defining the environment of the child and the environment of the family. As we have pointed out elsewhere in this volume, many measures of family and child overlap in their coverage (stress, support, resources, etc.), but the review of formal measures of the environment seems appropriate here, given the emphasis of these measures on environmental assessment per se.

Graphic Representation

A simple, uncomplicated method of assessing the family's physical environment is a graphic representation by means of pictures, drawings, or schematics. Although assessment at this level is most likely to be informal, the content and physical arrangement of a family's environment can be documented. Such representation will not only portray the environment unique to a family but, if repeated, can document changes in the environment over time. Such changes could reflect the effects of developmental or spontaneous events, but could also reflect the effects of planned intervention. An illustration of this approach might be a schematic representation of the living room and kitchen of the home of a family with a motor-impaired infant. An initial assessment might indicate, for example, that the arrangement of furniture and appliances limits the child's mobility. As a result of direct or indirect intervention efforts, the family makes environmental alterations that facilitate the child's mobility. These alterations are evident in the schematic of the home made during a follow-up assessment.

Systematic Observation

A second method of assessing family environments are through systematic observations. Two major approaches to systematic observation each represent a different theoretical view of environments. Ethology and ecological/psychological strategies study the relationships of environments to behavior. Both share a common focus on the assessment of behavior in actual environments (Berkson, 1978) and rely on nonintrusive documentation of context and behavior characteristics. An alternate approach is tied to the methodology of the functional analysis of behavior (Bijou & Baer, 1961), which assumes that specific environmental stimuli elicit or reinforce behavior. Assessment based on this model would thus be the method of choice if there were interest in documenting the role of environmental contingencies on children or families. The contrasting

TABLE 8.1
Characteristics of Ecological and Behavioral Strategies Relevant to Assessment

	Ecological	**Behavioral**
Goal of assessment	Defining situational context of behavior	Defining stimulus–behavior relationships
Method of assessment	"Naturalness" Nonobtrusive observation	Observation of behavior under different conditions of experimental control
Level of inference	Inferences about interdependence of behavior environment drawn after recording completed	Behavior operationalized before observation of stimulus–behavior relationships
Unit of analysis	Patterns and sequences of behavior	Frequency/duration of behavior
Example	Pattern of play of motor handicapped infant with sibling	Frequency of contingent maternal behavior on infant play

features of ethological/ecological and behavioral approaches to the assessment of environments are summarized in Table 8.1. Reviewing these features may be useful in selecting an assessment procedure appropriate to a particular referral problem. The ethological approach, for example, has been used by Richer (1979) to demonstrate that stereotyped behavior of handicapped children was relatively independent of environmental factors. Assessment based on the functional analysis of behavior, on the other hand, could demonstrate that environmental contingencies contributed to change in behavior. Assessment of environments could thus serve to identify behaviors that are likely to be amenable to environmental modification and those that are not.

Formal Measures of Environment

A variety of formal measures can be used to assess environments. We will consider separately those measures that focus on children and those that focus on families.

Assessing the Child's Environment. The role of the environment in mediating outcomes of children has been increasingly recognized (Sameroff & Chandler, 1975), and this recognition has led to a strong interest in assessing environmental characteristics that may influence children's behavior and development. Four useful measures focusing primarily on the home setting are summarized in Table 8.2. Although the measures vary in content, all share a common focus of documenting the extent to which the environment stimulates or promotes the child's development. The Purdue Home Stimulation Inventory (Wachs, Francis, & McQuiston, 1978) includes items that document specific physical features (mobile over crib) as well as a range of psychological characteristics (rate of maternal speech). The Characteristics of the Inanimate Environment (Yarrow, Rubenstein, & Pedersen, 1975) is an observational measure that documents the environment of the child in terms of responsiveness, complexity, and variety. The Home Observation for the Measurement of the Environment (Caldwell, 1972) is perhaps the best known instrument for assessing environments of infants (birth–3 years) and young children (3–6 years). The HOME consists of a number of true/false items. There are two levels involving such subscales as emotional and verbal responsivity of the mother; avoidance of restriction and punishment; organization of physical and temporal environment; provision of appropriate play materials; maternal involvement with child; and opportunities for variety in daily stimulation. Items tap both the physical features (child has a push or pull toy) and the psychological features (mother spontaneously praises child's qualities or behavior twice during visit) of the environment. These measures can provide appropriate means for examining the relationship of the environment to the development progress of handicapped infants. The study by Best and Roberts (1976), referred to

TABLE 8.2
Assessment of Child Environments

Measure	Number of Items	Subscales	Format	Reliability	Validity
Home Observation for the Measurement of the Environment (Caldwell, 1972) 2 Levels: 1. HOME Inventory for Families of Infants and Toddlers (birth–3 years) 2. HOME Inventory for Families of Pre-school Age Children (3–6 years)	Level 1: 45 Level 2: 55	Level 1: Emotional and verbal responsivity of mother Acceptance of child's behavior Organization of the physical and temporal environment Provision of appropriate play materials Maternal involvement with the child Opportunities for variety Total Level 2: Stimulation through toys, games, and reading materials Language stimulation Physical environment Pride, affection, and warmth Stimulation of academic behavior Modeling and encouragement of social maturity Variety of stimulation Physical punishment Total	Items scored as yes or no during a nonstandard interview	Level 1: Internal consistency: .44–.89 for subscales .89 for total score Test/retest reliability: .27–.77 for subtests .62–.77 for total score Level 2: Internal consistency: .53–.88 for subscales .93 for total score Test/retest reliability: .05–.70 for subscales with one subscale, physical punishment being below .20	Level 1: With SES measures moderate correlation HOME scores at 24 months with 36-month Binet IQ .72 Level 2: With SES measures moderate correlation

Instrument	Number	Areas/Content	Scoring	Reliability	Validity
Early Childhood Environment Rating Scale (Harms & Clifford, 1980)	37	7 areas: Personal-care routines of children; Furnishings and display for children; Language-reasoning experiences; Fine and gross motor activities; Creative activities; Social development; Adult needs	Each item is rated on a 7-point scale with 1 as inadequate, 3 as minimal, 5 as good, and 7 as excellent	Interrater reliability: by item .94 by classroom .79 to .90 Internal consistency: .22 to .87 for subscales .83 for total score	Criterion or "predictive" validity not available
Purdue Home Stimulation Inventory (Wachs, 1979; Wachs, Francis, & McQuiston, 1978)	30	*Section I*: Aspects of child's rearing environment; *Section II*: Stimulus characteristics of home; *Section III*: State of the home	Scores based on questions and observation	Mean interobserver agreement 85%	Significant male-female differences found in relationship of development and physical environment
Characteristics of the Inanimate Environment (Yarrow, Rubenstein, & Pedersen, 1975)	19 observation categories	Responsiveness; Complexity; Variety	Ratings based on observation (time-sampling)	Interobserver reliability r = .88–.99	Significant univariate and multivariate correlations found between input measures and environmental variables

earlier, demonstrated the use of the HOME Inventory in showing associations between developmental attainment of hearing-impaired infants and the environmental characteristics of their homes. The major environment of young handicapped children outside the home is the day care or pre-school setting, which can be assessed with the Early Childhood Environment Rating Scale (Harms & Clifford, 1980). A number of other measures of preschool environments may be applicable in the transition of handicapped infants from home- to center-based programs. Bailey and Wolery (1984) have described a number of these measures. The usefulness of assessing environments of handicapped preschool children was illustrated in a comparison study of settings for handicapped and nonhandicapped children by Bailey, Clifford, and Harms (1982). Results revealed that settings for non-handicapped preschoolers were rated significantly better than those of handicapped children in terms of desirable features on 12 of 37 items. Although the research described reflected findings about groups of handicapped infants and young children, the results can be applied to the role of setting variables for the individual child as well. However, using these formal measures to make reliable assessments often requires training and the establishment of interobserver reliability.

Assessing the Family's Environment.   The assessment of family environments has been approached primarily through an analysis of their psychological climate. Such analyses have resulted in a wide variety of typologies of families reflecting underlying psychological climates. Mink (1986) has reviewed many of these typologies in terms of their heuristic or empirical derivation. Heuristic typologies are derived from a theoretical base that has been proposed to describe the psychological climates of different groups: nonproblem families, lower-class families, and families seen in clinical contexts. Heuristic typologies that describe families with handicapped children include Farber's (1960) classification of child-oriented, home-oriented, and parent-oriented families and a classification of seven deviant families and one nondeviant family proposed by Ackerman and Behrens (1956). Empirically derived typologies, on the other hand, are drawn from data and have been described for problem and nonproblem families. A major contribution to typologies of families of handicapped and nonhandicapped children has been made by Moos and his colleagues (Moos, 1974; Moos, Insel, & Humphrey, 1974). Moos has developed his approach to the assessment of family environments by drawing on the concept of environmental press as a determiner of behavior. In this instance environmental press means that the environment exerts its influence in several ways. Moos has drawn on Murray's (1938) original formulation of alpha press (objective characteristics) and beta press (characteristics perceived by participants) in the development of assessment tools for environments. In this context, Moos emphasized the fact that environments, like people, can be distinguished by their personalities (Moos, 1974). These environments could be described in terms of these family dimensions: independence, structure, achievement, expression, moral/religious emphasis, or conflict.

Three formal measures may be appropriate in assessing environments of families with handicapped children. These measures are based by and large on the concept of beta press—that is, characteristics of the environment as perceived by the members of that environment. A summary of these three measures is presented in Table 8.3. The Henderson Environmental Learning Process Scale (Henderson, Bergan, & Hurt, 1972) measures the perceived characteristics of the home relative to child-aspiration level, parental-reinforcement practices, and educational opportunities. The HELPS has been used by Mink (1986) in a classification of families of slow learners and mildly mentally retarded children. The Home Quality Rating Scale (Meyers, Mink, & Nihira, 1977) was developed to portray the psychological climate of families of handicapped children as it pertained to child-rearing attitudes and practices. A factor analysis of the scale items yielded five main factors: harmony of the home and quality of parenting, concordance in parenting and marriage, openness and awareness of respondent, quality of the residential environment, and quality of the residential area. Although the first three factors reflect perceived characteristics of the environment (beta press), the last two seem to incorporate elements of the objective environment (alpha press). The Family Environment Scale (Moos, Insel, & Humphrey, 1974) has been used in a wide variety of applications. The 90 items cover nine subscales: cohesion, expressiveness, conflict, independence, achievement orientation, intellectual-cultural orientation, moral/religious emphasis, organization, and control.

The use of these three family environment measures in assessing unique characteristics in different families was illustrated in a study comparing 115 families with trainable mentally retarded children and 218 families with slow-learning children (Mink, 1986). The results revealed that the combined information of these measures yielded five family types in families with trainable mentally retarded children (cohesive, harmonious; control-oriented, somewhat unharmonious; low disclosure, unharmonious; child-oriented, expressive; disadvantaged with low morale). In families with slow-learning children, seven types were identified on the basis of combined information about family environments (child-oriented, cohesive; learning-oriented, high residential quality; low disclosure, unharmonious; disadvantaged, noncohesive; achievement-oriented, low residential quality; expression-oriented with low sociocultural interests; outer-directed with little achievement orientation). The value of this type of assessment is that it emphasizes the distinctive structure of families rather than assuming homogeneity of families of handicapped children. Mink recognizes that these typologies are tentative and must be validated through further research. The possibility of distinguishing family types that are not influenced by characteristics of the child from those that are disability-specific would have important implications for intervention. Specifically, "knowledge of family

TABLE 8.3
Assessment of Family Environment

Measure	Number of Items	Subscales	Format	Reliability	Validity
Henderson Environmental Learning Process Scale (Henderson, Bergan, & Hurt, 1972)	55	Quantifiable information on the aspiration level of the home Range of environmental stimulation available to the child Parental guidance or direct-teaching provided in the family Range (variability in occupational and educational status) of adult models available for emulation by the child Nature of reinforcement practices used in the home to influence the child's behavior Total score	Structured interview employing Likert-type scale	Internal consistency: .71 for Anglo sample .74 for Mexican-American sample .85 for middle-class Mexican-American families .74 for lower-class Anglo families .79 for Papago native American families	Predictive validity: Highly significant predictions of performance of Mexican-American and Anglo first graders on the Stanford Early Achievement Test and Boehm Test of Basic Concepts

Instrument	Number of items	Factors/Subscales	Format	Reliability	Validity
Home Quality Rating Scale (Myers, Mink, & Nihira, 1977)	33	5 factors: Harmony of the home and quality of parenting; Concordance in parenting and marriage; Openness and awareness of the respondent; Quality of the residential environment; Quality of the residential area	Interviewer ratings employing a variable format including 5-point rating scales and fixed choice responses	Internal consistency: .56–.83 for subscales	Not available
Family Environment Scale (Moos, Insel, & Humphrey, 1974)	90	Relationship domain—cohesion, expressiveness, conflict; Personal growth domain—independence, achievement orientation, intellectual-cultural orientation, moral/religious emphasis; System maintenance domain—organization, control; Derived nonprofiled family incongruence score	Items answered in a true/false manner using pencil-and-paper method	Internal consistency: .61–.78 for subscales; Test/retest reliability: .68–.86—8-week; .52–.89—12-month	Not available

patterns would enable a treatment program to be designed for those families in need that would be consistent with family functioning style and thus become effective" (Mink, 1986, p. 28).

In closing this section on assessment of family environments, it is necessary to point out that a number of the measures reviewed in Chapter 5 on stress, in Chapter 6 on critical events, and in Chapter 7 on support are also applicable in varying degrees to the assessment of family environments as perceived by family members. Such measures, while not primarily identified as measures of child or family environments, contain items or subscales that pertain to the family's physical and psychological environment. Measures that come to mind are the Parenting Stress Index (Abidin, 1986), the Impact-on-Family Scale (Stein & Reissman, 1980), the Questionnaire on Resources and Stress (Holroyd, 1973), and the Family Needs Survey (Bailey & Simeonsson, in press). Also, a number of measures of social support and family behavior compiled by Dunst and Trivette (1985) are applicable in assessing family environments. The use of such measures should be based on a clear conceptualization of the relationship of the environment to family functions and to the purpose of assessment.

ASSESSMENT AND INTERVENTION

Translating assessment findings on family environments into intervention plans may be approached in two ways, depending on whether the environment was assessed in terms of physical objective qualities (alpha press) or subjective psychological qualities (beta press). Physical assessment may reveal environments that are inadequate in terms of space or physical props. Environments may also be arranged or structured in ways that fail to enhance family functioning. Such findings may lead to intervention plans that focus on alterations or additions to the environment. Applications such as space expansion, space reduction, and increasing material availability can be carried out to enhance the behavior or development of handicapped children and their families. (Simeonsson, 1986). Psychological assessment may reveal dimensions of the family climate that have implications for intervention. A major reason for assessing environments and identifying their characteristics is to better understand the impact on the members of those environments. In such assessments it is important to recognize that the impact of environmental variables is a result of this interaction (Landesman-Dwyer, 1985). The degree to which environmental intervention can affect the development and functioning of children and families is unclear, but the potential impact seems high. Although the nature of environmental variables in family function is not well researched, the role that parents play in interventions in environmental organization has been explored. From a behavioral standpoint, environmental organization can (1) provide a setting for behavior, (2) provide contingencies to increase or decrease behavior, and (3) create conditions to maintain or generalize behavior (Twardosz, 1984). Environmental assessment within a behavioral framework might thus lead to a family goal to design a setting in which a sibling can reinforce specific behaviors of a handicapped child (Cash & Evans, 1975). In a more general sense, parents can play a vital role in the selection, delivery, and regulation of appropriate stimulation for children at various points in their development (Powell, 1981). This premise is supported by MacPhee, Ramey, and Yeates (1984), who see parents as the architects of the home environment. From this perspective, the parent may make the environment of a physically handicapped child interesting by increasing the variety of toys and more accessible by using props to position the child to allow manipulation of those toys. The implications for intervention may thus be to identify strategies to arrange environments so that they become more contingent or responsive, more cohesive, more structured, or more facilitative of efficient functioning. Although these are only a few of many possible levels of intervention, they point to the potential importance of enhancing family adaptation and development through systematic environmental intervention.

SUMMARY

This chapter has reviewed representative procedures and methods to assess the environments of handicapped children and their families. Assessment of the objective physical characteristics of environments was distinguished from assessment of the subjective psychological characteristics as that distinction pertains to measurement tools and implications for intervention planning. Family environments may differ substantially as a function of cultural or ethnic values. Such differences must be considered as part of early intervention efforts. The assessment of family environments constitutes an important component of family-focused intervention because the reciprocal influence of the environment and persons can be seen as major factors influencing family functioning. The identification of environmental determinants of child and family functioning may thus be an effective, efficient, and underused strategy in early intervention.

REFERENCES

Abidin, R. R. (1986). *Parenting stress index* (2nd ed.). Charlottesville, Va.: Pediatric Psychology Press.

Ackerman, N. W., & Behrens, M. D. (1956). A study of family diagnosis. *American Journal of Orthopsychiatry, 26,* 66–78.

Bailey, D. B., Clifford, R. M., & Harms, T. (1982). Comparison of preschool environments for handicapped and non-handicapped children. *Topics in Early Childhood Special Education, 2*, 9–20.

Bailey, D. B., & Simeonsson, R. J. (in press). Assessing the needs of families with handicapped infants: The family needs survey. *Journal of Special Education.*

Bailey, D. B., & Wolery, M. (1984). *Teaching infants and preschoolers with handicaps.* Columbus, Oh.: Merrill Publishing Company.

Berkson, G. (1978). Social ecology and ethology of mental retardation. In G. P. Sackett (Ed.), *Observing behavior, volume I: Theory and applications in mental retardation.* Baltimore: University Park Press.

Best, B., & Roberts, G. (1976). Early cognitive development in hearing impaired children. *American Annals of the Deaf, 121*, 560–564.

Bijou, S. W., & Baer, D. M. (1961). *Child development: Vol. 1. A systematic and empirical theory.* New York: Appleton-Century-Crofts.

Bronfenbrenner, U. (1979). *The ecology of human development: Experiments by nature and design.* Cambridge, Mass.: Harvard University Press.

Brooks, P. H., & Baumeister, A. A. (1977). A plea for consideration of ecological validity in the experimental psychology of mental retardation. *American Journal of Mental Deficiency, 81*, 407–416.

Burgess, J. W. (1981). Development of spacing in normal and mentally retarded children. *Journal of Nonverbal Behavior, 6*, 89–95.

Caldwell, B. (1972). *HOME Inventory.* Little Rock, Ark.: University of Arkansas.

Cash, W. M., & Evans, I. M. (1975). Training preschool children to modify their retarded siblings' behavior. *Journal of Behavioral Therapy and Experimental Psychiatry, 6*, 13–16.

Doherty, W. J. (1986). Quanta, quarks, and families: Implications of quantum physics for family research. *Family Process, 25*, 249–264.

Dunst, C. J., & Trivette, C. M. (1985). *A guide to measures of social support and family behaviors.* Chapel Hill, N.C.: TADS, Frank Porter Graham Child Development Center, University of North Carolina.

Farber, B. (1960). Family organization and crisis: Maintenance of integration in families with a severely mentally retarded child. *Monographs of the Society for Research in Child Development* (Serial No. 75).

Gehring, T. M. (1985). Socio-psychosomatic dysfunctions: A case study. *Child Psychiatry and Human Development, 15*, 269–280.

Harms, T., & Clifford, R. M. (1980). *Early childhood environment rating scale.* New York: Teachers College Press.

Henderson, R. W., Bergan, J. R., & Hurt, J., Jr. (1972). Development and validation of the Henderson environmental learning process scale. *Journal of Social Psychology, 88*, 185–196.

Holroyd, J. (1973). *Manual for the questionnaire on resources and stress.* Los Angeles: UCLA Neuropsychiatric Institute.

Kazak, A. E. (1986). Families with physically handicapped children: Social ecology and family systems. *Family Process, 25*, 265–281.

Kazdin, A. E., & Matson, J. L. (1981) Social validation in mental retardation. *Applied Research in Mental Retardation, 2*, 39–53.

Landesman-Dwyer, S. (1985). Describing and evaluating residential environments. In R. H. Bruininks & K. C. Lakin (Eds.), *Living and learning in the least restrictive environment* (pp. 185–196). Baltimore: Paul H. Brookes.

MacPhee, D., Ramey, C. T., & Yeates, K. O. (1984). Home environment and early cognitive development: Implications for intervention. In A. W. Gottfried (Ed.), *Home Environment and Early Cognitive Development* (pp. 343–369). New York: Academic Press.

Mink, I. T. (1986). Classification of families with mentally retarded children. In J. J. Gallagher & P. M. Vietze (Eds.), *Families of handicapped persons—Research, programs, and policy issues* (pp. 25–43). Baltimore: Paul H. Brookes.

Moos, R. H. (1974). *Family Environment Scale.* Palo Alto, Calif.: Consulting Psychologists Press.

Moos, R. H., Insel, P. M., & Humphrey, B. (1974). *Family, work and group environment scales manual.* Palo Alto, Calif.: Consulting Psychologists Press.

Murray, H. (1938). *Explorations in personality.* Oxford: Oxford University Press.

Myers, C. E., Mink, I., & Nihira, K. (1977). *Home quality rating scale.* Pomona, Calif.: UCLA/Neuropsychiatric Institute—Pacific State Hospital Research Group.

Powell, M. L. (1981). *Assessment and management of developmental changes and problems in children.* St. Louis, Mo.: C. V. Mosby.

Richer, J. (1979). Human ethology and mental handicap. In F. E. James & R. P. Smith (Eds.), *Psychiatric illness and mental handicap* (pp. 103–113). London: Gaskell Press.

Sameroff, A. J., & Chandler, M. J. (1975). Reproductive risk and the continuum of caretaking casualty. In F. D. Horowitz, M. Hetherington, S. Scarr-Salapatek, & G. Siegel (Eds.), *Review of child development research,* (vol. 4, pp.187–244). Chicago: University of Chicago Press.

Scott, M. (1980). Ecological theory and methods for research in special education. *Journal of Special Education, 14,* 279–294.

Simeonsson, R. J. (1986). *Psychological and developmental assessment of special children.* Boston, Mass.: Allyn & Bacon.

Stein, R. E. K., & Reissman, C. K. (1980). The development of an impact-on-family scale: Preliminary findings. *Medical Care, 18,* 465–472.

Twardosz, S. (1984). Environmental organization: The physical, social, and programmatic context of behavior. In M. Hersen, R. M. Eisler, & P. M. Miller (Eds.), *Progress in behavior modification,* (pp. 123–161). New York: Academic Press.

Wachs, T. D. (1979). Proximal experience and early cognitive-intellectual development: The physical environment. *Merrill-Palmer Quarterly, 25,* 3–41.

Wachs, T. D., Francis, J., & McQuiston, S. (1978). *Psychological dimensions of the infant's physical environment.* Paper presented to the Midwestern Psychological Association, Chicago.

Yarrow, L. J., Rubenstein, J. L., & Pedersen, F. A. (1975). *Infant and environment: Early cognitive and motivational development.* Washington, D.C.: Hemisphere Publishing.

9

The Family-Focused Interview: An Assessment Measure and Goal-Setting Mechanism

T wo assumptions underlie effective family assessment, planning, and service delivery: (1) the solutions to any family problem lie within the family's own definition of reality (Berger, 1986); and (2) intervention should help the family increase its own abilities to cope with parenting a handicapped child (Dunst, 1985). These assumptions require interventionists to gather valid assessment data and to collaborate with family members to set family goals. This chapter describes the rationale, structure, and format of an interview that will accomplish these ends.

THE RATIONALE FOR AN INTERVIEW IN FAMILY ASSESSMENT

As described thus far, family assessment generally embraces a multimethod approach to determining family needs (Hetherington, 1984; Winton, 1986). However, an interview may be the only means to uncover information about (1) family characteristics, (2) family strengths, and (3) family perceptions of situations, events, goals, or services.

This chapter was contributed by Pamela J. Winton, University of North Carolina at Chapel Hill.

Clarifying Family Characteristics

Certain family characteristics may be misinterpreted if information is gathered solely from traditional paper-and-pen measures. Two such characteristics are *family roles* (who functions in what roles and what meaning that has for other family members) and *family membership* (who is in and who is out of the family). According to Minuchin (1974), each family is composed of subsystems whose boundaries are defined by the functions and interactions of its various members. Because family members have simultaneous membership in different subsystems (e.g., a woman may be a spouse in the marital subsystem, a mother in a parental subsystem, and a daughter in the subsystem containing her own mother and father), an event that seems to impact only one family member directly in reality may affect others. The notion of "ripple effect" underscores the importance of assessing each individual family member and how he or she fits within the family's subsystems.

Roles. Family subsystems operate according to functions rather than strictly according to the chronological age of family members. For example, in some two-parent families one parent may actually function as a child, therefore being a member of the sibling rather than the parental subsystem. In such cases, the void in the parental subsystem may be filled by a powerful intergenerational alliance with a grandparent or by one of the siblings functioning in a parental role. Aponte (1986) illustrated how a dysfunctional family organization can be masked as a problem residing in an individual family member; he provided a case study of a single-parent family in which the mother had withdrawn from her parenting role because she was overwhelmed by familial and social problems. The teenage daughter, who initially was the identified client for therapy, had tried to fill the leadership vacuum created by her mother's abdication but did not have the power or authority to do so. This placed her in the difficult situation of being unable to function well in her role as a teenager at school and in the neighborhood and also unable to function in her role as a parent at home. Although the family problems were manifest primarily through this teenager's school difficulties, the solutions clearly resided in helping the family deal with broader issues related to parenting responsibilities and community supports. Because some research with siblings of handicapped children suggests that older daughters may be susceptible to taking on parental responsibilities (Simeonsson & Bailey, 1986), an appreciation of these perspectives by professionals working with families may be particularly important. An interview procedure increases the likelihood of gathering accurate information on who functions in what roles.

A related issue is the importance of understanding family members' perspectives on family roles and functions. With the increasing emphasis on family involvement has come the recognition that fathers have, for the most part, been left out of intervention efforts. The natural response has been to make up for this shortcoming by providing more opportunities for paternal involvement in program efforts (Meyer, 1986; Vadasy, Fewell, Greenberg, Dermond, & Meyer, 1986). Although the intent to broaden intervention to include fathers is meritorious, interventions based on a simplistic understanding of the father's role in the family may do more harm than good. Research on social support reveals that spousal support may be the most important mitigator of stress in families of handicapped children; however, the *perception* of such support rather than the actual amount of support is significant (Dunst, Trivette, & Cross, 1986). In a study of allocation of domestic tasks in families of handicapped children, Gallagher, Scharfman, and Bristol (1984) found that marital satisfaction was associated with *spousal agreement* about who was to perform what task rather than with actual patterns of task distribution. Kazak (1986) and Kazak and Marvin (1984) found in their samples that parents of handicapped children were more rigidly traditional in their enactment of roles than were parents of nonhandicapped children. Yet they also found that parents who functioned in this rigid style exhibited high levels of marital satisfaction. They concluded that for these families this was an adaptive coping strategy for handling stresses, particularly financial ones, associated with parenting a handicapped child. The father's lack of involvement in caregiving activities (a weakened father-child subsystem) was compensated for by his involvement in employment-related activities, which was his way of lending support to his spouse and strengthening the marital subsystem. Without a careful assessment of the meaning underlying a family's allocation of roles and tasks and the satisfaction of family members with these roles, false assumptions might be made that in turn might ensure the failure of intervention efforts. An interview provides an opportunity for interventionists to gather this sort of information.

Membership. Family members are those individuals who are regarded as a part of the family. Family membership information may be available only from a family interview—for example, when the presence or absence of a parent is not truly acknowledged. This phenomenon, which has been called boundary ambiguity (Boss & Greenberg, 1984), may occur in families with an alcoholic member or in families in which a parent or parental figure has died. In the case of the alcoholic, for example, the family may simply function as if the person does not exist, although theoretically and demographically the person is considered a family member. In the case of the deceased family member, the family may continue to respect that person's authority, making decisions in accordance with what the family believes that person's wishes would be. In conducting interventions, professionals may not realize that they are dealing with the values and expectations of absent family members unless a careful assessment of family membership that goes beyond the usual demographic forms is conducted.

An interesting variation on this theme involves families in which God operates as a powerful and respected family member, offering therapeutic possibilities often untapped and unappreciated by professionals. In assessing families along this dimension, Griffith (1986) emphasized the importance of understanding the family's interpersonal relationship with God, as opposed to religious affiliations or abstract theological beliefs. In addition, he described the importance of avoiding making judgments about theological beliefs. Rather, the important task is to understand the ways in which the God-family relationship affects family functioning, with the ultimate goal being to use this resource in intervention efforts.

Another example in which standardized demographic forms may not yield complete information about family characteristics is the case of the single-parent black family. Stack's (1975) ethnographic study of a low-income black community provided evidence that fathers more often than not acknowledge paternity even without marriage. Not only are they involved in child care, but their extended family is likely to provide support and physical assistance to the single mother and child. A pilot study by Bristol (1987) corroborated that fathers, boyfriends, and other nonparent caregivers assist single mothers with child-care tasks.

The family-focused interview provides an opportunity to assess who functions in what roles in the family, family members' satisfaction with these arrangements, and possible changes that might facilitate family adaptation.

Family Strengths

Many assessment measures used with families of handicapped children focus on pathology, stress, problems, and the burden of care. In part, this approach relates to the negative attitudes that professionals have historically held toward parents of handicapped children—in some instances, in fact, blaming the parents for creating the child's handicap. An example is considering mothers the "cause" of autistic children's problems owing to cold and unfeeling maternal behavior (Bristol & Schopler, 1984). Although these attitudes have shifted dramatically over the last several decades, the idea of focusing on family strengths is still relatively new in special education. Turnbull (1985) noted that the professional literature has failed to recognize the positive contributions that a handicapped child makes on a family. She described how research results suggesting positive contributions were interpreted as reflecting a methodological problem rather than reality.

What effects are observed when families are approached from an essentially negative perspective? Tomm (1987), a psychiatrist and family therapist, made the point that intervention with a family begins with the first encounter; if the interventionist initially assumes that problems exist, that assumption is likely to color how families define their situations. He suggests asking questions designed to strengthen what the family is doing right.

Public Law 99-457 further supports an assessment approach that considers family strengths. This legislation mandates that individualized family service plans must be developed as the basis for intervention efforts with young handicapped children and that these plans must include an assessment of family strengths. An interview in which families have the opportunity to describe their situation, including the positive aspects, would provide interventionists with useful information about family strengths.

Family Perceptions

The importance of family perceptions and definitions of events is exemplified in Hill's (1958) ABCX Model of family functioning and its extension by McCubbin and Patterson (1983). Hill, a sociologist, was intrigued originally by the question of why different families responded in such different ways to a natural disaster, such as a tornado, that theoretically did equal damage to every family in its path. Why did some families come through the devastation with the capacity to survive and, in some cases, to thrive, while other families disintegrated and never recovered? That question and the information Hill generated to answer it formed the basis for his model, which simply stated that the capacity to adapt (X) to crisis (A) depended on an interaction between a family's resources (B) and its perceptions of the crisis event (C). Acceptance of this theoretical model calls for an assessment strategy that emphasizes strengths, resources, and perceptions rather than problems, pathology, and stress. As stated earlier, an interview offers families the opportunity to describe their definition of events and what has worked for them in the past.

Research by family sociologists with families of normally developing children has documented the importance of perceptual coping strategies in dealing with stress (Olson et al., 1983). Olson and his associates found that families dealt with stress in two ways: (1) "passive appraisal," a type of denial or avoidance of the problem, and (2) "reframing," the family's ability to identify the aspects of a problem they can control and to redefine those aspects beyond their control in a way that makes the stress easier to accept. The authors emphasized that the family's ability to define the stressor event as a challenge that could be overcome (through reframing) or ignored for the present time (through passive appraisal) kept the family from being overwhelmed by the crisis. An understanding of these strategies may be particularly relevant in light of the professional literature's emphasis on families overcoming parental denial to "accept" the handicap. The research by Olson et al. emphasized that denial may play an important role in protecting the family from being overwhelmed and should be recognized as an adaptive strategy rather than a condition to be eradicated.

Overall, in terms of family assessment, the field is shifting away from sole reliance on descriptions and observations of behavioral patterns and easily observable and measurable facts. The subjective meaning that these phenomena have for family members is recognized as having critical importance. A family interview is an effective means of collecting this information.

THE RATIONALE FOR AN INTERVIEW IN GOAL SETTING

With regard to the role of the interview in goal setting, one might ask initially, "Isn't such a mechanism already in place in the form of the conference to determine the individualized educational plan?" Public Law 94-142 did mandate a meeting between professionals and parents to decide on the best educational plan for the handicapped child. The intent of the law was to make parents equal partners with professionals in the decision-making process. However, reviews of the research on IEP conferences have concluded that parents are typically passive recipients of information rather than active decision makers in goal setting (Brinckerhoff & Vincent, 1986; Turnbull & Winton, 1984). In part, this may result from professional indifference to parents' contributions. Gilliam (1979) found that professionals ranked parents' contributions to team meetings as only ninth in importance of 16 categories of contributions. Research on IEP meetings by Fenton, Yoshida, Maxwell, and Kaufman (1979) indicated that 79% of the placement teams surveyed were either unaware or unclear that communication with parents was a goal of interdisciplinary teams. In a review article, Witt, Miller, McIntyre, and Smith (1984) concluded that "parent input and understanding is not a major goal, is not highly valued by other interdisciplinary team members, and the parental role preferred by most professional team members is that of passive participant" (p. 32). This research indicates that, contrary to the intent of the policy, the IEP meeting has not evolved as a means for collaborative goal setting.

A second point should be made about comparisons between parent involvement policy as defined in Public Law 94-142 and the assumptions underlying parent involvement as defined in this text. The law's intent was to involve parents in the IEP process to ensure development of the best possible educational plan for the child. The child was the primary target of intervention, and parents were seen as having valuable information to help determine intervention goals. In contrast, the assumption underlying this text is that the family, as a powerful and mediating social system within which the child resides, must be understood if meaningful intervention goals are to be generated. As pointed out by Shapiro (1983), various aspects of an illness or a disability may require different coping strategies; within an individual or a family, coping strategies that are successful in one area may be harmful in another area. Likewise, intervention efforts meeting narrowly defined goals may have unintended consequences on other aspects of family functioning. Unfortunately, these side effects of intervention are rarely considered in the training programs provided for interventionists (Doernberg, 1978). For these reasons, an understanding of the family context, as described in preceding chapters, is a critical step in goal setting.

These differences between Public Law 94-142 and current trends in early intervention make it clear that one cannot look to the literature, training, and practices associated with the IEP meeting for a model that could be extended downward to families with handicapped infants and preschoolers. A more effective mechanism is needed that includes parents' values, beliefs, and priorities in goal setting. Research by Cadman, Shurvell, Davies, and Bradfield (1984) on the issue of parental compliance with intervention goals suggests that failure to incorporate parental values is the primary reason parents ignore professionals' recommendations. Research from the business literature (e.g., Bass & Leavitt, 1963; Latham & Locke, 1979) and the clinical judgment of many therapists support the notion that "ownership" of goals, which is only possible when a person is meaningfully involved in setting his or her own goals, is the most effective way to ensure that goals are successfully met. A family interview has the potential for enabling families to engage truly in collaborative goal setting with professionals.

THE FOCUSED INTERVIEW

The interview as a research, assessment, and problem-solving tool has been described extensively in the psychiatric, social work, sociological, and anthropological literature (Benjamin, 1969; Gorden, 1969; Hepworth & Larsen, 1982; Ivey, 1971; Weber, McKeever, & McDaniel, 1985). From this information, two broad objectives of an interview can be identified. The first is *to create a trusting and respectful relationship* with the individual or family by expressing empathy and accepting their definition of events. Within the psychiatric literature, this is sometimes called "joining" the family (Weber et al., 1985); it is essentially rapport building, without which the second broad purpose—*to gather information*—cannot be achieved. The interviewer must be able to pursue the content goals of the interview objectively while evaluating the adequacy of the information to the ultimate purpose of the interview. Research in medicine and psychology (Adler, Ware, & Enelow, 1970; Helfer & Hess, 1970; Evans, Hearn, Uhlemann, & Ivey, 1984; Ivey, 1971; Meadow & Hewitt, 1972) has demonstrated that the communication skills essential for accomplishing these broad purposes can be taught. A fairly extensive body of literature that cuts across many disciplines broadly identifies what constitutes an effective interview and the skills necessary for conducting one (Gorden, 1969; Hepworth & Larsen, 1982; Ivey, 1971; Weber et al., 1985).

Recently, within the field of special education, the interview has been used with families as a data-collection and problem-solving technique. For example, it has been used where the task was understanding family needs and perceptions associated with certain events, such as transitions (Johnson, Chandler, Kerns, & Fowler, 1986); diagnosing developmental delays (Shuster, Guskin, Hawkins, & Okolo, 1986); mainstreaming preschool children (Turnbull & Winton, 1983); involving parents in preschool programs (Winton & Turnbull, 1981); and setting goals in both adult life planning (Turnbull et al. 1984) and home-based intervention efforts (Bailey et al., 1986). Although these interviews have been developed and used to address diverse topics, they share certain important characteristics: they are open-ended and semistructured and therefore can be tailored to the needs and demands of each situation; yet at the same time, certain topics are identified in advance to be covered with each respondent. From this literature on interviews with families of handicapped children, two characteristics associated with effective interviews can be identified: flexibility and structure. The drawback to the studies cited is the absence of specific detail about the structure and format of the interviews employed. The remainder of this chapter will describe the focused interview, which is characterized by both flexibility and structure, and will present a specific structure for conducting a family-focused interview to assess family needs and set family goals collaboratively. Chapter 10 discusses communication skills identified in the literature that enable an interviewer to conduct a focused interview successfully.

Description

The focused interview—which has its philosophical origins in the sociological tradition, where it was used for research purposes—has been described by many authors (Denzin, 1970; Gorden, 1969; Maccoby & Maccoby, 1954; Merton, Fiske, & Kendall, 1946; Selltiz, Jahoda, Deutsch, & Cook, 1965) and is considered particularly well suited when information is sought about complex, emotionally laden topics or about values, beliefs, or attitudes underlying an expressed opinion or behavior (Richardson, Dohrenwend, & Klein, 1965; Selltiz et al., 1965). When conducting a focused interview, the interviewer identifies in advance certain broad topics that he or she would like all respondents to cover. The interviewer may use an interview guide listing specific questions and objectives to ensure that this information is covered, but within this framework, the interviewer has considerable flexibility, and each interview is therefore tailored to the particular situation. Because the most effective sequence of topics for any respondent is determined by that respondent's readiness and willingness to approach a topic

(Denzin, 1970; Richardson et al., 1965), allowing respondents this freedom is likely to result in the raising of important issues not anticipated by the interviewer (Selltiz et al., 1965). The interviewer may also find that the respondent will summarize entire topics in one long sequence of statements if allowed this opportunity (Denzin, 1970). These are the characteristics that contribute to the great flexibility of the focused interview, making it possible to obtain breadth, depth, and richness of information. At the same time, the use of an interview guide provides a degree of structure to the interview. This combination of flexibility and structure supports the focused interview.

Structure and Format

Although much has been written about the focused interview, there is an absence of specific detail about the actual steps to follow in interviewing an individual or family. Because professionals from a variety of disciplines, including some that do not presently emphasize interviewing skills or strategies, should be able to use the methods of assessment described, it is important to outline specifically a structure and format for conducting a family-focused interview. To develop the format that will be presented here, we turned to the psychological (Evans et al., 1984; Gorden, 1969; Ivey, 1971) and psychiatric (Weber et al., 1985) literature on clinical interviewing. From this information, we derived five phases of the interview process, as displayed in Table 9.1.

Preliminary Phase. Before the interview is conducted, the assessment information already gathered should be consolidated and summarized. Each standardized measure should be examined and high-priority needs specified. Such analysis might identify the following:

1. Items rated as areas of need by mother or father on a family needs assessment scale
2. Items or clusters of items receiving low scores on a parent-child observational rating scale
3. Child behaviors, demand characteristics, or temperament styles with potential family impact
4. Current or upcoming critical events

It is particularly important to note discrepancies that might emerge as measures are examined. For instance, a parent may receive a very low rating on the appropriateness of his or her play interaction with the child, indicating a misunderstanding of the child's abilities or developmental level; the parent might be expected to indicate a need for information on the child's developmental status on a survey of family needs. However, if the parent does *not* rank this as an area of need, a discrepancy exists. During the interview the interventionist would want to explore reasons for the discrep-

TABLE 9.1
A Model for Conducting a Family-Focused Interview

Interview Phase	Purpose
1. Preliminary Identify high-priority needs Identify difficulties in parent-child interaction Specify child characteristics that have potential family impact Note upcoming critical events	Prepare for interview by summarizing assessment data
2. Introduction Explain purpose of the interview Confirm time allotted and format Discuss confidentiality Structure physical environment (if possible)	Reduce parents' anxiety and create appropriate listening environment
3. Inventory Make opening statement Allow parents to do most of the talking	Validate and elaborate information from assessment Identify additional areas of family needs, strengths, and resources
4. Summary, priority, and goal setting Make summarizing statements Explore family's priorities Set goals collaboratively	Clarify consensus and disagreement between parents Agree on definition of family needs Establish priorities and set goals
5. Closure Express recognition and appreciation of parents' contribution Ask if family members have additional concerns or thoughts about interview	Recognize parents' efforts Allow concerns about interview to emerge

ancy (e.g., the parents may be unaware of or unwilling to acknowledge difficulties in their interactions with their child, or the difficulties might be related to issues other than misunderstandings or a lack of information about the child's developmental level).

Discrepancies might also indicate that the measures were not valid in the situation. For instance, if a mother receives a low rating on acceptance and enjoyment of play on an observational measure, yet does not indicate a need for help in areas pertaining to interaction with her child, additional observations or data collection may be needed. Perhaps the parent does not feel comfortable displaying warmth and positive affect within the context of a structured observation. Informal observations would shed light on this hypothesis. Contextual variables must also be considered when interpreting assessment data. For instance, certain children are temperamentally adverse to a great deal of physical direction and handling, especially when they are busily engaged in play. What might be interpreted as lack of warmth could be a parent's sensitivity to the child's temperamental idiosyncrasies.

Discrepancies will also exist in how mothers and fathers respond to the assessment measures. The interviewer should address those areas in which differences are great. For instance, if the mother indicates on a family needs survey that she does not need help in finding babysitters yet the father indicates that this is an area of great need, a discrepancy is suggested in how they view the issue. The interview would offer a means of assessing the extent to which the parents are aware of this discrepancy, the extent to which the discrepancy is a problem for each of them, and, if applicable, how they have tried to solve the problem. A clear understanding of a situation by the parents and the interventionist is necessary before solutions and goals can be effectively generated.

A family planning guide, such as the one provided in Table 9.2, can be used to consolidate assessment information in preparation for conducting the interview. The planning guide in Table 9.2 is divided into two sections. Section 1 deals with information generated by the interventionist after careful analysis of the standardized measures. This includes identifying initial hypotheses about family goals and areas needing further exploration during the focused interview. Section 2 deals with information gathered during the focused interview, and includes family resources, family perceptions, and the final goals set in collaboration with families.

Introductory Phase. During the introductory phase important details about the purpose, format, and structure of the interview are confirmed with the family. This includes explaining the purpose of the interview, confirming the time allotted and the format to be followed, discussing confidentiality issues such as who will have access to the information and under what conditions, and structuring the physical environment to limit interruptions, reduce distractions, accommodate young children, and create a facilitative seating arrangement.

Some of these issues should be discussed when the interview is arranged. For instance, setting a mutually agreed on time for the interview when both parents and other interested family members and caregivers can be present may be a major task. Interventionists will need flexible work schedules, perhaps including some weekend and evening work, to permit true collaboration with families on interview times.

TABLE 9.2
An Example of a Family Planning Guide

Topics	Section 1 Summary—Standardized Assessment Data		Section 2 Summary—Interview Data		
	Initial Hypotheses	Areas to Explore	Family Resources	Family Perceptions	Collaboratively Set Goals
Family needs		Discrepancy between mother and father regarding need for babysitting	Grandmother is eager to babysit	Mother is concerned that grandmother can't manage; father disagrees	Family meeting, including grandmother, will be held to discuss grandmother's involvement in intervention visits
Family roles	Father will help with evening child care and mealtime	Father's perspective on involvement with feeding and evening child care responsibilities	Father is available most evenings	Father is eager and skillful playmate but doesn't enjoy or feel competent at feedings—he is willing to learn; mother would like a break from feeding	Father will become involved with feeding program set up by interventionist; he will take over evening feedings two times a week when trained

Category					
Family supports	Involve maternal grandmother to greater extent	Parent's perspective on grandmother's involvement	Grandmother is eager to learn more about care of child	Parents would like grandmother to be involved, although mother is concerned about grandmother's competence	Grandmother will become involved in intervention visits if she is willing
Critical events		Are there any critical events upcoming not covered on measures?		Mother is contemplating returning to work part-time but is concerned about child care	Provide information on day care options to mother; provide opportunities for further discussion
Parent-child interactions	Provide mother with information on developmentally appropriate play activities	Mother's perspective on interactions with child	Father models appropriate play interactions	Mother is frustrated by constant demands on her time; is not enjoying time with child	Father and grandmother will provide opportunities for mother to have time away from home
Home environment	No concerns				
Child characteristics	Child will improve sitting and eating	What is impact on family of child's low functioning?		Child's inability to sit makes independent play and eating difficult; this is frustrating for mother	Physical therapist will help family with sitting and feeding program
Other					

Exhibiting this sort of flexibility before the interview may be essential to the success of the interview. Gorden (1969) listed "competing demands on time" as a major inhibitor of effective communication. Time is likely to be a precious commodity for families with children because of "role strain," or escalation in role demands (Rollins & Galligan, 1978). This may be especially true in dual-career families (Skinner, 1983). Making sure that the time scheduled is convenient for the family is critically important in getting the interview off to a good start. It is a way of letting families know at the beginning that their perspective is important in the process.

Even when preliminary information has already been discussed before the interview, repeating this information is worthwhile. Misunderstandings about issues such as interview purpose and confidentiality may distort the information families are willing to share. The ultimate goal for the interviewer during this phase is to reduce the family's anxiety and to create an appropriate and facilitative listening environment.

Inventory Phase. The inventory phase could be considered the needs-assessment portion of the interview. The interviewer's purpose is to validate and elaborate on the assessment information already gathered from the family, while at the same time remaining open to unanticipated issues, needs, and strengths that were not revealed during the standardized assessment process. During this phase the type of information discussed earlier in this chapter on family membership characteristics, roles, perceptions, and strengths might be explored. Also at this time the family's basic beliefs and values underlying their behaviors and opinions might emerge.

The interviewer's opening statement sets the tone for the entire interview and is therefore very important. It should be clearly related to the stated purpose of the interview, open-ended, nonthreatening, and designed to allow the family members to start with a topic they feel comfortable discussing. The interviewer's major task at the beginning of the inventory stage is to establish rapport and to convey to the family that he or she is there to listen, not to lecture or give advice. The family members should do most of the talking during this phase. By using carefully worded responses and questions as well as the communication skills described in Chapter 10, the interviewer should subtly guide the interview to ensure that all the important topics identified are covered.

The Summary, Priority, and Goal-Setting Phase. The fourth phase begins when the interviewer concludes that all the topics identified before the interview have been covered and that the family has had ample opportunity to introduce additional issues important to them. At this point the interviewer succinctly summarizes what has been discussed in a way that allows the family members to hear and reflect on what they have said. The interviewer then translates this information into meaningful and practical goals whose importance to all parties is clearly recognized. Goals should be formulated in such a way that success is probable. This builds a family's confidence and sense of competence and demonstrates the interventionist's ability to be a family helper and ally (Aponte, 1976; Berger, 1986; Bryant, 1984).

Closure. The final interview phase, closure, takes place after the formal portion of the interview is over. During this phase the interviewer expresses appreciation and recognition of the family's time and effort, makes plans for future meetings, possibly reiterates objectives to be reached before the next meeting, and gives the family a chance to reflect on feelings about the interview. Our clinical experiences suggest that families sometimes use this time to bring up important information that did not emerge during the more formal phases of the interview. In addition, if parents have shared very personal and emotionally laden information, they might be having second thoughts about their candor. For these reasons, some time should always be reserved for closure, and the interviewer should be sensitive and receptive to final thoughts, concerns, and questions from family members. Gorden (1969) suggested a follow-up phone call to family members if the interview has been particularly difficult or emotional. Doubts about sharing intimate information and releasing unpleasant tensions might grow when the interviewer is not there to make assurances of confidentiality or to display a nonjudgmental attitude. A phone call may allay these concerns.

Examples of statements that might be used during various phases of the interview are displayed in Table 9.3 (pp. 200–201).

SUMMARY

The development of the family-focused interview as a mechanism to serve the dual purposes of assessment and collaborative goal setting has been based on a substantial body of theoretical, clinical, and research information. The rationale is compelling for including a method to assess family variables not traditionally examined, such as strengths, values, and definitions. Data have recently been described (Winton & Bailey, in press) that support the impact of the interview on trained interventionists and on intervention goals set for families and children, and suggest that the interview is an effective and practical component to intervention efforts. The success of any approach, however, lies in the hands of those who implement it; therefore, training is a critical variable in considering the effectiveness and practicality of the interview. An interventionist cannot successfully conduct the kind of interview described in this chapter without a command of certain communication skills. Chapter 10 focuses on those skills and issues related to parent and professional communication.

TABLE 9.3
Sample Statements Used During the Family-Focused Interview

Purpose	1. You have already filled out several forms for us. We appreciate the time you've spent on those, and that information has been helpful in getting to know [*child's name*] and your family. But we feel the best way to get an overall picture of your family is to have a chance to sit down with the two of you so you can share with us the way you see things now with [*child's name*]. In this way we can plan together the services and programs that will be most helpful to you and [*child's name*]. That is the purpose of today's visit.
	or
	2. The purpose of today's visit (interview) is for us to be able to learn from you about [*child's name*], about your family, and about concerns and needs that you might have. We have asked you to fill out a number of forms as a first step in getting this information, and we appreciate the time you spent on those. We feel this second step, sitting down and talking together, is a good way for us to plan for the best kinds of services that will meet your needs as a family.
Format	During the first part of the interview it would be helpful if you shared with me a little bit about what life is like with [*child's name*] right now. Then during the second part we could talk about goals that you might have that we could work on together. As I mentioned on the phone, I expect that we'll spend about 45 minutes to an hour together today.

TABLE 9.3
Continued

Confidentiality	You might remember filling out a permission slip when you agreed to be involved in this project. There was a confidentiality statement attached to it [or there was a statement with it assuring you that the information would be kept confidential and would not be given out to other people]. The same thing is true of this interview. The information we talk about today will be shared with other members of the intervention team only. It will not be shared with other family members or professionals unless you agree that this would be helpful to you.
Opening statement	Could you tell me a little bit about what life is like with [*child's name*] right now? [This statement will depend upon the number and type of previous contacts with the family. The opening statement should have the following characteristics: 1. It should be nonthreatening and something parents can answer. It sets the tone for the entire interview. 2. It should be open-ended. This allows parents to start where they are most comfortable. 3. It should be related to purpose of the interview.]
Covering areas of need identified in standardized assessments	I noted that on one of the forms you [fill in content]. Could you tell me a little bit about that?
Recognizing of parents' contribution	I feel that you've given me a very clear picture of how things are going for you and [*child's name*] right now. I so much appreciate the time you've spent helping us understand things about [*child's name*] and your family so we can plan together with you.

REFERENCES

Adler, L., Ware, J., & Enelow, A. (1970). Changes in medical interviewing style after instruction with two closed-circuit television techniques. *Journal of Medical Education, 45,* 21–28.

Aponte, H. (1976). Underorganization in the poor family. In P. Guerin (Ed.), *Family therapy: Theory and practice* (pp. 432–448). New York: Science Press.

Aponte, H. (1986). "If I don't get simple, I cry." *Family Process, 25,* 531–548.

Bailey, D. B., Simeonsson, R. J., Winton, P. J., Huntington, G. S., Comfort, M., Isbell, P., O'Donnell, K. J., & Helm J. M. (1986). Family-focused intervention: A functional model for planning, implementing, and evaluating individualized family services in early intervention. *Journal of the Division for Early Childhood, 10,* 156–171.

Bass, B. M., & Leavitt, H. J. (1963). Some experiments in planning and operating. *Management Science, 9,* 574–585.

Benjamin, A. (1969). *The helping interview.* Boston: Houghton-Mifflin.

Berger, M. (1986). Contributions of family therapy to the development of early childhood special education services that enhance individual and family development. *Training professionals to interact with families* (Monograph 2). (Available from the Parent/Family Support Series, University of Idaho, Moscow, ID 83843.)

Boss, P., & Greenberg, J. (1984). Family boundary ambiguity: A new variable in family stress theory. *Family Process, 23,* 535–546.

Brinckerhoff, J. L., & Vincent, L. J. (1986). Increasing parental decision-making at the individualized educational program meeting. *Journal of the Division for Early Childhood, 11,* 46–58.

Bristol, M. (1987). Methodological caveats in the assessment of single-parent families of handicapped children. *Journal of the Division for Early Childhood, 11,* 135–142.

Bristol, M., & Schopler, E. (1984). A developmental perspective on stress and coping in families of autistic children. In J. Blacher (Ed.), *Severely handicapped young children and their families.* Orlando, Fla.: Academic Press.

Bryant, C. (1984). Working for families with dysfunctional children: An approach and structure for the first family therapy interview. *Child and Adolescent Social Work, 1,* 102–117.

Cadman, D., Shurvell, B., Davies, P., & Bradfield, S. (1984). Compliance in the community with consultants' recommendations for developmentally handicapped children. *Developmental Medicine and Child Neurology, 26,* 40–46.

Denzin, N. (1970). *The research act: A theoretical introduction to sociological methods.* Chicago: Aldine Publishing.

Doernberg, N. (1978). Some negative effects on family integration of health and educational services for young handicapped children. *Rehabilitation Literature, 39,* 107–110.

Dunst, C. J., (1985). Rethinking early intervention. *Analysis and Intervention in Developmental Disabilities, 5,* 165–201.

Dunst, C. J., Trivette, C. M., & Cross, A. H. (1986). Mediating influences of social support. *American Journal of Mental Deficiency, 90,* 403–417.

Evans, D., Hearn, M., Uhlemann, M., & Ivey, A. (1984). *Essential interviewing: A programmed approach to effective communication* (2nd ed.). Monterey, Calif.: Brooks/Cole Publishing.

Fenton, K., Yoshida, R., Maxwell, J., & Kaufman, M. (1979). Recognition of team goals: An essential step toward rational decision making. *Exceptional Children, 45,* 638–644.

Gallagher, J. J., Scharfman, W., & Bristol, M. (1984). The division of responsibilities in families with preschool handicapped and nonhandicapped children. *Journal of the Division for Early Childhood, 8,* 3–12.

Gilliam, J. (1979). Contributions and status rankings of educational planning committee participants. *Exceptional Children, 45,* 466–468.

Gorden, R. (1969). *Interviewing: Strategies, techniques and tactics.* Homewood, Ill.: Dorsey Press.

Griffith, J. L. (1986). Employing the God-family relationship in therapy with religious families. *Family Process, 25,* 609–618.

Helfer, R., & Hess, J. (1970). An experimental model for making objective measurements of interviewing skills. *Journal of Clinical Psychology, 26,* 327–331.

Hepworth, D., & Larsen, J. (1982). *Direct social work practice: Theory and skills.* Homewood, Ill.: Dorsey Press.

Hetherington, E. M. (1984). Stress and coping in children and families. In A. Doyle, D. Gold, & S. Moskovitz (Eds.), *Children in families under stress* (pp. 7–33). *New Directions for Child Development,* no. 24. San Francisco: Jossey-Bass.

Hill, R. (1958). Social stresses on the family. *Social Casework, 39,* 139–150.

Ivey, A. (1971). *Microcounseling: Innovations in interview training.* Springfield, Ill.: Charles C. Thomas.

Johnson, T. E., Chandler, L. K., Kerns, G. M., & Fowler, S. A. (1986). What are parents saying about family involvement in school transitions? A retrospective transition interview. *Journal of the Division for Early Childhood, 11,* 10–17.

Kazak, A. E. (1986). Families with physically handicapped children: Social ecology and family systems. *Family Process, 25,* 265–281.

Kazak, A. E., & Marvin, R. S. (1984). Differences, difficulties, and adaptation: Stress and social networks in families with a handicapped child. *Family Relations, 33,* 67–77.

Latham, G., & Locke, E. (1979). Goal-setting: A motivational technique that works. *Organizational Dynamics,* 45–54.

Maccoby, E., & Maccoby, N. (1954). The interview: A tool for social service. In G. Lindzey (Ed.), *Handbook of social psychology* (vol. 1). Cambridge, Mass.: Addison-Wesley.

McCubbin, H., & Patterson, J. (1983). The family stress process: The double ABCX model of family adjustment and adaptation. In H. McCubbin, M. Sussman, and J. Patterson (Eds.), *Advances and developments in family stress theory and research.* New York: Haworth.

Meadow, R., & Hewitt, C. (1972). Teaching communication skills with the help of actresses and videotape simulation. *British Journal of Medical Education, 6,* 317–322.

Merton, R., Fiske, M., & Kendall, P. (1946). *The focused interview: A manual of problems and procedures.* Glencoe, Ill.: Free Press.

Meyer, D. (1986). Fathers of children with special needs. *The family of the handicapped infant and young child* (Monograph 1). (Available from the Parent/Family Support Services, University of Idaho, Moscow, ID 83843.)

Minuchin, S. (1974). *Families and family therapy.* Cambridge, Mass.: Harvard University Press.

Olson, D., McCubbin, H., Barnes, H., Larsen, H., Muxen, M., & Wilson M. (1983). *Families: What makes them work.* Beverly Hills, Calif.: Sage Publications.

Richardson, S., Dohrenwend, B., & Klein, D. (1965). *Interviewing: Its forms and functions.* New York: Basic Books.

Rollins, B., & Galligan, R. (1978). The developing child and marital satisfaction of parents. In R. Lerner & G. Spanier (Eds.), *Child influences on marital and family interaction: A life-span perspective* (pp. 71–102). New York: Academic Press.

Selltiz, C., Jahoda, M., Deutsch, M., & Cook, S. (1965). *Research methods in social relations.* New York: Holt, Rinehart & Winston.

Shapiro, J. (1983). Family reactions and coping with physically ill or handicapped children. *Social Science Medicine, 17,* 913–931.

Shuster, S., Guskin, S., Hawkins, B., & Okolo, C. (1986). Views of health and development: Six mothers and their infants. *Journal of the Division for Early Childhood, 11,* 18–27.

Simeonsson, R. J. & Bailey, D. B. (1986). Siblings of handicapped children. In J. J. Gallagher & P. N. Vietze (Eds.), *Families of handicapped persons* (pp. 67–77). Baltimore: Paul H. Brookes.

Skinner, D. (1983). Dual-career families: Strains of sharing. In A. McCubbin & C. Figley (Eds.). *Stress and the family, Vol. II: Coping with catastrophe* (pp. 90–101). New York: Brunner/Mazel.

Stack, C. (1975). *All our kin.* New York: Harper & Row.

Tomm, K. (1987). Interventive interviewing: Part I. Strategizing as a fourth guideline for the therapist. *Family Process, 26,* 3–13.

Turnbull, A. (1985, May). *Positive contributions that members with disabilities make to their families.* Paper presented at the meeting of the American Association for Mental Deficiency, Philadelphia, Pa.

Turnbull, A., Brotherson, M., Bruinicks, G., Benson, H., Houghton, J., Roeder-Gorden, C., & Summers, J. (1984). *How to plan for my child's adult future: A three-part process to future planning.* Lawrence, Kan.: Future Planning Project, Bureau of Child Research, University Affiliated Faculty, University of Kansas.

Turnbull, A., & Winton, P. (1984). Parent involvement policy and practice: Current research and implications for families with young severely handicapped children. In J. Blacher (Ed.), *Severely handicapped young children and their families: Research in review* (pp. 377–397). New York: Academic Press.

Vadasy, P., Fewell, R., Greenberg, M., Dermond, N., & Meyer, D. (1986). Follow-up evaluation of the effects of involvement in the father program. *Topics in Early Childhood Special Education, 6*(2), 16–31.

Weber, T., McKeever, J. E., & McDaniel, S. H. (1985). A beginner's guide to the problem-oriented first family interview. *Family Process, 24,* 357–364.

Winton, P. (1986). The developmentally delayed child within the family context. In B. Keogh (Ed.), *Advances in special education: Vol. 5. Developmental problems in infancy and the preschool years.* (pp. 219–255). Greenwich, Conn.: JAI Press.

Winton, P. J., & Bailey, D. B. (in press). The family-focused interview: A collaborative mechanism for family assessment and goal-setting. *Journal of the Division for Early Childhood.*

Winton, P. J., & Turnbull, A. P. (1981). Parent involvement as viewed by parents of preschool handicapped children. *Topics in Early Childhood Special Education, 1,* 11–19.

Witt, J., Miller, C., McIntyre, R., & Smith, D. (1984). Effects of variables on parental perceptions of staffings. *Exceptional Children, 51,* 27–32.

10

Effective Communication Between Parents and Professionals

P rofessionals and parents of handicapped children have much vital information to share. Both Public Law 94-142 and Public Law 99-457 emphasize the importance of collaboration between parents and professionals in formulating effective individualized plans. A cornerstone of collaboration is *communication*, or the sharing of information and feelings with another person. This chapter describes barriers to effective communication with parents and presents key skills necessary for effective communication. Although the importance of these skills in the focused interview is emphasized, these skills are also important in continued *interaction* with family members.

BARRIERS TO COMMUNICATION

Attitudes, perceptions, cultural beliefs, and assumptions clearly affect communication patterns. The following section describes how these variables affect communication between parents and professionals.

This chapter was contributed by Pamela J. Winton, University of North Carolina at Chapel Hill.

Attitudinal Barriers

Descriptions in the literature (Bristol & Schopler, 1984; Turnbull & Turnbull, 1986; Turnbull & Summers, 1985) of some professional attitudes toward parents of handicapped children (parents as scapegoats; parents as deviants; parents as patients; parents as adversaries; parents as "denying," "hostile," or "emotionally upset") suggest the communication styles that have characterized some professionals' interactions with parents. Correspondingly, an indication of parents' general opinion of professionals was presented by Simpson (1982). Parents have observed these deficiencies in some educators:

1. They seem preoccupied while parents are talking; they obviously have something else on their minds.
2. They seem to be listening, but their responses make it apparent that they do not understand.
3. They respond critically to what parents say or make suggestions when the parent only wants (and needs) an opportunity to talk.
4. They listen with one ear, waiting for the parents to finish speaking so that they can make their point or explain the way it "really" is.

From a systems perspective, both parents and professionals play a role in the communication difficulties that have existed over time. An examination of some current attitudinal barriers may identify new directions to facilitate interaction.

Parents' Attitudes Toward Professionals. Historically, parents have most frequently criticized medical professionals for communicative shortcomings, particularly in terms of how doctors convey the diagnosis of a handicap. Given the extent of the literature on the importance of sensitively communicating this information (Klaus & Kennell, 1976; Guralnick & Richardson, 1980; Olson & Kroth, 1986; Wolraich, 1982), one might presume this issue to be of historical interest rather than of contemporary concern. However, current research has documented that parents still perceive medical personnel as doing a less than adequate job in communicating. In a survey of 59 families of Down syndrome infants conducted by Cunningham, Morgan, and McGucken (1984), 59% of parents reported dissatisfaction with how the diagnosis was given. Parents were specifically dissatisfied with the timing (delays in getting the information), the manner (lack of sympathy, with an emphasis on the negative aspects or the condition), and the format (couples not told together). This dissatisfaction was further substantiated in an interview study by Gowen, Johnson-Martin, and Goldman (1987), in which parents identified the following problems with the way doctors conveyed the diagnosis: (1) parents were not treated with respect and listened to; (2) doctors did not respect the individuality of the handicapped child, but treated the child as a "diagnostic category"; and (3) doctors did not provide adequate information or referrals for services but conveyed a "give up" attitude. Parents in this study emphasized the importance of honest information presented in a way that offered some hope, in the form of a positive direction (i.e., referral or intervention). The validity of this information is reinforced by the finding described in Chapter 9 that reframing—identifying an aspect of a stressor event over which some control is possible—is an effective coping strategy used by families faced with crisis (Olson, et al., 1983).

The argument that diagnosis will always engender dissatisfaction with the person conveying the bad news was dispelled in a small intervention study by Cunningham et al. (1984). They developed and implemented a "model service" for delivering diagnostic information to families of Down syndrome infants and evaluated its effectiveness using an experimental design. All the families in the experimental group ($N = 7$) were satisfied with how diagnostic information was delivered, compared to a 20% satisfaction rate in the control group ($N = 25$). Although small in scale, this study suggests that communication of difficult and emotionally laden information can be done in a way that parents perceive as sensitive and helpful.

Simpson (1982) suggested that educators are in an excellent position to avoid the difficulties encountered by other professionals, because they are less likely to be involved in the initial diagnosis. If they are involved, they may be able to provide a more positive perspective because of their knowledge of intervention programs and services. In addition, because they are often in contact with the family over a period of time, they have more opportunities to establish rapport and develop a helping relationship.

The challenge for educators may be to avoid or ameliorate problems inherent in the tangled system of agencies and professionals with whom parents interact. Based on their study of the use of formal support networks by families with handicapped children, Suelzle and Kenan (1981) concluded that these networks are "uncoordinated, uninformed about the complete range of resources available and unable to supplement diagnosis with specific advice about parenting a retarded child" (p. 268). Harrison (1983) illustrates the personal frustration that can result when parents deal with a number of professionals, each having a different opinion:

> When we first consulted developmental specialists, we hoped for answers about Edward's condition and suggestions for helping him. What we got instead was confusion. Yes, Edward was ready for toilet training. No, he wasn't. Yes, heel cord surgery would help him walk better. No, that was the worst thing we could do. We soon learned that there was no right answer to any question about Edward's care and upbringing. We began to rely more and more on our own judgment. We continued to seek professional insight, but we tried to find doctors and therapists with whom we felt compatible; people whose advice made sense to us. (p. 221)

Parents seem to be saying that they need a professional operating as a "case manager" who can help them coordinate and understand the various perspectives presented by the different professionals with whom they have contact. Unger and Powell (1980) used the term *linkage approach* in describing a program in which nurses act as "links" among high-risk parents bearing their first child, formal health care and community services, and informal support networks and resources. Functioning in such a role requires skills in networking, interagency collaboration, communication, and group dynamics. These skills are not traditionally emphasized in training programs for interventionists; however, as the field moves in the direction of a systems approach, preservice (Dale, 1986; Bailey, Farel, O'Donnell, Simeonsson, & Miller, 1986) and inservice (Bailey, Simeonsson, et al., 1986) training programs are beginning to be developed that reflect the importance of considering the various contexts in which the handicapped child resides.

Professionals' Attitudes Toward Parents. The troublesome aspects of the parent-professional relationship may partly account for the finding by Bensky et al. (1980) that teachers rank communications with parents as a major source of job stress. If teachers are compelled by law to engage in an activity (communicating with parents) that they do not value or for which they lack skill, their attitudes are likely to contribute to an unproductive and unfulfilling experience.

Recent approaches to intervention with families (Bailey, Simeonsson, et al., 1986; Berger, 1984, 1986; Dunst, 1985; Foster & Berger, 1979; Turnbull & Turnbull, 1986) deemphasize the pathological or negative interpretations of family behavior and focus on a greater understanding of how and why families operate as they do. For example, the "shopping behavior" observed in parents and negatively connoted at one point (Anderson, 1971) has been reinterpreted as a potentially adaptive response to the difficulties in obtaining a diagnosis when the child's handicap is ambiguous (Bernheimer, Young, & Winton, 1983). Parental denial, which had been described in the past as an obstacle to acceptance of the handicap—the desired state—is now understood to be a potential coping strategy that can protect the family from being overwhelmed (Olson et al., 1983). The parents' choice to bypass traditional parent activities (parent-support groups, parent-training programs, etc.) of the intervention program can be understood in the context of other demands on their time and energy and their involvement at home with the child and his or her siblings rather than as a professional or parental failure (Winton & Turnbull, 1981). As research and clinical practice become grounded in theories and models of family functioning, the integral role of parents' perspectives in effective programming is increasingly apparent.

Perceptual Barriers

For several reasons, the ability of parents and professionals to share perceptions about the child is an important aspect of intervention. First, research has shown high correlations between mothers and professionals in their overall developmental assessments of handicapped infants and children (Gradel, Thompson, & Sheehan, 1981; Sexton, Miller, & Murdock, 1984). This finding suggests that both parties have areas of agreement that could form the basis of effective programming and demonstrates to doubting professionals that parents have credibility when describing what their child can and cannot do.

In addition to recognizing similarities, it is important to look at how perceptions of parents and professionals differ and to recognize that these differences will affect assessment, implementation, and intervention outcomes. In terms of assessment, existing discrepancies have been described as either parental overestimation or professional underestimation of the child's abilities (Gradel et al., 1981). As pointed out by Shuster, Guskin, Hawkins, and Okolo (1986) and Gradel et al. (1981), these differences in perception may be due to different opportunities and contexts in which to observe the child. The parent sees the child in a much broader array of situations, which makes it more likely that she or he will notice newly emerging skills or irregularly occurring symptoms than will the professional. In addition, Shuster et al. (1986) observed that physicians are more likely to notice behaviors that fit diagnostic categories, whereas parents are apt to react to behaviors with emotional impact, such as screaming or irritability.

Another area in which parents' and professionals' perceptions clearly differ is the impact of various interventions (Battle, 1974; Doernberg, 1978; Shuster et al., 1986). An example from Shuster et al. (1986) is the case of the physician whose primary interest is an accurate diagnosis even if there are no advantages in terms of treatment. For the family, the pain and disruption of additional diagnostic procedures may be unwanted inconveniences. Another example is the case of the family dealing with a large array of specialists, each suggesting a simple home-therapy program or exercise. From the family's point of view, each recommendation may add up to an overwhelming number of tasks.

The third area in which perceptual differences affect intervention is ultimate outcomes. A study by Cadman, Goldsmith, and Bashim (1984) comparing parental and professional values placed on seven different functions or attributes related to child well-being indicated that the two groups differed in priorities for outcome. Parents placed the greatest overall value on prognosis for normal role fulfillment in later years, whereas professionals rated family interaction (which parents ranked sixth in importance out of seven) as most important, followed by normal role fulfillment.

Two points should be made regarding implications of perceptual differences for family assessment and communication. First, parents' information on assessment, implementation, and outcome, which is not available to the professsional by any means other than direct communication, is critical for program success. If parental values are not taken into account, compliance with intervention goals is less likely (Cadman, Shurvell, Davies,

& Bradfield, 1984; Dunst & Leet, 1987). In the words of Dunst and Leet, "Whenever there is a mismatch between what a family and professional see as child, parent and/or family needs, the probability of a family adhering to professional prescriptions would be diminished" (p. 112).

Second, communication skills play an important role in obtaining information on parents' perspectives. Shuster et al. (1986) observed that, ironically, the stress experienced by families at the point of diagnosis and evaluation makes it harder for them to share the information that professionals so vitally need. At this point the skills of hearing parents and speaking their language become critical in demonstrating a true desire to understand their viewpoint (Berger, 1986; Gorden, 1969; Gowen et al., 1987).

Cultural Barriers

The foregoing discussion of attitudes and perceptions has focused on differences between families of handicapped children and professionals. An inherent danger in this kind of discussion is that false assumptions may be made about the homogeneity of families of handicapped children. The *individuality* of each family is of great importance. The most compelling and visible way in which within-group differences may be manifest is through cultural differences. Cultural style has been described as containing four major components: ethnicity, religion, socioeconomic status, and geographic location (Turnbull, Brotherson, & Summers, 1986). The present discussion focuses on ethnicity and socioeconomic status because of the large number of families affected by these two factors. For example, according to the U.S. Census Bureau, more than one-third of Americans were non-Anglo in 1980; today that number is even higher. One out of every four children under the age of 6 is living in poverty (Schweinhart & Koshel, 1986), and a higher percentage of children of low socioeconomic status are handicapped.

At the simplest level, language differences associated with cultural style limit communication between professionals and families. Words such as *retardation, mainstreaming,* or *intervention* may have different meanings for different cultural groups. At a more complex level, differences in values, beliefs, social structures, and practices color the meaning and effectiveness of relationships with interventionists. A closer look at how ethnicity and socioeconomic status affect (1) reactions to handicaps and (2) attitudes and beliefs about intervention clearly illustrates the implications of such differences.

Reactions to Handicaps.   Lynch (1986) and Turnbull and Turnbull (1987) provide descriptions and case examples of non-Anglo values relating to child rearing and family support that differ tremendously from traditional Anglo views. For example, the Anglo-American emphasis on independence, which shapes many intervention goals, is not shared by Central and South American cultures. The permissiveness and indulgence shown to children within these cultures is likely to be interpreted as "spoiling" by interventionists. The values of some cultures encourage passivity and ascribe events to fate or outside uncontrollable sources. For these families, a simple acceptance of the handicapped child may be their natural response; reliance on outside help may be minimal.

Farber (1960) was one of the first to study how differences in socioeconomic status (SES) affected reaction to the birth of a handicapped child. He concluded that middle-SES families experienced the birth as a "tragic crisis" that shattered dreams and expectations for their child's future; whereas lower SES families reacted more to the actual caregiving and financial demands of the situation. His conclusions are corroborated by the research of Dunlap and Hollingsworth (1977). In a survey of predominantly poor families in the South, they found that families tended to perceive the problems associated with the handicapped child in terms of physical and financial demands rather than emotional ones.

Beliefs About Intervention. In addition to differences in perception, a family's cultural style may affect its level of cooperation and participation with intervention efforts. Lynch (1986) provides case examples and Shapiro (1983) describes the kinds of cultural factors that interfere with the successful implementation of intervention. They include (1) strong family pride; (2) the need for approval for any treatment by the community, religious, or spiritual leaders; and (3) superstitions related to illness and medical technology. In her ethnographic study of low-income, urban black families, Stack (1975) observed a distrust of all representatives of social service agencies, a consideration in the planning of intervention with families from this cultural group.

Because most intervention efforts are planned and implemented by white middle-class professionals, the demands on families with different cultural styles to adapt are particularly high (Allen, Affleck, McGrade, & McQueeney, 1984). For instance, families with limited verbal skills are less likely to benefit from parent-training programs and parent-support groups with a middle-class orientation. Documented differences between middle- and lower SES maternal interaction styles require lower SES mothers to make greater accommodations to meet the standards promoted by interventionists. A study by Granger cited in Wright, Granger, and Sameroff (1984) indicated that for mothers lacking a sophisticated understanding of child development, involvement with an intervention program may be associated with greater stress. Wright et al. surmised the stress could be attributed to the conflicting (more sophisticated) beliefs to which mothers were exposed in intervention.

Dunst and Leet (1987) suggested using a needs-hierarchy perspective when providing intervention to families with different cultural styles. This approach is based on Maslow's (1954) notion that basic (physiological and intrapersonal) needs must be met before more complicated (interpersonal and growth-oriented) needs can be addressed. Dunst and Leet (1987) provided data indicating that mothers who reported inadequacies in family resources were less likely to see the child's educational and therapeutic needs as immediately important. They contended that families with inadequate basic resources are primarily interested in meeting those needs and are less likely to comply with interventionists' recommendations. These data support Dunlap and Hollingsworth's (1977) survey information that low-income families perceive the impact of their handicapped children in terms of physical and financial, rather than emotional, demands.

Clearly, attitudes, beliefs, perceptions, and cultural styles are interrelated critical variables that must be considered if intervention efforts are to be successful. In the past, intervention goals and programmatic decisions have been based on professional beliefs and attitudes about what is important. The flaws in this approach require broader theoretical frameworks and increased knowledge to make efforts more meaningful and effective with a larger and more diverse group of families. If one accepts the linguists' premise that language is the most significant feature differentiating cultural styles (Lynch, 1986), then effective communication is a key to intervention success. "Every social group has its own special vocabulary which is not always understood by outsiders" (Gorden, 1969, p. 52). Effective communication involves learning to use the modes of expression and specific words that have meaning for the families being interviewed. This approach builds rapport and ensures that the information shared is clear and understood by all parties.

TEACHING COMMUNICATION SKILLS

The issues associated with communication between parents and professionals are so complex that a simple discussion or recognition that they exist is unlikely to bring about dramatic improvements. In fact, research by Carkhuff, Kratochvil, and Friel (1968) suggests that a didactic approach to teaching interview skills may have a negative impact. They studied clinical psychology graduate students at the beginning and end of their four-year graduate programs and found a decline in communication skills. Even more surprising, they found a negative correlation between effective communication skills and academic grades. In trying to understand why successful graduate students, in programs that seemingly value and teach interviewing skills, would decline in their abilities, the authors examined the communication skills and the methods of teaching of the professors in the program. They found that the professors exhibited lower than average levels of communication skills and that their instructional methods emphasized conceptual abilities and mastery of content. They concluded that training programs without effective models and experiential opportunities for learning skills would not create effective interviewers. This finding suggests that simply providing information on communication and interviewing to interventionists is not likely to improve communication between parents and professionals. An interactive, experiential training approach is needed.

Fortunately, a body of literature within the medical and psychological disciplines relates to the development and evaluation of experiential methods for teaching communication skills (Adler, Ware, & Enelow, 1970; Helfer, Black, & Helfer, 1975; Helfer & Hess, 1970; Higgins, Ivey, & Uhlemann, 1970; Ivey, Normington, Miller, Morrill, & Haase, 1968; Iwata, Wong, Riordan, Dorsey, & Lau, 1982; Matarazzo, Phillips, Wiens, & Saslow, 1965; Meadow & Hewitt, 1972; Stillman, Sabers, & Redfield, 1977). Two critical components to training emerge from this literature:

1. The broad area of communication is broken down into component skills that are taught separately, primarily through a combination of programmed text material and videotaped or live examples of each component skill.
2. The trainees practice interview skills in a role-play situation (with another trainee, an actor playing a certain role, or a mother trained to respond in a standardized fashion). The interview is either audio- or videotaped to facilitate feedback and evaluation.

"Microtraining" Techniques

The most thoroughly developed and empirically tested training approach is the "microtraining" method developed and evaluated by Ivey (1971). He described microtraining as "a structural method which can be used by any of a variety of theoretical persuasions to impart their constructs and interviewing strategies" (p. 6). He developed a multimedia, multifaceted experiential approach that used several aspects of learning theory. The procedures involve cue discrimination and video models (Bandura, 1969), written materials, and operant techniques (Skinner, 1953), with an emphasis on positive reinforcement. Although many variations of the basic training model have been successfully implemented, Ivey (1971) has identified four critical microtraining variables: instructions, modeling, feedback, and supervision.

Instructions. The single most important instructional element in the microtraining approach is the breakdown of the broad area of communication into specific and discrete skills that can be presented and taught individually. Each skill area is initially introduced through written materials. In fact, one outgrowth of the microtraining approach has been the development of a programmed text (Evans, Hearn, Uhlemann, & Ivey, 1984) that can be used as an instructional component.

This single-skills approach is akin to the teaching strategy of task analysis, which interventionists and special educators have been using successfully for years and which has the same obvious advantages. The learner is not immediately overwhelmed by the enormity of the task or the absence of skills. Focusing on one skill at a time provides the learner with a sense of mastery early in the learning process and allows him or her to build on newly acquired skills.

Modeling.   Two modeling components are important in the microtraining approach. One is the presentation of video models of each skill to be learned; providing both a bad example and a good example of each skill is thought to enhance the learning process. The other component is the modeling of each skill by the supervisor or trainer during the course of the training.

Feedback.   Providing trainees with opportunities for self-observation and feedback through an audio- or videotape of their performance of the individual skills is a vital aspect of the approach. In this way, supervisors can help trainees identify for themselves areas in which improvements are needed.

Supervision.   An integral part of each component is the presence of a supportive and highly skilled supervisor who has a cognitive understanding of the process, is able to model the skills, and is able positively to reinforce the trainees' learning of the skills through objective and supportive feedback.

In summing up the research conducted on the microtraining approach and its many variations, Ivey (1971) concluded that different trainees respond most favorably to different parts of the training. He suggested that the question is not "which combination of methods works best, but which method, with what individuals and under what conditions" (p. 22) is most effective. He cites research supporting the need for follow-up supervision and practical experiences that reinforce the communication skills if behaviors are to be maintained over time. He also suggested a "do-use-teach" method, whereby trainees eventually keep in practice by teaching the skills to others.

Pilot Study: Training Early Interventionists in Communication Skills

Several microtraining components identified by Ivey (1971), along with other information from the clinical and behavioral literature on interviewing (Gorden, 1969; Hepworth & Larsen, 1982; Weber, McKeever, & McDaniel, 1985) were incorporated by this author in a training workshop on interviewing conducted for interventionists in two states. A total of 124 interventionists in North Carolina and Maine were trained to use the family-focused interview as part of a larger training effort in family-focused intervention (Bailey, Simeonsson, et al., 1986). The eight hours of interview training consisted of two components: the five-phase interview structure for conducting a family-focused interview described in Chapter 9; and the four basic communication skills described in a later section of this chapter. The training strategies used included the following: (1) an *instructional* component, consisting of lectures, discussion, and written materials focusing on the single-skills approach; (2) a *modeling* component, consisting of live and videotaped positive and negative examples of specific skills; (3) an *experiential* and *feedback* component, consisting of role-play activities with other trainees; and (4) a *supervision* component during role-play activities provided by trainers circulating through role-play groups.

Critical elements identified by Ivey (1971) but not present in this pilot training effort were opportunities for self-observation and follow-up supervision to ensure maintenance of skills. These absences were a function of logistical constraints. However, the training was evaluated in two respects. First, the interventionists in North Carolina were assessed pre- and post-training to determine their knowledge of interviewing skills, and all interventionists were assessed at post-training to determine their opinions of the usefulness of the training for clinical practice. Second, the effects of conducting a family-focused interview on the intervention goals they set for children and families were examined.

The results of a 10-item measure assessing the interventionists' knowledge of communication and interviewing skills administered before and after the training to the interventionists in North Carolina indicated that they increased their knowledge as a result of training ($N = 49$, pretest $X = 6.05$; post-test $X = 8.94$). Interventionists in North Carolina and Maine rated the training on a Likert-type scale in response to two questions:

1. How useful will the training be in your work with children and families?
2. To what extent did you gain new information as a result of the interview training?

The results indicated that they found the training useful ($N = 111$, $X = 4.5$, with 1 being "not at all useful" and 5 being "very useful") and felt they learned new information ($N = 112$, $X = 4.16$, with 1 being "none" and 5 being "a lot").

An indirect assessment of the training was made by examining how conducting the family-focused interview affected the intervention goals generated by interventionists for families and children. The interventionists were asked to list the child and family goals set before and after they conducted the family-focused interview. Of the original 235 goals devised after collecting information from families through standardized assessment measures but before conducting the interview, 36 (15%) were deleted, 35 (14%) were modified, and 32 new goals were generated. In terms of overall impact, 64 (28%) of the final 231 goals were affected by the family-focused interview.

This information does not document the extent to which the interventionists used effective communication skills, but it does provide evidence that interventionists learned something from the training, perceived that learning to be useful, and applied it in a way that affected the goals set with families. This pilot study represents an attempt to apply to training efforts with early interventionists the work of Ivey (1971), Gorden (1969), Weber et al. (1985), and others who have reviewed, developed, implemented, and evaluated the communication skills necessary for effective interviewing.

WHAT ARE THE CRITICAL COMMUNICATION SKILLS?

Research has indicated that certain communication skills are critical in determining the nature and effectiveness of the interview (Ivey, 1971; Hepworth & Larsen, 1982; Maccoby & Maccoby, 1954; Matarazzo et al., 1965; Morganstern & Tevlin, 1981; Weber et al., 1985; Wiens, 1976). One of the most systematic examinations of interviewing skills was provided by Ivey (1971) in his development of the microtraining approach. With regard to the interview skills he identified as critical, he stated, "All the microcounseling skills developed to date have been empirically related to either verifiable outcome criteria or to changes in counselee behavior which are in turn related to outcome criteria" (p. 22). The following skills and their descriptions are based on a compilation of the work of Ivey and the others referenced. A version of this description also appears in Winton and Bailey (in press).

Effective Listening

The first and most important step in conducting an effective interview is conveying a listening and nonjudgmental attitude toward the family and any behavior they report. This "consists of showing interest in the information, appreciation for the respondent's efforts in giving it, interest in the respondent as a person and a critical assessment of the relevance of this information" (Gorden, 1969, p. 76). In addition to expressing interest, it is important to convey a nonjudgmental attitude. Tomm (1987a) described this as "neutrality," a stance in which the interviewer avoids taking sides and accepts everything that is said or that occurs. Cecchin (1987) cautioned that "neutrality" should not be confused with noninvolvement or failing to take responsibility when necessary. He proposed that neutrality is associated with curiosity, which leads to exploration with the family of their view of events and situations.

Listening or attending behaviors are both nonverbal and verbal. The nonverbal components include eye contact (natural and varied), body language and posture (relaxed and attentive), and voice modulation (warm and well modulated). Although communication is typically viewed as a verbal activity, some estimates suggest that 86% of our communication skills are nonverbal (Evans et al., 1984). Many clues to feelings and attitudes are evident through a person's nonverbal behavior. For instance, a mother may speak calmly and exhibit a neutral facial expression while twisting her hands or gripping her chair in an anxious manner. Gorden (1969) emphasized the importance of looking at the total bodily response when evaluating nonverbal behavior rather than simply focusing on the facial expression, which is generally more easily and readily controlled. Gorden also made the following suggestions:

1. People vary in their normal range of expressive behavior. Because agitation in one person may be normal fidgeting for another, look at *changes* in levels of expressive behavior.
2. Be alert to inconsistencies in verbal and nonverbal behavior; this is often how conflict is manifest.
3. Be aware of the context in which the behavior is occurring and interpret accordingly.

One advantage the interview offers interventionists is the opportunity to evaluate the validity of the standardized assessment data; by carefully observing nonverbal reactions to the topic being discussed, the interventionists are able to gather information that is not available in any other way.

The verbal components of listening include making responses that are relevant and follow from family member's comments. As mentioned earlier, using the language and speech patterns family members use is an important way of conveying a listening and accepting attitude. One of the greatest problems for interventionists is their tendency to offer sympathy and solutions before family members have a chance to explain their situation in detail. This can be attributed in large measure to training and years of practice as child care specialists who are expected to offer expert opinions to families. In our experience it takes training and objective feedback before many interventionists are even aware of this tendency. By maintaining a noncritical stance and refraining from giving advice, sermonizing, analyzing, or persuading, the interventionist has a greater likelihood of finding out information necessary for effective problem solving.

The skills of listening that are so critical to the success of the interview are the skills that novice interviewers are least likely to possess. A training study conducted by Matarazzo et al. (1965) with medical students indicated that three of the five most common errors before training were interrupting, focusing on irrelevant material, and awkwardness (consisting of long speeches or abruptness). These skills are all related to listening. Listening skills build trust and a working relationship, they help family members relax and focus on the purposes of the interview, and they increase the likelihood that the family's perspectives on events are elicited and understood. As such, they are critical in getting the interview off to a good start and in ensuring that the goals of the interview are met.

Effective Questioning

An underlying goal of the interview is to gather information; therefore, the interviewer should have skills that direct the discussion toward topics of interest. The act of questioning, in and of itself, may constitute an intervention with the family (Tomm, 1987a). Therefore, questioning must be considered as both a way of collecting information and a form of intervention.

Those who consider questioning primarily an information-gathering mechanism usually describe the following kinds of questions: open-ended questions, closed-ended questions, minimal encouragements, and silent probes. A considerable body of research has examined these interview skills, largely focusing on the association between the kinds of questions asked and the kinds of information elicited. For instance, novice interviewers often use a large number of closed-ended questions (Gorden, 1969; Matarazzo et al., 1965). *Closed-ended questions* are associated with restricted responses or simple yes or no answers, whereas *open-ended questions* are associated with expanded responses that allow respondents to express what is relevant and important to them. Open-ended questions can be more or less structured. For example, "What time does Mary go to bed?" is more structured and limiting than "Can you tell me about bedtime with Mary?" A general guideline offered in terms of questioning for information is to use a "funnel approach" (Gorden, 1969; Maccoby & Maccoby, 1954; Oppenheim, 1966), in which the interviewer starts with a broad question and narrows the scope of questions until all important points related to that issue have been covered. Starting with a broad, open-ended question that will be fairly easy for family members to answer is thought to increase the probability of getting information through a spontaneous reply. Strategies recommended when more specific information is sought are to provide a context (place, time, etc.) as part of an open-ended question and to use wording that reflects the family's way of describing events (e.g., "You mentioned feeling as if you were getting the runaround when you called the school system last month about preschool programs. Could you tell me more about what they told you?").

Minimal encouragements are another means of gathering information. These include head nods, expectant facial expressions that convey the message "Tell me more," or silence. *Silent probes* create a thoughtful mood and allow family members to control the direction of the next step of the discussion. Gorden (1969) found a positive correlation between the amount of silence used by an interviewer and the respondent's general level of spontaneity.

Very different kinds of questions are described by those who conceptualize questioning in terms of its therapeutic possibilities, in addition to its information-gathering function. This approach to questioning has been described in the family therapy literature (Selvini-Palazzoli, Boscolo, Cecchin, & Prata, 1980; Tomm, 1987a, b), is based on clinical experience rather than empirical research, and is rooted in a particular conceptual approach to family therapy known as the Milan approach to systemic family therapy.

Of particular relevance to the kind of interview described in this text is the work of Tomm (1987b). He has described several types of questions that may be used to motivate families to generate solutions to problems or situations they face. These include *future-oriented questions,* which he defined as helpful in getting families to consider future alternatives and choices. An example of this type of question that Tomm provided is "Are there any goals that you all agree on and see yourselves working toward together right now?" If families are vague in stating goals, Tomm suggested asking "How will you know when that goal has been achieved?" The content of that answer will be important in operationalizing the goal (i.e., establishing conditions and criteria for success); in addition, Tomm has contended that of greater importance is that family members begin thinking of goals and generating solutions or means of reaching them.

Other types of future-oriented questions that Tomm described include the following: *exploring anticipated outcomes* (e.g., "How much progress do you think your child will make in the next month?"); *highlighting potential consequences* that might result from continuing in the same patterns when these patterns are not working for the family (e.g., "If you do not get respite help, what do you expect will happen to you, to your relationship with other family members, etc.?"); and *exploring catastrophic expectations* so that hidden fears and anxieties can be dealt with openly (e.g., "What are you worried might happen if your child was left with a respite care provider?"). Tomm suggested that if parents are reluctant to provide answers to this last type of question, the interviewer might ask questions that *introduce hypothetical possibilities.* He described these as questions that encourage families to consider new possibilities and solutions that they have not previously thought of but that are consistent with their values and beliefs. An example of this kind of question is: "Can you imagine that if you did find the right kind of respite care provider, it might not only provide you with a break from constant care but also enlarge your child's world and provide another person who knows and loves your child?" Tomm has contended that future-oriented questions like the ones described can instill hope in the family. Research with families has suggested that families desire that professionals provide hope as part of their recommendations (Gowen et al., 1987). This approach to interviewing seems to ensure that the hope is based on real possibilities and alternatives that emerge from the families in the interview situation.

The two approaches to questioning described are not incompatible, and both bodies of literature offer appropriate guidelines for professionals in terviewing families. The information from the family therapy literature on questioning as a therapeutic intervention is particularly relevant to the goal-setting phase of the interview process.

Reflection of Feelings

Reflecting feelings, or the ability to respond empathetically, consists of two components (Evans et al., 1984): (1) the ability to perceive accurately and sensitively a person's inner feelings, and (2) the ability to communicate understanding of those feelings in appropriate language. Because people learn to hide clues to certain feelings or attitudes, perceiving feelings is not as easy as it may appear. A prerequisite skill is the ability to convey basic acceptance of a person so he or she will feel comfortable sharing feelings. Another component to reflecting feelings is being closely attuned to nonverbal and verbal behaviors that provide the clues to mixed emotions. For example, a mother may say with tears in her eyes, "I'm so glad that my child has been accepted into the intervention program." This mother is expressing her ambivalence toward the situation, and the interventionist should recognize and reflect both aspects of her feelings.

Reflecting feelings back to family members allows them to evaluate their appropriateness. For example, parents may express a great deal of anger or hostility toward a doctor who insensitively provided the family with the diagnosis of their child's handicap; when hearing their anger reflected back, they may be able to relinquish it. Awareness of feelings is often a prerequisite to solving problems. When family members realize how upset or dissatisfied they are with a situation, they are more likely to take steps to deal with it. In addition, by reflecting feelings, an interventionist lets the family know that he or she can perceive the world as they perceive it. This is important in building rapport, trust, and a good relationship.

Reflection of Content

Two components of reflecting content are (1) paraphrasing the main idea in a family member's message and (2) restating and summarizing what has been said (Evans et al., 1984). This skill is important for several reasons. It clarifies for the family members what they have said, thus giving them a chance to ponder their situation and consider various problem-solving approaches. It conveys to the family members that their message has been heard and understood, thus building rapport and increasing their respect for the interventionist as a helper and ally. It secures consensus among family members or helps identify areas of family disagreement. Finally, it is a way of connecting relevant aspects of the discussion and summarizing and highlighting what has been discussed and decided. This helps families see their situations more clearly, identify available options, and determine possible family goals (Bryant, 1984). As Turnbull (1987) pointed out, many families have not had the chance to reflect on their needs and strengths, coping strategies, and resources before early intervention. She has described the opportunity provided in early intervention to engage in this process as the "linchpin of problem solving" and as an experience that can serve the family well throughout the life cycle.

Integrating and Maintaining Skills

Although certain communication skills are best used at certain points during the interview (e.g., the interview should be started with a broad, open-ended question; the skills of summarizing are particularly useful when a parent is talking in a disorganized and rambling fashion), there are no rigid rules dictating their use. Just as each person will respond to different aspects of training in communication, each person will adapt and use the skills according to his or her own sense of style and personality. Through practice the skills will blend so that *empathy and an acceptance of the world as the family defines it* are conveyed and *information necessary for generating intervention goals* is collected.

Little research has been conducted on the degree to which communication skills are maintained beyond the training period. A study by Haas, DiMattia, and Guttman (1970) suggested that there is some maintenance of skill level. However, Ivey (1971) recommended that follow-up supervision and opportunities to practice skills on a routine basis are necessary to reinforce the communication skills learned in training.

SUMMARY

Clearly, the tasks of interviewing and communicating with families raise questions about the nature of the interventionist's job. Not only are interventionists expected to assimilate new knowledge and incorporate new skills, but they are also being asked to expand their focus from the child to the family. This raises many issues, including:

- What are the boundaries between intervention with families and family therapy?
- Under what circumstances does the family focus become overly intrusive?
- Are early interventionists qualified to deal with family issues?
- Should only certain members of intervention teams, such as social workers or psychologists, deal with family issues?

A quote from Turnbull (1987) is relevant to these issues. She stated:

> I like to use the term "family support" rather than "family services," because I think many kinds of family support do not require a service but, perhaps, a particular *communication style.* For example, parents may gain insight into the

future needs of their child not only from formal workshops or printed material but from an offhand comment from a teacher about the expectations of elementary teachers. Thus, we need to start thinking about every interaction with a family being an opportunity for support, as contrasted to discrete and separate services." (p. 6)

The point to be made here is that intervention efforts affect families, whether or not interventionists consciously adopt a family focus or receive special training in working with families. Because every interaction conveys information that reflects underlying attitudes and values, all early interventionists have an obligation to further their understanding of families to ensure that their interactions are as supportive as possible.

In many respects, legal and professional trends in working with families promise that intervention efforts will be more successful and will reach a broader and more diverse group of families. Because of the complexities of the systems within which professionals work, however, caution is necessary, because there is the danger that one might cause more harm than good. A critical ingredient in working with families in the collaborative ways described in this text is the development and maintenance of effective communication skills.

REFERENCES

Adler, L., Ware, J., & Enelow, A. (1970). Changes in medical interviewing style after instruction with two closed-circuit television techniques. *Journal of Medical Education, 45,* 21–28.

Allen, D., Affleck, G., McGrade, B., & McQueeney, M. (1984). Factors in the effectiveness of early childhood intervention for low socioeconomic status families. *Education and Training of the Mentally Retarded, 19,* 254–260.

Anderson, K. (1971). The "shopping" behavior of parents of mentally retarded children: The professional person's role. *Mental Retardation, 9,* 3–5.

Bailey, D., Farel, A., O'Donnell, K., Simeonsson, R., & Miller, C. (1986). Preparing infant interventionists: Interdepartmental training in special education and maternal and child health. *Journal of the Division for Early Childhood, 11,* 67–77.

Bailey, D. B., Simeonsson, R. J., Winton, P. J., Huntington, G. S., Comfort, M., Isbell, P., O'Donnell, K. J., & Helm, J. M. (1986). Family-focused intervention: A functional model for planning, implementing, and evaluating individualized family services in early intervention. *Journal of the Division for Early Childhood, 10,* 156–171.

Bandura, A. (1969). *Principles of behavior modification.* New York: Holt, Rinehart & Winston.

Battle, C. V. (1974). Disruptions in the socialization of a young severely handicapped child. *Rehabilitation Literature, 35,* 130–140.

Bensky, J., Shaw, S., Gouse, A., Bates, H., Dixon, B., & Beane, W. (1980). Public Law 94-142 and stress: A problem for educators. *Exceptional Children, 47*, 24–29.

Berger, M. (1984). Special education. In M. Berger & G. Jurkovic (Eds.), *Practicing family therapy in diverse settings* (pp. 142–179). San Francisco: Jossey-Bass.

Berger, M. (1986). Contributions of family therapy to the development of early childhood special education services that enhance individual and family development. *Training professionals to interact with families* (Monograph 2). (Available from the Parent/Family Support Series, University of Idaho, Moscow, ID 83843.)

Bernheimer, L. P., Young, M. S., & Winton, P. J. (1983). Stress over time: Parents with young handicapped children. *Developmental and Behavioral Pediatrics, 4*, 177–181.

Bristol, M., & Schopler, E. (1984). A developmental perspective on stress and coping in families of autistic children. In J. Blacher (Ed.), *Severely handicapped young children and their families* (pp. 91–134). Orlando, Fla.: Academic Press.

Bryant, C. (1984). Working for families with dysfunctional children: An approach and structure for the first family therapy interview. *Child and Adolescent Social Work, 1*(2), 102–117.

Cadman, D., Goldsmith, C., & Bashim, P. (1984). Values, preferences, and decisions in the care of children with developmental disabilities. *Developmental and Behavioral Pediatrics, 5*, 60–64.

Cadman, D., Shurvell, B., Davies, P., & Bradfield, S. (1984). Compliance in the community with consultants' recommendations for developmentally handicapped children. *Developmental Medicine and Child Neurology, 26*, 40–46.

Carkhuff, R., Kratochvil, D., & Friel, T. (1968). Effects of professional training: Communication and discrimination of facilitative conditions. *Journal of Counseling Psychology, 15*, 68–74.

Cecchin, G. (1987). Hypothesizing, circularity, and neutrality revisited: An invitation to curiosity. *Family Process, 26*(4), 405–414.

Cunningham, C. C., Morgan, P. A., & McGucken, R. B. (1984). Down's syndrome: Is dissatisfaction with disclosure of diagnosis inevitable? *Developmental Medicine and Child Neurology, 26*, 33–39.

Dale, D. (1986). Training professionals in the special needs of the 0–3 population. *Training professionals to interact with families* (Monograph 2). (Available from the Parent/Family Support Series, University of Idaho, Moscow, ID 83843.)

Doernberg, N. (1978). Some negative effects on family integration of health and educational services for young handicapped children. *Rehabilitation Literature, 39*, 107–110.

Dunlap, W., & Hollingsworth, J. (1977). How does a handicapped child affect the family? *Family Coordinator, 26*(3), 286–293.

Dunst, C. J. (1985). Rethinking early intervention. *Analysis and Intervention in Developmental Disabilities, 5*, 165–201.

Dunst, C. J., & Leet, H. E. (1987). Measuring the adequacy of resources in households with young children. *Child: Care, Health and Development, 13*, 111–125.

Evans, D., Hearn, M., Uhlemann, M., & Ivey, A. (1984). *Essential interviewing: A programmed approach to effective communication* (2nd Ed.). Monterey, Calif.: Brooks/Cole Publishing.

Farber, B. (1960). Family organization and crisis: Maintenance of integration in families with a severely mentally retarded child. *Monographs of the Society for Research in Child Development* (Serial No. 75).

Foster, M., & Berger, M. (1979). Structural family therapy: Application in programs for preschool handicapped children. *Journal of the Division for Early Childhood, 1,* 52–58.

Gorden, R. (1969). *Interviewing: Strategies, techniques and tactics.* Homewood, Ill.: Dorsey Press.

Gowen, J., Johnson-Martin, N., & Goldman, B. (1987). The parent-child reciprocity project. Symposium presentation at Council for Exceptional Children Annual Conference, Chicago, Ill.

Gradel, K., Thompson, M., & Sheehan, R. (1981). Parental and professional agreement in early childhood assessment. *Topics in Early Childhood Special Education, 1,* 31–39.

Guralnick, M., & Richardson, H. (1980). *Pediatric education and the needs of exceptional children.* Baltimore: University Park Press.

Haas, R. F., DiMattia, D. J., & Guttman, M. A. (1972). Training of support personnel in three human relations skills: A systematic one-year follow-up. *Counselor Education and Supervision, 11,* 278–291.

Harrison, H. (1983). *The premature baby book: A parents' guide to coping and caring in the first years.* New York: St. Martin's Press.

Helfer, R., Black, M., & Helfer, M. (1975). Pediatric interviewing skills taught by nonphysicians. *American Journal of Diseases of the Child, 129,* 1053–1057.

Helfer, R., & Hess, J. (1970). An experimental model for making objective measurements of interviewing skills. *Journal of Counseling Psychology, 26,* 327–331.

Hepworth, D., & Larsen, J. (1982). *Direct social work practice: Theory and skills.* Homewood, Ill.: Dorsey Press.

Higgins, W., Ivey, A., & Uhlemann, M. (1970). Media therapy: A programmed approach to teaching behavioral skills. *Journal of Counseling Psychology, 17,* 20–26.

Ivey, A. (1971). *Microcounseling: Innovations in interview training.* Springfield, Ill.: Charles C. Thomas.

Ivey, A., Normington, C., Miller, C., Morrill, W., & Haase, R. (1968). Microcounseling and attending behavior: An approach to prepracticum counselor training. *Journal of Counseling Psychology, 15,* 1–12.

Iwata, B., Wong, S., Riordan, M., Dorsey, M., & Lau, M. (1982). Assessment and training of clinical interviewing skills: Analogue analysis and field replication. *Journal of Applied Behavior Analysis, 15,* 191–203.

Klaus, M., & Kennell, J. (1976). *Maternal-infant bonding.* St. Louis, Mo.: C. V. Mosby.

Lynch, E. (1986). Families from different cultures. In the Family Network Series (Monograph 1): *The family of handicapped infants and young children.* University of Idaho, Moscow: Family Involvement with At-Risk and Handicapped Infants Project.

Maccoby, E., & Maccoby, N. (1954). The interview: A tool for social service. In G. Lindzey (Ed.), *Handbook of social psychology* (vol. 1). Cambridge, Mass.: Addison-Wesley.

Maslow, A. (1954). *Motivation and personality.* New York: Harper & Row.

Matarazzo, R., Phillips, J., Wiens, A., & Saslow, G. (1965). Learning the art of interviewing: A study of what beginning students do and their patterns of change. *Psychotherapy: Theory, Research and Practice, 2,* 49–60.

Meadow, R., & Hewitt, C. (1972). Teaching communication skills with the help of actresses and videotape simulation. *British Journal of Medical Education, 6,* 317–322.

Morganstern, K., & Tevlin, H. (1981). Behavioral interviewing. In M. Hersen & A. Bellack (Eds.), *Behavioral assessment: A practical handbook* (2nd ed.). New York: Pergamon Press.

Olson, D., McCubbin, H., Barnes, H., Larsen, A., Muxen, M., & Wilson, M. (1983). *Families: What makes them work.* Beverly Hills, Calif.: Sage Publications.

Olson, J., & Kroth, R. (1986). Training early interventionists in the delicate art of delivering sensitive information. In *Training professionals to interact with families* (Monograph 2). (Available from the Parent/Family Support Services, University of Idaho, Moscow, ID 83843).

Oppenheim, A. (1966). *Questionnaire design and attitude measurement.* New York: Basic Books.

Schweinhart, L. J., & Koshel, J. J. (1986). *Policy options for preschool programs.* (High Scope Early Childhood Policy Papers, No. 5) Ypsilanti, Mich.

Selvini-Palazzoli, M., Boscolo, L., Cecchin, G., & Prata, G. (1980). Hypothesizing-circularity-neutrality: Three guidelines for the conductor of the session. *Family Process, 19,* 3–12.

Sexton, D., Miller, J., & Murdock, J. (1984). Correlates of parental-professional congruency scores in the assessment of young handicapped children. *Journal of the Division for Early Childhood, 8,* 99–109.

Shapiro, J. (1983). Family reactions and coping with physically ill or handicapped children. *Social Science Medicine, 17,* 913–931.

Shuster, S., Guskin, S., Hawkins, B., & Okolo, C. (1986). Views of health and development: Six mothers and their infants. *Journal of the Division for Early Childhood, 11,* 18–27.

Simpson, R. (1982). *Conferencing parents of exceptional children.* Rockville, Md.: Aspen.

Skinner, B. F. (1953). *Science and human behavior.* New York: Macmillan.

Stack, C. (1975). *All our kin.* New York: Harper & Row.

Stillman, P., Sabers, D., & Redfield, D. (1977). Use of trained mothers to teach interviewing skills to first year medical students: A follow-up study. *Pediatrics, 60,* 165–169.

Suelzle, M., & Kenan, V. (1981). Changes in family support networks over the life cycle of mentally retarded persons. *American Journal of Mental Deficiency, 86,* 267–274.

Tomm, K. (1987a). Interventive interviewing: Part I. Strategizing as a fourth guideline for the therapist. *Family Process, 26*(1), 3–14.

Tomm, K. (1987b). Interventive interviewing: Part II. Reflexive questioning as a means to enable self-healing. *Family Process, 26*(2), 167–184.

Turnbull, A. (1987). Accepting the challenge of providing comprehensive support to families. Paper presented at Early Childhood Development Association of Washington, Annual Conference, May, 1987, Seattle, Washington.

Turnbull, A., Brotherson, M., & Summers, J. (1986). The impact of deinstitutionalization on families: A family systems approach. In R. Bruinicks (Ed.), *Living and learning in the least restrictive environment* (pp. 26–52). Baltimore: Paul H. Brookes.

Turnbull, A., & Summers, J. (1985). *From parent involvement to family support: Evolution to revolution.* Paper presented at the Down Syndrome State-of-the-Art Conference, Boston, Mass.

Turnbull, A., & Turnbull, R. (1986). *Families, professionals, and exceptionality: A special partnership.* Columbus, Oh.: Merrill Publishing Company.

Turnbull, H., & Turnbull, A. (1987). *The Latin American family and public policy in the United States: Informal support and transition into adulthood.* Lawrence, Kan.: University of Kansas, Bureau of Child Research.

Unger, D., & Powell, D. (1980). Supporting families under stress: The role of social networks. *Family Relations, 29,* 566–574.

Weber, T., McKeever, J. E., & McDaniel, S. H. (1985). A beginner's guide to the problem-oriented first family interview. *Family Process, 24,* 357–364.

Wiens, A. (1976). The assessment interview. In I. Weiner (Ed.), *Clinical methods in psychology* (pp. 3–60). New York: John Wiley & Sons.

Winton, P. J., & Bailey, D. B. (in press). The family-focused interview: A collaborative mechanism for family assessment and goal-setting. *Journal of the Division for Early Childhood.*

Winton, P. J., & Turnbull, A. P. (1981). Parent involvement as viewed by parents of preschool handicapped children. *Topics in Early Childhood Special Education, 1,* 11–19.

Wolraich, M. (1982). Communication between physicians and parents of handicapped children. *Exceptional Children, 48,* 324–329.

Wright, J., Granger, R., & Sameroff, A. (1984). Parental acceptance and developmental handicap. In J. Blacher (Ed.), *Severely handicapped young children and their families: Research in review* (pp. 51–90). New York: Academic Press.

11

Considerations in Developing Family Goals

F amily assessment is a process designed to help interventionists and families jointly identify family strengths and needs to determine potentially helpful services and comprehensive support for families. At present, services are often provided without individualized goals having been specified. For example, a parent-support group could have several broad aims: developing a social support network, providing information, strengthening advocacy efforts, and training parents. Parents may elect to attend and participate in such a group without specifying the goals for attending. The group is viewed as an experience that provides the site for many possible outcomes to occur. The actual effects of the group will vary depending on the activities provided, parents' expectations, and level of participation.

However, there are several reasons to specify the expected individual outcomes of the service provided. This chapter reviews the rationale for goal setting and discusses issues related to specifying family outcomes in early intervention. It concludes with a discussion of procedural and ethical considerations in writing individualized family service plans.

This chapter was contributed by Donald B. Bailey, Jr., University of North Carolina at Chapel Hill.

WHY SPECIFY GOALS AND OBJECTIVES?

A goal or objective specifies the expected end results of a given activity. Usually, goals and objectives are differentiated by time span and specificity. Typically, a *goal* is a long-term target that often consists of a general statement of expected outcome. For example, a child might be expected to achieve independent use of the toilet or to communicate basic needs to parents or other adults, a mother might be expected to increase the extent to which her expectations are consistent with a child's developmental abilities, or a sibling might be expected to interact more positively with his handicapped sister.

An *objective* is typically viewed as a short-term intervention target and is a more specific statement of expected outcome than a goal. A well-written behavioral objective consists of at least four components (Mager, 1962):

1. Identification of the *target individual*—the person expected to accomplish the objective
2. An operational statement of the precise *behaviors* the individual is expected to perform
3. A description of the *conditions* under which the behavior is expected
4. Specific *criteria* to evaluate attainment of the objective, including projected dates for accomplishment

The specification of objectives meets legal requirements, provides a focus for intervention and enhances its effectiveness, evaluates progress, and communicates expectations.

Meeting Legal Requirements

Writing goals and objectives for handicapped children is now a familiar and routine activity for special educators and related service professionals. Public Law 94-142 mandated that an individualized educational plan (IEP) be developed for each handicapped student, with long-term (annual) goals and short-term instructional objectives related to those goals. Public Law 99-457 has expanded that mandate with respect to services for handicapped infants, toddlers, and preschoolers. For handicapped infants and toddlers (through age 2), interventionists must now write an individualized family services plan (IFSP) that includes, in addition to the usual child-oriented content, a statement of family strengths and needs related to enhancing the development of the handicapped infant or toddler and a statement of the major outcomes expected and the services to be provided for both child and family. The statement of outcomes must include the criteria, procedures, and timelines used to determine progress toward achieving the specified outcomes. The committee report accompanying the legislation for handicapped 3- and 4-year-olds affirmed the importance of family services in preschool programs for this age group as well and stated that the IEP for handicapped preschoolers, when appropriate and desired by parents, should provide for parent instruction. The specifics of these requirements are detailed in subsequent sections of this chapter. The point to be made here is that one reason for writing goals and objectives is to fulfill a legislative mandate. Although historically this mandate has been child-focused, current legislation requires the additional specification of family goals and objectives in the context of early intervention.

Facilitating Intervention Effectiveness

A second rationale for specifying goals and objectives is to enhance the effectiveness of intervention. This rationale is based primarily on the assumption that objectives provide a specific focus for intervention efforts. This focus reminds interventionists of the primary purpose of services and thus guides the choice of areas or activities in which primary effort should be expended. Also, specification of goals and objectives provides a concrete target for clients as they participate in and contribute to their own treatment. Research from the world of business has demonstrated that specifying objectives for employees, work groups, and companies can significantly improve performance, productivity, and worker satisfaction (McConkie, 1979); when employees participate in the process of specifying objectives, positive outcomes are enhanced (Latham & Locke, 1979). Likewise, studies have indicated that the use of instructional objectives enhances student performance (Hartley & Davies, 1976) and that the involvement of handicapped students in goal planning can enhance goal attainment and work effort (Kelley & Stokes, 1984; Tollefson, Tracy, Johnsen, Farmer, & Buenning, 1984).

Monitoring Progress

A third rationale for specifying goals and objectives is to provide concrete markers or indices for evaluating client progress. When clients and interventionists know the specific outcomes expected of a given treatment or intervention service, they can determine whether outcomes have been achieved or whether progress is occurring. In work with handicapped children and their families, measuring attainment of individualized goals to indicate progress and program success is often considered superior to more traditional evaluation procedures, such as standardized testing. Standardized developmental or achievement tests have been criticized because they lack instructional relevance and cannot reflect progress in handicapped children, particularly those with severe and multiple handicaps (Simeonsson, Huntington, & Parse, 1980). Likewise, with regard to families, the use of family assessment tools such as those described in this text have serious limitations when used to evaluate program effectiveness. Thus, the attainment of goals has been suggested as an important indicator of client progress and program effectiveness with both children and families (Lloyd, 1983; Simeonsson, Huntington, & Short, 1982; Woodward, Santa-Barbara, Levin, & Epstein, 1978).

Communicating Expectations

A final rationale for specifying goals and objectives is to facilitate communication and agreement. Goals and objectives provide other professionals on the interdisciplinary team with a statement of agreed-on outcomes toward which all should be working in their interactions with children and families. Furthermore, parents have a right to know the value orientation and priorities of professionals with whom they are working. To establish covert goals for clients without explicitly informing them raises serious ethical and legal issues in intervention (Margolin, 1982).

ISSUES IN WRITING FAMILY GOALS

Although professionals working with handicapped infants and preschoolers generally agree that family involvement is important, concerns have been raised about actually writing down family goals and objectives. Many of these concerns have also surfaced regarding writing objectives for children, as described in reviews by Lovitt (1977), Vargas (1972), and Wolery, Bailey, and Sugai (1988). In fact, the mandate to write family goals and objectives raises significant professional issues that must be addressed.

Professional Training

A primary concern is whether professionals currently working in early intervention and preschool handicapped programs have the skills and training necessary to write family goals and provide family services. As described in Chapter 1, most teachers and professionals in related services receive very little preservice training in family assessment, communication, goal setting, or services. When such training is provided, it is likely to be in the form of coursework rather than actual clinical experiences, because intervention-program personnel are reluctant to allow students opportunities for significant involvement with families.

Appropriate skills and training are essential if family services are to be provided in an effective and acceptable fashion. Interestingly, it has been argued in the therapy literature that family therapy is very different from individual therapy. In fact, Margolin (1982) states that "for a person untrained and unsupervised in family therapy to invite a number of family members into a therapy session would be construed as practicing beyond that person's area of competence" (p. 800). This statement is addressed to licensed therapists or clinical psychologists with extensive training in therapeutic skills but no specialized training in family therapy. Given this position, it could be argued that professionals with considerably less training in either therapeutic skills or family therapy, such as special educators, speech pathologists, or physical therapists, lack the qualifications to write family goals or provide family services.

It would be neither possible nor appropriate, however, for early interventionists to disregard family needs or to inform families that they cannot deal with certain problems beyond their expertise. Having a handicapped child is undeniably a family issue, and therefore working with such a child necessarily takes place in a family context. To ignore both the issues and the context is inappropriate and is likely to result in ineffective interventions. Thus, the ecological characteristics of the early intervention context make it inevitable that family issues will arise and will need to be addressed. The question is not *whether* early interventionists should be concerned with family involvement, but rather *how* professionals from multiple disciplines can optimize the relationships they will inevitably develop with families. Specifying family goals is a mechanism for clarifying the relationship between professionals and families and the expectations for that relationship.

The importance and inevitability of family involvement in early intervention enhance the need for further training of professionals. Extensive training efforts are clearly required. Attempts to meet this need are evident in efforts by the United States Department of Education to fund preservice and in-service training programs that focus specifically on preparing professionals from multiple disciplines to work with handicapped infants and preschoolers and their families. An early childhood research institute has been funded to develop and study procedures for such training. Furthermore, state agencies will need to provide comprehensive in-service training programs to assist currently employed professionals in expanding their family focus.

Also, more work is needed in defining the boundaries of professional skills and treatments. What is the difference between a helping relationship and a therapeutic relationship? When does talking about depression related to daily stresses become a mental health issue rather than one adult sharing feelings with another? Should early interventionists attempt to address systems-level issues such as father involvement and support? Of ultimate importance is the professional's ability to differentiate which goals and services he or she can provide and which should be addressed by other specialists.

Imposition of Values

Lovitt (1977) reports that some have argued against the specification of goals because the process inherently results in one person imposing values upon another. Clearly, this assumption is true in professional-client relationships in which the professional plays a dominant role in goal specification and the client is allowed little if any input. But the argument is not valid when professionals and clients engage in collaborative goal setting. The strong influence of value systems, however, cannot be ignored.

The role of values in the professional-client relationship has been discussed in the family therapy literature (Aponte, 1985; Margolin, 1982). For example, Margolin describes the dilemma of a therapist working with family members who agree that they want to attain goals or maintain roles that the therapist considers sexist (e.g., wife stays home and has exclusive child care responsibility):

> By attempting to remain nonjudgmental about the client's objectives, the therapist may unwittingly reinforce these sexist attitudes. But by attempting to reorient them to an egalitarian viewpoint, the therapist might thwart the family from attaining their goals and alienate those individuals whose socialization is such that they are happy with traditional roles. (p. 798)

Early interventionists are inevitably faced with values that conflict with those observed in families with whom they are working (Bailey, 1987). These conflicts include different perceptions of parent involvement, discipline, and decisions regarding what is best for the handicapped infant or preschooler. Consider the following examples:

☐ Susie is 3 years old and has Down syndrome. Her parents believe that she should be in a highly structured, academically oriented preschool program. Staff feel that Susie needs to focus on learning social and communication skills.

☐ Mrs. Byrnes refuses to follow through on home instructional activities for her son Jimmy, who has spina bifida, saying she does not feel they are important. Moreover, she is too busy taking care of her other three children. Staff feel that follow-up activities are essential if Jimmy's skills are to be maintained.

☐ Marty is 4 and displays behavioral and emotional problems. His father yells at him for any small infraction and tells Marty that he is a bad boy. The staff feel that his father's behavior is contributing to Marty's difficulties.

These brief examples demonstrate only a few of the innumerable value conflicts that may arise between families and interventionists. Some are due to differences in culture, religious background, or socioeconomic status. Others stem from parents' present levels of acceptance of the situation or the professional's philosophical orientation. Such conflicts are inevitable. How does the interventionist meet professional requirements for writing family goals and satisfy personal value systems in such situations?

Aponte (1985) argues that "the therapist should attempt to exercise no more influence over the family's values than is required adequately to address the family's problems" (p. 335). To accomplish this maxim, he recommends four basic abilities necessary for the professional. They are discussed here because they seem applicable to early interventionists as well.

Values, Structures, and Functions. The effective interventionist must be able to understand and differentiate among values, structures, and functions. Aponte describes a family as a social unit, "an aggregate of people who join together in patterned structures to carry out a function or complex of functions in accord with a framework of standards or values" (1985, p. 329). *Values* are those standards by which families or family members make decisions. *Structure* refers to the way a family is organized, whereas *function* refers to the purposes or activities the family must achieve or accomplish. Aponte argues that the professional's primary responsibility is to *help clients improve functioning.* Thus, family assessment should be directed primarily toward helping interventionists and families identify functions with which families need help. Frameworks for conceptualizing family functions, such as respite, financial management, child care, or housekeeping, were described in Chapter 7 of this text.

Professional Values. Aponte's (1985) second suggestion is that professionals examine their own personal and professional values. Professionals invariably bring a set of values to the intervention context. But how often are those values articulated or recognized? Explicit recognition of personal values can help prevent the unwitting imposition of personal values on families (Margolin, 1982).

Individualized Family Values and Structures. Interventionists must be aware of the values embraced by individual families for whom they have a professional responsibility and the structures in which those values operate. When existing values and structures are recognized, functional interventions can be designed that fit, rather than conflict with, those values and structures.

Negotiating Values. The most complex, nebulous, yet important skill of all is the ability to negotiate value differences between professionals and families. This skill is needed when the professional believes that a change in a family's values is necessary to solve a problem. Aponte (1985) believes such a change is necessary in the following instances:

> *(a)* when a conflict about values between members of a family or between a family and its community is a significant pathological force. . . .
> *(b)* when the family's values are *not compatible* with the function the family intends to carry out or the structures through which it is to operate. . . .
> *(c)* if the family or its members have *not developed* the values necessary to guide the evolution of structures necessary to deal with the functional issues with which the family is contending. . . .
> *(d)* to the extent that the family and the therapist are struggling to agree on a value framework for addressing the family's dysfunction. (pp. 333–334)

The changing of family values must be negotiated with family members and will necessitate a long-term therapeutic process.

Implications for Early Interventionists. This brief discussion highlights the role and importance of values in family goal setting in early intervention. Setting goals is necessarily a value-laden activity. The extent to which goals are in concert with family value systems will determine the degree of family acceptance of and follow-through on goals. To this end, interventionists should follow these guidelines in family goal setting:

1. Attempt to articulate personal and professional values, particularly as they relate to issues that may arise in the context of parent-professional relationships
2. Acknowledge the powerful influence of values on both individual and family lifestyle and decision making and recognize the impact of communicating to someone else that values are wrong or inappropriate
3. Seek to understand the value systems and organizational structures of families with whom they are working
4. Work collaboratively with families to identify goals related to achieving specific *functions*, rather than goals related to changing family values or family organizational structures, with an understanding that the achievement of these functional goals is best accomplished when they fit with existing family values and structures
5. Learn to identify situations in which family values are destructive to either the handicapped child or the family
6. Recognize that interventions that focus on changing family values and organizational structures are beyond the expertise of most early interventionists and should not be attempted without professional help from trained therapists

To explore their own values in working with families, interventionists may want to engage in small-group discussions and role-playing activities with colleagues to discuss value conflicts and their implications for service delivery.

Who Is the Intervention Target?

Historically, the handicapped child has been the primary target of goals in the individualized educational plan. Public Law 99-457 has broadened this focus to include the child's family. But who will be the targets of this family-focused goal setting?

Figure 11.1 displays examples of varying targets for goals. For example, Figure 11.1a shows the traditional model of a goal written for the handicapped child. The next level, displayed in Figure 11.1b, represents goals specified for other family members. For example, a mother might attend and

FIGURE 11.1
Varying Targets for Goals

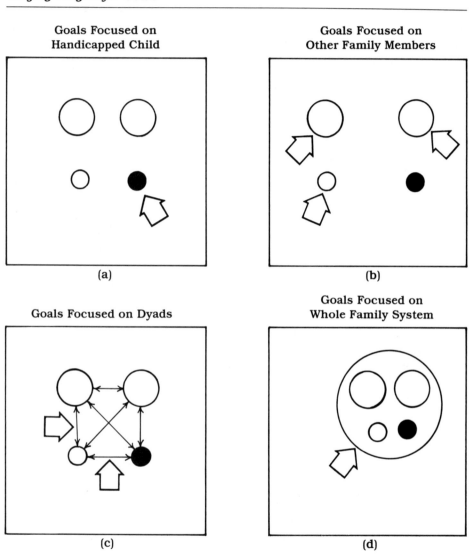

Goals Focused on
Handicapped Child

(a)

Goals Focused on
Other Family Members

(b)

Goals Focused on Dyads

(c)

Goals Focused on
Whole Family System

(d)

become involved in a parent-support group, a father might learn more about his son's disability, or a sibling might learn strategies for responding when peers make insensitive comments about the handicapped child. The third level, displayed in Figure 11.1c, represents goals involving dyads or pairs of family members. For example, a mother might learn strategies for handling her infant's fussiness, a husband might learn to listen more attentively when his wife discusses decisions regarding the handicapped child, or a sibling might learn to interact with his handicapped sister in a more developmentally appropriate fashion. The fourth level, displayed in Figure 11.1d, represents goals involving the entire family system. For example, a family might learn how to include the handicapped child in family vacations, help grandparents become more accepting of the handicapped child, or establish a more predictable family routine during a disruptive and stressful time of day, such as early mornings.

Each level represents a different degree of complexity in both goal setting and intervention. The level at which goals are specified and services provided will depend in part on individual family needs. But as early interventionists move away from goals and treatments focused on the handicapped child to goals and treatments focused on the family system, they move increasingly farther from their professional expertise. Who, then, are the legitimate targets of services in early intervention? The idea that the family is the primary target has quite different implications from the notion that the handicapped child is the primary target. The family represents multiple clients, and as Margolin (1982) suggests, "the dilemma with multiple clients is that in some situations an intervention that serves one person's best interests may be countertherapeutic to another" (p. 789). For example, introducing a mother to a parent-support group may help her but disrupt her relationship with her husband if he resents her evenings away from home. According to Margolin, when the family becomes the target for treatment, the professional must take great care to ensure that helping one person does not hurt another family member or negatively affect the family system.

Public Law 99-457 does provide some guidelines about the target for services. The opening portions of Part H state that one purpose of the law is "to enhance the capacity of families to meet the special needs of their infants and toddlers with handicaps." The IFSP must include "a statement of the family's strengths and needs relating to enhancing the development of the family's handicapped infant or toddler." These statements imply that the handicapped child is the primary target of concern for the interventionist. A narrow interpretation is that family needs should be addressed primarily to the extent that they will benefit the handicapped child's development. However, because allowable services listed in the legislation include family counseling, a broader definition of the target for goals is clearly intended.

An unresolved issue is whether a goal should target a change in the professional's behavior. For example, the following goals are conceivable:

■ The special educator will provide information about locally available respite services.

■ The nurse will start a parent-support group and run the first three meetings.

■ The social worker will help the parent apply for SSI benefits.

These are examples of the "family" goals we have seen on individual program plans. Because this is a new area in early intervention, no definitive guidelines are available, and it is thus impossible to answer definitively whether professional behavior should be targeted for change. The present thinking of the authors of this text is that writing goals for professional behavior change is generally inappropriate and should *not* be incorporated as standard practice, for several reasons. First, professional behavior essentially represents the service aspect of early intervention. Professional behavior is often the means by which goals are achieved but not the reason that the individual plan is being written. Second, each example cited has an eventual goal aimed at the parent: respite, social support, or financial support. If those are the actual goals of intervention, those are the goals that should be specified. For example, the respite goal could be rewritten as "Parent selects best option from several respite possibilities and uses option at least three times." Third, professional behavior may change without subsequent benefits for parents. For example, a parent-support group is initiated but only one parent attends. In this scenario the stated goal is accomplished, but the parents for whom the goal was intended do not benefit. An objective should target the ultimate change desired, and its attainment should be the basis for evaluating the effectiveness of services. Finally, targeting the family rather than the professional is in keeping with Dunst's (1985) suggestion that a primary goal of early intervention is to "empower" parents to act on their own behalf. Targeting professional behavior change does little to foster parent empowerment.

Stating Performance Outcomes

What are the expected outcomes of family services? If a major reason for writing objectives is to specify the precise outcomes expected from treatment, then statements regarding those outcomes should be as clear as possible. However, some have argued that such specificity results in objectives that state simple, knowledge-level skills rather than the more complex, sophisticated skills needed for performing important tasks in the real world. Furthermore, it is virtually impossible to predict accurately a client's level of achievement for a given skill at the end of a certain time period.

The following examples illustrate difficulties in writing family goals and objectives.

Mrs. Inman experiences numerous sources of stress: a demanding handicapped infant with an unpredictable pattern of feeding and sleeping; a husband who must work overtime at the local textile mill to make ends meet; 3-year-old twin boys; and her husband's mother, sick with cancer, who lives with them. She tells the interventionist that she feels overwhelmed and needs a regular break from daily demands. At what level of specificity should objectives for Mrs. Inman be written? Following are some examples of varying outcomes:

- Mrs. Inman will get out of the house alone at least one hour, three days per week (function only specified).

- Mrs. Inman will use the respite services program sponsored by the local parents' association (use of a specific service required for achievement).

- Mrs. Inman will place her children in day care and get a job, and the couple will place her husband's mother in a nursing home (specific behaviors and radical reshifting of life required).

- Mrs. Inman will report less stress (ultimate outcome only specified, means for accomplishment left open).

Mr. Oldham's interactions with his 18-month-old handicapped son, Rodney, are generally too verbal and therefore developmentally inappropriate. Furthermore, the skills Rodney learns in a developmental center are not being reinforced at home. Following are some examples of varying outcomes in this case:

- Mr. Oldham's interactions with Rodney will be developmentally appropriate approximately 75% of the time (general qualitative outcome, no specific behaviors required).

- Mr. Oldham will accurately implement in-home activities recommended by the center staff (specific outcome required).

- Mr. Oldham will think of new activities at home to reinforce skills Rodney learns at the center (specific targets for instruction specified, generalized outcome required).

As can be seen, many different levels of outcome can be specified and the effects can be "near" (short-term, specific) effects or "far" (long-term, generalized) effects.

In stating desired performance outcomes, the interventionist should (1) be as specific as necessary to evaluate attainment, but not so specific as to be trivial, and (2) address skill maintenance and generalization as well as skill acquisition.

Specificity. Behavioral objectives must include specific criteria to document attainment of goals. Usually these criteria include a statement of rate of performance, percent accuracy, duration, latency, or frequency. However, being *too* specific may have disadvantages. Specifying outcome in terms of rate may not reflect qualitative aspects of behavior. In addition, overspecificity can result in the assessment of quantifiable but meaningless outcomes.

Two basic rules govern outcome specification. First, the measurement criteria should fit the intent of the goal. If, for example, parental accuracy in implementing a therapeutic technique is the desired outcome, measures such as number or percent of steps correctly performed may be appropriate. Second, there should be agreement as to whether the objective has been met. If two people cannot agree, then the objective has not been written well. Thus, a criterion statement such as "some of the time" is acceptable if it can be reliably scored. Exactly who should evaluate goal attainment depends on the goal; for some goals (e.g., parent teaching skills), two professionals should be able to agree, whereas for other goals (e.g., parent participation in a support group), the professional and the parent should be able to agree.

Skill Maintenance and Generalization.   Recent reviews on helping parents to be more effective teachers of their children suggest that although parents generally learn the basic skills taught them, those skills often are not likely to maintain (endure over time) or generalize (be adapted to new situations) (Breiner & Beck, 1984; Howlin, 1984; O'Dell, 1985). Maintenance and generalization are essential, however, if parents are to apply skills independently in new situations (Reese & Serna, 1986). Maintenance and generalization are important to all family objectives, ranging from respite to transitions. The ultimate goal of intervention is to help families develop and use resources that allow them, on their own, to solve problems and adapt to new situations throughout the family life cycle.

Bloom, Englehart, Furst, Hill, and Krathwohl (1956) described a taxonomy of behavioral objectives consisting of six levels in an assumed hierarchical order. The most basic level is *knowledge,* or the ability to repeat information provided. The *comprehension* level seeks to determine if the individual understands the information well enough to restate it in a different form. At the *application* level, the individual must apply the information learned to a new but similar problem. *Analysis* requires the individual to break down and analyze the components of a problem. *Synthesis* involves the generation of new solutions to a problem, and *evaluation* is the ability to judge and select from competing options.

Interventionists should consider a taxonomy such as Bloom's when writing family goals and services. Clearly the lower-level skills are fundamental and must be learned first. However, if the ultimate goal is to help parents learn functional independence skills, higher levels of the taxonomy must be addressed. Examples of family goals written at each level of Bloom's taxonomy are displayed in Table 11.1.

GOAL ATTAINMENT SCALING

Goals can be written and evaluated in early intervention in a variety of ways. For several years we have used and studied a procedure that facilitates goal writing and evaluation. The procedure, goal attainment scaling (GAS), evolved from efforts to evaluate outcomes in clients with diverse problems participating in mental health programs (Kiresuk & Sherman, 1968). GAS consists of six steps:

TABLE 11.1
Sample Family Goals Based on Bloom's Taxonomy

Level	Definition	Example 1 Parent Teaching Skills	Example 2 Parent Involvement in Transitions	Example 3 Parent Use of Respite
Knowledge	Memorizes and repeats information presented	Memorizes and performs 10-step instructional sequence for teaching spoon feeding, 90% accuracy	Visits one potential preschool placement and gathers five pieces of information as recommended by interventionist	Knows name and phone number of one agency that provides respite services
Comprehension	Demonstrates understanding well enough to paraphrase information or state it in another form	Describes, in own words, teaching sequence and rationale for each step	Describes importance of planning for transitions	Describes process for qualifying for and securing respite services
Application	Uses information, method, rule, or principle in new but similar situations	Uses at home skills in teaching spoon feeding, with accuracy and without reminders, at least one time per day	Without prompting, visits additional potential placement sites and gathers essential information	Contacts respite agencies and private sitters to determine availability, costs, and basic competencies
Analysis	Identifies components of a problem	When faced with the need to teach a new skill, can independently break skill down into its components	Observes in placement option to determine skills that appear to be expected of children	Identifies aspects of respite options that correspond to predetermined criteria for acceptability
Synthesis	Generates new solutions to a problem	If a given instructional strategy does not work, generates and attempts a new strategy	Generates new questions that need to be answered to decide among placement options	If one respite option is not satisfactory, independently generates new options and explores their feasibility
Evaluation	Decides whether a given strategy or solution meets specified criteria, or compares two alternative strategies, solutions, or decisions	When presented two options for teaching a skill, decides which option would be better	Independently evaluates placement options and identifies placement that will best meet both child and family needs	Selects among alternative respite options and uses most acceptable option

1. A set of goals is specified for the client.
2. Each goal is weighted according to priority.
3. A continuum of possible outcomes by the end of an intervention period is determined. The continuum typically consists of five steps, each with a descriptive label and a numerical value: best expected outcome (2), more than expected outcome (1), expected outcome (0), less than expected outcome (-1), and worst expected outcome (-2).
4. The current or initial performance level is assessed for each goal.
5. Intervention services are provided.
6. Attained performance on each objective after the specified intervention period is determined.

A sample goal attainment scale demonstrating a variety of family goals is displayed in Table 11.2.

The advantages of goal attainment scaling are its flexibility and applicability in evaluating goal attainment of clients with highly variable needs. Recent papers have described the usefulness of GAS in evaluating goals and services provided to handicapped children (Maher, 1983; Maloney, Mirrett, Brooks, & Johannes, 1978; Shuster, Fitzgerald, Shelton, Barber, & Desch, 1984; Simeonsson et al., 1982). It has also been used to evaluate family therapy outcome (Woodward et al., 1978) and to plan services for pregnant teenagers (Enos & Hisanaga, 1979). We have suggested its use in planning and evaluating family goals and services in early intervention as a part of family-focused intervention (Bailey et al., 1986).

Use of GAS for evaluation is described in Chapter 12. As with any formal evaluation procedure, the usefulness of GAS depends on several factors, including staff training and commitment. In a study of its use with severely handicapped clients, we found that interdisciplinary treatment teams were not very accurate in predicting client outcome (Bailey & Simeonsson, in press), although the teams found the procedure useful in providing feedback about the progress of individual clients. Woodward et al. (1978) emphasized the importance of extensive training for psychotherapists in the use of GAS to evaluate family therapy, reporting greater prediction accuracy after such training. Maloney et al. (1978) reported that therapists generally become more accurate in their predictions over time.

GOAL SETTING AND THE IFSP

Generating family goals is an activity that is likely to increase in the coming years because Public Law 99-457 mandates the writing of an individualized family services plan for handicapped infants, toddlers, and their families. Family goals are also encouraged in individualized plans written for handicapped preschoolers. What does a good IFSP look like? This question will be discussed for some time. It is tempting to develop specific examples in this text. However, given the newness of this facet of early intervention and the

TABLE 11.2
Sample Goal Attainment Scale for Family-Related Goals

Program Families Project		Goal Attainment Scale for Jason		Date of Program Plan 9/23/84	
Scale Attainment Levels	Goal 1 Quality of Handling (W1 = 3)	Goal 2 Awareness of State (W2 = 2)	Goal 3 Community Resources (W3 = 3)	Goal 4 Implementing Training (W4 = 3)	Goal 5 Sibling Relationship (W5 = 1)
2 Best expected outcome	Father almost always handles child in sensitive fashion. Never rough or abrupt	Mother almost always differentiates states when child is receptive for social/educational interactions	Family always accesses needed community resources independently	Mother follows training program steps with accuracy of at least 90% (A)	Sibling often participates in a positive fashion in interactions between handicapped sibling and parents
1 More than expected outcome	Usually sensitive handling of child	Usually differentiates states (A)	Usually accesses community resources independently. Occasionally needs help	Mother follows training program steps with accuracy of at least 80%	Sibling sometimes participates in a positive fashion in interactions between handicapped sibling and parent
0 Expected outcome	Sometimes sensitive handling; about half the time (A)	Sometimes differentiates states; about half the time	Sometimes accesses needed community resources; about half the time (A)	Mother follows training program steps with accuracy of at least 70%	Sibling rarely interferes with parent-child interactions (A)
−1 Less than expected outcome	Occasionally sensitive handling	Occasionally differentiates states and responds appropriately	Family rarely accesses community resources independently	Mother follows training program steps with accuracy of at least 60%	Sibling sometimes interferes with parent-child interactions
−2 Worst expected outcome	Father never handles child in sensitive fashion; almost always rough or insensitive (I)	Mother never differentiates states when child is receptive for social/educational interactions (I)	Family always depends on others to access community resources (I)	Mother follows training program steps with less than 60% accuracy (I)	Sibling almost always interferes with parent-child interactions (I)

W = weights, I = initial performance, A = attained performance

From D. B. Bailey, R. J. Simeonsson, P. J. Winton, G. S. Huntington, M. Comfort, P. Isbell, K. J. O'Donnell, & J. M. Helm. Family-focused intervention: A functional model for planning, implementing, and evaluating individualized family services in early intervention. *Journal of the Division for Early Childhood, 10,* 1986, 156–171. Reprinted by permission.

current paucity of research and policy development pertaining to Public Law 99-457, caution is necessary. For example, in a recent study we demonstrated that in-service training in family assessment and collaborative goal setting increased interventionists' use of family assessment tools and increased the proportion of family goals written as part of a comprehensive plan (Bailey et al., 1988). The proportion of family goals varied across families and within families across time, raising questions about the number of family goals that should be included in the IFSP and whether an IFSP without family goals is appropriate. Also, although more family goals were written after training, were those goals appropriate? This section examines each component of the IFSP as specified in the legislation and addresses issues related to it.

Individualized Plans for Infants and Toddlers

In general, each infant, toddler, and family must receive a multidisciplinary assessment of needs and a written individualized family services plan. The plan must be evaluated yearly and reviewed at six-month intervals. Seven components of the IFSP are specified:

1. *A statement of the infant's or toddler's present levels of physical development, cognitive development, language and speech development, psychosocial development, and self-help skills, based on acceptable objective criteria.* Early intervention has been, and will continue to be, a child-focused service. This part of the IFSP corresponds to the traditional IEP in its statement of the child's developmental and behavioral skills. The multidisciplinary team should ensure that information regarding the child's abilities is based on appropriate assessment instruments, uses multiple sources of information (including parents), and is nondiscriminatory (Bailey & Wolery, in press). Following are recommendations for this component:
   a. State the child's strengths as well as needs
   b. Emphasize functional abilities rather than test scores
   c. Place abilities within a developmental context
   d. Describe abilities in all relevant developmental domains
   e. Include less traditional child-related information such as behavioral characteristics
   f. Describe functional limitations of the child (e.g., sensory impairment, motor impairment, chronic health problem) likely to be relevant to intervention planning
2. *A statement of the family's strengths and needs related to enhancing the development of the family's handicapped infant or toddler.* This component is analogous to the first except that it focuses on the family's strengths and needs rather than the child's. As described in this text, the multidisciplinary team should ensure that information regarding family needs is based on appropriate assessment instruments and draws

heavily on parent perceptions. Recommendations for this component, for the most part, parallel those suggested for children:
a. Emphasize family strengths and resources (see Chapter 7)
b. Focus on functional family needs
c. Include information in relevant family domains
d. Avoid negative statements about families, focusing instead on strengths, resources, and identified needs

3. *A statement of major goals for the infant or toddler and the family, and the criteria, procedures, and timelines used to measure progress toward these goals and determine if modifications of goals or services are necessary.* This is the major section of the IFSP because it describes the specific goals of family and child services. These goals should be developed collaboratively with families. The following recommendations pertain to this section:
a. Draw goals and objectives from family needs stated in item 2
b. Target the child, a family member, or an interactional system within the family for services
c. Clearly describe objectives with measurable outcomes
d. Focus on functional objectives
e. Include objectives aimed at higher-level skills as well as basic skills
f. Specify projected dates for accomplishment

4. *A statement of specific early intervention services necessary to meet the unique needs of the infant or toddler and the family, including the frequency, intensity, and method of delivering services.* This section describes the means by which goals are to be attained and the services to be provided by the intervention team. The team should ensure that services are available and are designed to benefit the family. An underlying principle of these services is that they should strengthen rather than undermine family authority, competence, and self-esteem. The following recommendations are offered for this section:
a. State the specific services to be provided and their frequency
b. Describe what family members will do to accomplish goals

5. *The projected dates for initiation of services and the anticipated duration of such services.* This requirement is straightforward and requires no explanation.

6. *The name of the case manager from the profession most immediately relevant to the infant's or toddler's and the family's needs, who will be responsible for implementing the plan and coordinating with other agencies and persons.* Different states will likely adopt different policies for case management. The legislation specifies only that the IFSP include the name of the case manager. The case manager's authority and role in treatment provision are not required to be specified. However, to protect the family's interests and to clarify responsibilities, we offer the following suggestions:
a. State each professional's responsibility in provision of family services

b. Describe the specific authority of the case manager in decision making, treatment provision, and resource allocation

7. *The steps to be taken supporting the transition of the handicapped toddler to services provided for preschoolers to the extent such services are considered appropriate.* This refers to part B of the legislation, requiring services for handicapped 3- and 4-year-old children. Guidelines for preparing for transitions were described in detail in Chapter 6 of this text. We assume that if a transition is not expected within the coming year, this section is not applicable. However, this issue has not been resolved. When included, this section should do two things:

a. Describe the options available for placement

b. Describe a sequence of steps necessary to determine the best option, identify requirements for transition, and plan for transition

We suggest that approximately six months before transition a more detailed transition plan be developed and implemented.

Individualized Plans for Preschoolers

The new legislation does not specify for preschoolers the family components indicated regarding infants. However, we believe that the same principles should apply to this age group. Parents should be engaged in a collaborative planning process and preschool programs should provide, when needed, both family and child services.

SUMMARY

The assessment process in early intervention culminates when the information gathered is used to help families and interventionists jointly determine the needs of both children and families, and subsequently provide services in response to those needs. The specification of intervention goals is important for reasons of legality, functionality, and communication. However, numerous problems and important professional issues are associated with the process. Interventionists must be aware of these issues and should recognize that goal setting can be a serious and meaningful activity, not simply a legal requirement.

REFERENCES

Aponte, H. J. (1985). The negotiation of values in therapy. *Family Process, 24*, 323–338.

Bailey, D. B. (1987). Collaborative goal-setting with families: Resolving differences in values and priorities for services. *Topics in Early Childhood Special Education, 7*(2), 59–71.

Bailey, D. B., & Simeonsson, R. J. (in press). Goal attainment scaling: An investigation of its use to evaluate individual progress of severely and profoundly retarded clients. *Mental Retardation.*

Bailey, D. B., Simeonsson, R. J., Isbell, P., Huntington, G. S., Winton, P. J., Comfort, M., & Helm, J. (1988). Inservice training in family assessment and goal-setting for early interventionists: Outcomes and issues. *Journal of the Division for Early Childhood, 12,* 126–136.

Bailey, D. B., Simeonsson, R. J., Winton, P. J., Huntington, G. S., Comfort, M., Isbell, P., O'Donnell, K. J., & Helm, J. M. (1986). Family-focused intervention: A functional model for planning, implementing, and evaluating individualized family services in early intervention. *Journal of the Division for Early Childhood, 10,* 156–171.

Bailey, D. B., & Wolery, M. (Eds.) (in press). *Assessing infants and preschoolers with handicaps.* Columbus, Oh.: Merrill Publishing Company.

Bloom, B. S., Englehart, M. D., Furst, E. J., Hill, W. H., & Krathwohl, D. R. (1956). *A taxonomy of educational objectives: Handbook I, the cognitive domain.* New York: McKay.

Breiner, J., & Beck, S. (1984). Parents as change agents in the management of their developmentally delayed children's noncompliant behaviors: A critical review. *Applied Research in Mental Retardation, 5,* 259–278.

Dunst, C. J. (1985). Rethinking early intervention. *Analysis and Intervention in Developmental Disabilities, 5,* 165–201.

Enos, R., & Hisanaga, M. (1979). Goal setting with pregnant teenagers. *Child Welfare, 58,* 541–551.

Hartley, J., & Davies, I. K. (1976). Preinstructional strategies: The role of pretests, behavioral objectives, overviews and advance organizers. *Review of Educational Research, 46,* 239–265.

Howlin, P. (1984). Parents as therapists: A critical review. In D. J. Muller (Ed.), *Remediating children's language: Behavioral and naturalistic approaches* (pp. 197–229). San Diego: College-Hill.

Kelley, M. L., & Stokes, T. F. (1984). Student-teacher contracting with goal-setting for maintenance. *Behavior Modification, 8,* 223–244.

Kiresuk, T. J., & Sherman, R. E. (1968). Goal attainment scaling: A general method for evaluating comprehensive community mental health programs. *Community Mental Health Journal, 4,* 443–453.

Latham, G., & Locke, E. (1979). Goal-setting: A motivational technique that works. *Organizational Dynamics,* 45–54.

Lloyd, M. E. (1983). Selecting systems to measure client outcome in human service agencies. *Behavioral Assessment, 5,* 55–70.

Lovitt, T. C. (1977). *In spite of my resistance, I've learned from children.* Columbus, Oh.: Merrill Publishing Company.

Mager, R. F. (1962). *Preparing instructional objectives.* Belmont, Calif.: Fearson.

Maher, C. A. (1983). Goal attainment scaling: A method for evaluating special education services. *Exceptional Children, 49,* 529–536.

Maloney, F. P., Mirrett, P., Brooks, C., & Johannes, K. (1978). Use of the goal attainment scale in the treatment and ongoing evaluation of neurologically handicapped children. *American Journal of Occupational Therapy, 32,* 505–510.

Margolin, G. (1982). Ethical and legal considerations in marital and family therapy. *American Psychologist, 37,* 788–801.

McConkie, M. E. (1979). Classifying and reviewing the empirical work on MBO: Some implications. *Group and Organization Studies, 4,*461–475.

O'Dell, S. L. (1985). Progress in parent training. *Progress in Behavior Modification, 19,* 57–108.

Reese, R. M., & Serna, L. (1986). Planning for generalization and maintenance in parent training: Parents need I.E.P.s too. *Mental Retardation, 24,* 87–92.

Shuster, S. K., Fitzgerald, N., Shelton, G., Barber, P., & Desch, S. (1984). Goal attainment scaling with moderately and severely handicapped preschool children. *Journal of the Division for Early Childhood, 8,* 26–37.

Simeonsson, R. J., Huntington, G. S., & Parse, S. A. (1980). Expanding the developmental assessment of young handicapped children. *New Directions for Exceptional Children, 3,* 51–74.

Simeonsson, R. J., Huntington, G. S., & Short, R. J. (1982). Individual differences and goals: An approach to the evaluation of child progress. *Topics in Early Childhood Special Education, 1,* 71–80.

Tollefson, N., Tracy, D. B., Johnsen, E. Q., Farmer, A. W., & Buenning, M. (1984). Goal setting and personal responsibility training for LD adolescents. *Psychology in the Schools, 21,* 224–233.

Vargas, J. S. (1972). *Writing worthwhile behavioral objectives.* New York: Harper & Row.

Wolery, M., Bailey, D. B., & Sugai, G. (1988). *Effective teaching: Principles and procedures of applied behavior analysis with exceptional students.* Boston: Allyn & Bacon.

Woodward, C. A., Santa-Barbara, J., Levin, S., & Epstein, N. B. (1978). The role of goal attainment scaling in evaluating family therapy outcome. *American Journal of Orthopsychiatry, 48,* 464–476.

12

Evaluating the Effects of Family-Focused Intervention

ntervention with families of handicapped children is predicated on the
assumption that it will effect some change. That change could be developmental achievement of the child, reduced stress for parents, or improved family relationships. Although such changes often are not measured
formally, a given intervention would not be continued unless some progress
could be attributed to it, even if that attribution was based primarily on the
family's or interventionist's personal judgment. This chapter discusses the
importance of evaluation in early intervention with families of handicapped
children. The fundamental issue underlying evaluation is clinical and program accountability. As used in this context, *clinical accountability* refers
to the effective provision of individualized services to a family with a handicapped child. *Program accountability* refers to the efficient use of resources at the program level to achieve broad intervention goals for children
and families. Accountability requires documentation of child and family
characteristics and evaluation of intervention effects. The sophistication
and rigor of evaluation methods as they pertain to broad questions about
the significance and impact of early intervention have been debated extensively in the literature (Dunst & Rheingrover, 1981; Simeonsson, Cooper, &

This chapter was contributed by Rune J. Simeonsson, University of North Carolina at Chapel
Hill.

Scheiner, 1982; Casto & Mastropieri, 1986). The purpose here is not to review experimental designs and statistical methodology in early intervention research. Instead, we present a rationale for evaluating early intervention efforts at clinical and program levels and identify applicable methods and procedures. Earlier efforts to evaluate early intervention have focused primarily on the child. The increasing focus on the family's role in early intervention calls for evaluation procedures that examine family outcomes.

THE RATIONALE FOR EVALUATION IN EARLY INTERVENTION

Although evaluation is perhaps the least understood and most difficult task faced by early interventionists, it is essential. The term *evaluation* is not synonymous with research and should not be equated with a particular method or statistical procedure. At the most basic level, evaluation refers to any effort that demonstrates real or perceived intervention impact. As we will review later in this chapter, a number of procedures can be adopted to demonstrate child or family changes as a function of intervention, ranging from basic anecdotal recording to more specific forms of evaluation methodology. Our contentions are that any evaluation effort is preferable to none and that every program providing early intervention services should adopt the most rigorous evaluation method possible, given the program objectives and resources. To this end, Wolery and Bailey (1984) have identified seven questions that can guide evaluation of an early intervention program. A review of these questions and associated strategies (see Table 12.1) for answering them may be useful in developing a comprehensive evaluation plan.

The rationale for evaluating intervention impact has two complementary components: formative evaluation and summative evaluation. *Formative evaluation* deals with ongoing monitoring of child and family progress. This can take the form of documenting child, family, and intervention characteristics as the intervention is implemented. Particular emphasis can be placed on the manner and extent to which specified intervention activities or objectives are carried out. Formative evaluation documents intervention impact by demonstrating that planned interventions were actually implemented, in the manner and for the duration specified. In reference to the questions listed in Table 12.1, formative evaluation addresses questions 2, 3, 4, and 6 in particular, as well as elements of the other questions. Activities that fall under the rubric of formative evaluation, such as record keeping of family contacts, stimulation objectives, and physical therapy sessions, are often documented in human service settings and can be readily incorporated into an overall evaluation plan.

The complementary component to formative evaluation is *summative evaluation*, the purpose of which is to demonstrate that the interventions caused or contributed to expected child or family change. For practical as

TABLE 12.1

*Questions and Strategies in Evaluation of Early Intervention (Wolery &
Bailey, 1984)*

Questions	Strategies
1. Can the program demonstrate that the methods, materials, and overall service delivery represent the best educational practice?	Describe program and philosophy Develop rationale for program components Document best practice Offer professional validation
2. Can the program demonstrate that the methods espoused in the overall philosophy are implemented accurately and consistently?	Generate record of services Generate record of implementation of services Provide evidence of replicability
3. Can the program demonstrate that it attempts to verify empirically the effectiveness of interventions or other individual program components for which the best educational practice has yet to be verified?	Analyze individual components of intervention program
4. Can the program demonstrate that it carefully monitors client progress and is sensitive to points at which changes in services need to be made?	Collect and monitor data to document provision of services and to facilitate decision making
5. Can the program demonstrate that a system is in place for determining the relative adequacy of client progress and service delivery?	Compare child progress with reference group Calculate gain relative to time in intervention Interpret gain relative to criteria Interpret gain relative to expectation
6. Can the program demonstrate that it is moving toward the accomplishment of program goals and objectives?	Specify program objectives in measurable terms Generate questions about program achievement of objectives Identify data sources; collect data Prepare report
7. Can the program demonstrate that the goals, methods and materials, and overall service delivery system are in accordance with the needs and values of the community and clients it serves?	Review needs assessment Subjectively evaluate program activities and child and family progress

well as methodological reasons, summative evaluation, involving pre/post testing or other systematic methods to assess child and family change, is not as easily incorporated into ongoing activities of an overall evaluation plan as is formative evaluation. However, evaluation plans should incorporate both components to document potential effects of early intervention.

Documenting the impact of early intervention with the family is part of a larger effort to show program accountability for effective and efficient use of resources to achieve stated program intervention objectives. In some instances, such documentation can involve describing the collective formative and summative evaluations of individual families in that program. In other instances, some analytical or statistical procedure may be applied to an aggregation of information to document achievement of program objectives. Such documentation is likely to be important to funding and oversight agencies responsible for human services.

PROCEDURAL CONSIDERATIONS IN EVALUATION

Typically, the evaluation of intervention impact, whether at the level of clinical services for an individual family or at the level of planned intervention research, is beset with a number of problems. These problems can be summarized in terms of the nature, adequacy, and interpretability of information used in evaluation. The nature and adequacy of assessment information have been addressed in most of the previous chapters; child and family characteristics most relevant to the program's intervention objectives should be assessed. The interpretability of information used in evaluation reflects concerns regarding the attribution, relevance, and significance of change (Simeonsson, 1986). *Attribution* of change concerns whether observed change in child or family functioning can logically be attributed to intervention effects. Alternative interpretations, such as maturation, test wiseness, or spontaneous change, are always possible. More detailed reviews of alternative explanations are often defined in formal research as threats to the validity of findings (Campbell & Stanley, 1966). The *relevance* and *significance* of change, while having theoretical and methodological aspects, reflect more practical concerns. In essence, these concerns focus on the degree to which change, if observed, is relevant to child and family needs and whether the observed change is in some sense significant or important in their lives. Relevance of change was touched on in Chapter 8 in terms of ecological validity of assessment; significance of change will be addressed later in this chapter.

Three procedural considerations are important in the evaluation of early intervention services: asking appropriate questions, using appropriate measures, and drawing appropriate conclusions.

Asking Appropriate Questions

The purpose of evaluation should determine the choice of appropriate evaluation questions. Evaluation seeks to infer a cause-and-effect relationship between intervention activities and family outcomes. Can change in the child or the family be attributed to intervention? This question requires careful and appropriate documentation of child and family characteristics and of the nature of intervention activities so that their scope and content is clear. In making a causal inference about the impact of intervention, one must consider the strength of alternative explanations for observed outcome. A second question that can be asked with regard to evaluation pertains to generalization. Are the observed intervention effects found in one family generalizable to other children and families? To ask this question, evaluators must document the characteristics of children and families in detail sufficient to establish their similarity with those of other families who may benefit from intervention.

Using Appropriate Measures

A second procedural concern pertains to the selection and use of appropriate measures. The use of appropriate measures should logically follow from the purpose of evaluation. If the purpose is to show that planned interventions resulted in family change (causal inference) or that intervention effects may be achievable in similar families (generalization), then appropriate measures are ones that assess child or family outcomes. In this case, child outcomes can be ascertained by many developmental and behavioral measures, including those described in Chapter 3. These measures range from assessment of gross motor skills to assessment of expressive communication or task orientation. Family outcomes may be assessed in a variety of ways, depending on the needs or problems targeted for intervention. Assessment of outcome for an individual family may thus focus on the reduction of stress (Chapter 5), changes in roles and supports (Chapter 7), or improvements in the parent-child relationship (Chapter 4).

Drawing Appropriate Conclusions

The third procedural concern involves drawing appropriate conclusions when evaluating early intervention effects. Evaluation will reveal that anticipated changes either occurred or did not occur. If evaluation provides evidence for change, at least two possible conclusions can be drawn about the role of early intervention. The obvious conclusion is that the intervention accounts for the change—that is, the intervention produced the desired effects. A competing conclusion is that the change is not directly attributable to the intervention but may be the result of other factors, such as the passage of time or the occurrence of unanticipated events. A definite determination about the causal relationship between intervention and change in the family and the child requires experimental procedures that are beyond the capabilities of most clinical service programs. Evaluation results should always be interpreted cautiously, with the recognition that alternate conclusions about intervention impact are possible. The careful design and implementation of evaluation activities should strengthen the conclusion that intervention produced family change.

If evaluation reveals little or no change, several interpretations are possible. The lack of change in children or families after a given period may imply that the intervention is not effective. An alternative conclusion, however, is that the intervention might have been effective but was not implemented correctly or for a long enough period to achieve the desired outcome. The effectiveness of the intervention might be masked or minimized by idiosyncrasies or spontaneous events beyond the control of the intervention program. As when conclusions are drawn regarding causality, evaluators should recognize that alternate factors might account for the lack of change, so that intervention activities are not prematurely terminated or their potential effects inappropriately discounted.

THE EVALUATION OF PARENT SATISFACTION

A related but distinct purpose of evaluation is to determine parent satisfaction. Although parent satisfaction is not likely to be independent of intervention effects, it may reflect the parents' broader view of the scope and quality of intervention services. Documenting satisfaction by recipients of care is an important issue in human service fields generally. It is also one of three identified criteria for the evaluation of health care systems, because of its association with treatment compliance, comprehension of medical information, and continuity of care (Lewis, Scott, Pantell, & Wolf, 1986). Despite its importance, client satisfaction is difficult to evaluate objectively, particularly in the case of parents of young handicapped children. Perhaps the major difficulty in evaluating parent satisfaction with intervention services is that such services are usually the only ones available, which means that parents must evaluate existing services against no services at all. Given the emotional and personal dimensions of raising a young handicapped child (Chapters 1 and 2), parents are unlikely to evaluate objectively the only available services. A second difficulty is that parents may not be in a position to determine a standard against which they should judge the services they are receiving. Neither parents nor interventionists are likely to have clear criteria of excellence regarding quantity, quality, and form of services and intervention activities. Concerns about these issues reinforce the importance of ascertaining shared values and negotiating priorities in intervention planning, as discussed in Chapter 10.

Despite these difficulties, or perhaps because of them, it is essential to evaluate family satisfaction with early intervention services to identify the perceived value of services and to provide feedback to families. Unfortunately, evaluating family satisfaction is an area that has not been explored extensively with families of handicapped children, and therefore suitable measurement strategies are lacking. Meyers and Blacher (1987) examined parent satisfaction with schooling as one outcome variable in a study of home-school relationships for 99 parents of severely impaired 3- to 8-year-old children. The format was based on the coding of parent interviews involving direct and indirect questions about school, the program, teachers, and communication between teachers and parents. Most parents indicated satisfaction, and level of satisfaction correlated with the perceived benefit of the program. General levels of satisfaction with an intervention program can be assessed with a generic satisfaction measure such as the Client Satisfaction Questionnaire (Larsen, Attkisson, Hargreaves, & Nguyen, 1979). This instrument includes only eight items, but they are broad in content (Table 12.2), which makes the questionnaire applicable in a variety of program settings and allows results to be compared across other human service delivery systems. If information about parent satisfaction with specific program components is desired, parents can be asked to rate or rank those components. Research on parent satisfaction with children's medical care may provide an approach that is applicable to evaluating satisfaction with early intervention services. The Parent Medical Interview Satisfaction Scale (Lewis et al., 1986) was developed to evaluate parent satisfaction with one aspect of medical care—namely, the physician's conduct during the medical visit. The scale consisted of 27 items distributed across four subscales: physician communication with the parents, physician communication with the child, distress relief, and adherence intent. Parent satisfaction was found to be significantly associated with objective observations of the physician's conduct during the interview. The format of the scale and the nature of most of the individual items makes the approach seem applicable to evaluating satisfaction of families with handicapped children. Findings by Lewis et al. showed that measurement of satisfaction in this manner can meet standards of internal consistency and construct validity. Furthermore, no significant associations were found between satisfaction and demographic characteristics or medical care variables (visits), suggesting that satisfaction is in fact an index of the parents' evaluation of the physician's behavior. Given the similarity of the relationship between service providers and families in early intervention to that of the physicians and parents studied, evaluation of parent satisfaction would seem to be feasible and productive.

Important elements in the evaluation of satisfaction by parents should most likely include communication, perceived competence of intervention staff, quality and appropriateness of services, and perceived empathy and sensitivity of staff. Some useful guidelines to consider in the assessment of

TABLE 12.2
The Client Satisfaction Questionnaire (CSQ)

Please help us improve our program by answering some questions about the services you have received at the _____. We are interested in your honest opinions, whether they are positive or negative. <u>Please answer all of the questions.</u> We also welcome your comments and suggestions. Thank you very much, we appreciate your help.

Circle Your Answer

1. How would you rate the quality of service you received?

4	3	2	1
Excellent	Good	Fair	Poor

2. Did you get the kind of service you wanted?

1	2	3	4
No definitely not	No not really	Yes generally	Yes definitely

*3. To what extent has our program met your needs?

4	3	2	1
Almost all of my needs have been met	Most of my needs have been met	Only a few of my needs have been met	None of my needs have been met

4. If a friend were in need of similar help, would you recommend our program to him/her?

1	2	3	4
No definitely not	No I don't think so	Yes I think so	Yes definitely

5. How satisfied are you with the amount of help you received?

1	2	3	4
Quite dissatisfied	Indifferent or mildly dissatisfied	Mostly satisfied	Very satisfied

6. Have the services you received helped you to deal more effectively with your problems?

4	3	2	1
Yes they helped a great deal	Yes they helped somewhat	No they really didn't help	No they seemed to make things worse

*7. In an overall, general sense, how satisfied are you with the service you received?

4	3	2	1
Very satisfied	Mostly satisfied	Indifferent or mildly dissatisfied	Quite dissatisifed

8. If you were to seek help again, would you come back to our program?

1	2	3	4
No definitely not	No I don't think so	Yes I think so	Yes definitely

Write Comments Below

*Can be used as a shorter scale

Reprinted with permission from *Evaluation and Program Planning*, 2, D. Larsen, C. Attkisson, W. Hargreaves, & T. Nguyen, Assessment of client patient satisfaction: Development of a general scale, Copyright 1979, Pergamon Journals Ltd.

family satisfaction are: (1) parents should rate individual aspects of the program separately rather than on a general basis, and (2) scales should require parents to rank-order services provided by the program. This approach ensures that parents will indicate their relative satisfaction with the services offered by the program, thereby providing information about aspects of the program that should be strengthened or perhaps eliminated.

EVALUATION PROCEDURES AND METHODS

A variety of methods and procedures can be adopted to evaluate the effects of early intervention with families of handicapped children. These range from informal and straightforward documentation to more formal and demanding methods. The selected methods and procedures that will be described begin with the simplest evaluative strategy of anecdotal records and proceed to increasingly more formal approaches of the case method, pre/post assessment, single-subject design, and goal attainment scaling technique. Although these approaches are also applicable to the documentation of child progress, such evaluation is described elsewhere (Bailey & Wolery, 1984); Simeonsson, 1986); the focus here will be on evaluating the effects of family intervention.

The selection of a particular evaluation strategy is likely to be based on several factors. The conceptual framework adopted by a program may influence its approach to evaluating intervention effects. Programs with a general view of family functioning may find anecdotal and case-method approaches most suitable to the evaluation of clinical data that are often gathered in such programs. A program based on behavior modification principles, on the other hand, will by definition be suited to some form of single-subject design methodology in which the family is seen as the subject. Programs oriented to precise goal setting may find goal attainment scaling (Kiresuk & Lund, 1976; Simeonsson, Huntington, & Short, 1982) the strategy of choice. The nature of assessment instruments and the form of data they yield may also influence the selection of an evaluation strategy, in that the availability of quantitative scores will permit the calculation of descriptive statistics, whereas nominal data are limited to qualitative summaries. A third important determinant in selecting an evaluation approach is the human and technical resources that a program can commit to evaluation. Carrying out a comprehensive evaluation plan is time consuming; the program's capabilities in this regard should be considered in designing and implementing such a plan.

Anecdotal Records

Using anecdotal records to evaluate intervention effects is the least formal and least rigorous approach. Documenting family responses to intervention through anecdotal data involves analyzing progress notes, clinical summaries, and other records that describe family behavior or achievements. Although anecdotal data constitute a rich source of information, they are often idiosyncratic in form and content, which limits their use in evaluation, particularly with respect to comparative analysis across families and the degree of confidence with which inferences can be drawn about the causal role of intervention in family change. The keeping of anecdotal records is, however, an approach that can provide at least a qualified evaluation of intervention effects, in that it involves documentation of child and family characteristics at different points in the intervention program.

Case Study

The case-study method may be well suited to documenting the effects of clinical interventions. The major difference between the case-study method and the collection of anecdotal data is that case study involves a planned approach that specifies the scope and contexts of documentation. As such, the case-study method can be considered a systematic method of recording observations and impressions about the responses of families to interventions. Because the case-study method involves planning what is to be recorded, similar data can be collected across families for comparative purposes. The case-study method is also rich in information that has been used to describe behavioral and developmental change of children and families in clinical contexts. Drawing on the case-approach procedures used in counseling and psychotherapy (Corey, 1986), the following is an outline of a case-method approach to evaluation:

1. Identify data
2. Take a developmental history
3. Present problems and concerns
4. Identify current situational factors
5. Set intervention goals
6. Initiate implementation of intervention
7. Manage the course of intervention
8. Summarize and formulate case

With careful planning, this method can yield qualitative-level data of reasonable rigor for evaluation purposes. Because data obtained by the case-study method are collected in sequence along with the implementation of intervention activities, a stronger basis exists for drawing inferences about the causal role of intervention in family outcome than when anecdotal records are used.

Pre/Post Assessment

The comparison of data from measures administered before and after interventions is often employed to document the impact of intervention in the form of change or progress. The issue of pre/post assessment as an evaluative approach in early intervention has been examined extensively, and the use of efficiency indices has been proposed to deal with some problems of this approach to documenting progress (Simeonsson, 1982). Pre/post assessment of mother-child interaction, for example, could show an increase in the quality as well as the appropriateness of a mother's verbal initiations with her handicapped infant. Similarly, pre/post assessment might also reveal that the level of perceived stress was reduced over the period of intervention. In many instances, it may be logical to conclude that observed changes are attributable to the intervention. However, findings derived by this method are susceptible to alternative explanations for observed change—that is, factors other than the intervention itself may account for the change. As discussed earlier in this chapter, the passage of time, unanticipated events, and familiarity with assessment measures may account for child or family change from one occasion to the next. To strengthen the conclusion that changes observed on the basis of pre/post assessment are a result of intervention, this evaluation method is best used in combination with other forms of documenting progress.

Single-Subject Design

The single-subject design has a long history as a method of evaluating the effects of behavioral interventions across a variety of applications involving child behavior and parent-child interactions. The single-subject design is the graphic form of documenting the functional relationship of behaviors with environmental contingencies. The key components of the classic *ABAB* single-subject design are (1) operational definition of the behavior or behaviors of interest; (2) establishment of a trend-free baseline of behavior; (3) documentation of change in the behavior during the intervention phase in which an environmental contingency is applied; (4) a discernible shift in behavior toward baseline levels with the removal of the contingency (reversal phase); and (5) a subsequent change in behavior with the reinstatement of the contingency. The logic of this classic *ABAB* design is that consistent changes in behavior in the four phases confirm the impact of the intervention on behavior. An example of an *ABAB* evaluation of family progress is displayed in Figure 12.1. The figure shows a functional relationship for Family X across the different phases, whereas there is no evidence of a functional relationship for Family Y. Although the *ABAB* design is best suited to evaluate interventions couched within a behavioral framework, the *AB* components (baseline, intervention phases) can be used to describe status at the end of the treatment. When only these first two phases are used, definite conclusions about intervention impact cannot be drawn. The *AB* design can describe whether a change has occurred, but cannot indicate a cause-and-effect relationship.

FIGURE 12.1

Functional and Nonfunctional Relationships between Caregiver Behavior and Contingent Intervention across Experimental Phases for Two Families

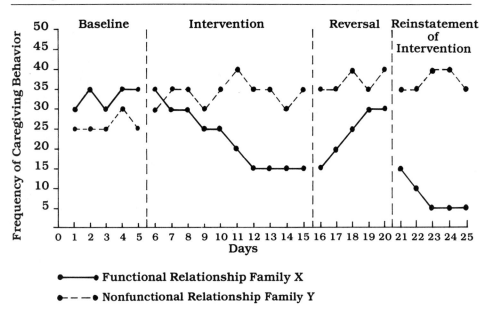

An alternative to the *ABAB* design is the multiple baseline approach, which is useful when the behaviors changed cannot or should not be reversed. Multiple-baseline designs require that baseline data be collected on several behaviors in several settings or across several individuals. Treatment is sequentially applied to one behavior, situation, or individual at a time while baseline conditions are simultaneously maintained in the other contexts. If change occurs only when the intervention is applied, a causal relationship is assumed to obtain between the intervention and the behavior. An example of the use of a multiple-baseline design is presented in Figure 12.2. Here changes in family behavior are shown to be reliably associated with the intervention across the three settings, suggesting a generalized effect of the intervention. Variations of the single-subject design may thus constitute an evaluation strategy that would be suitable for programs that conceptualize their interventions in a manner compatible with this approach.

Goal Attainment Scaling

Goal attainment scaling (GAS) is a planning and evaluation method that has been used extensively in the mental health field to document the at-

FIGURE 12.2

Multiple Baseline Procedure to Document Sibling Caregiving Behavior as a Function of Intervention in Three Settings

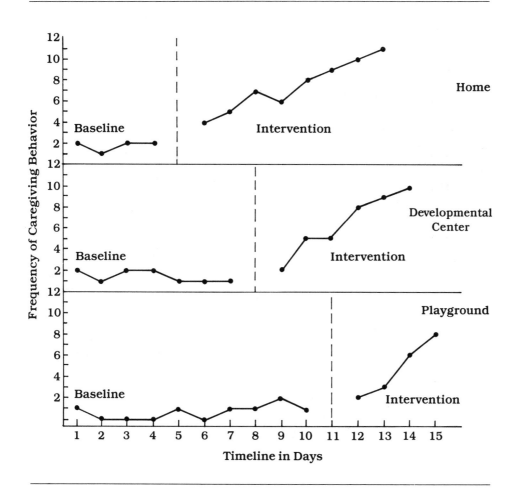

tainment of intervention goals. It is presented here as a relatively simple but precise method of comparing the extent to which planned goals are attained as a function of intervention. The format consists of scaling potential outcomes from the most unfavorable to the best expected, with the expected level of intervention success constituting the goal of intervention for the families, as illustrated in Figure 12.3. The applicability of GAS in early intervention has been detailed by Simeonsson, Huntington, and Short (1982) and is based on several features that make it particularly attractive for use in evaluating child and family change as a function of intervention.

FIGURE 12.3
Initial and Attained Goal Attainment Scores for Two Families in Early Intervention

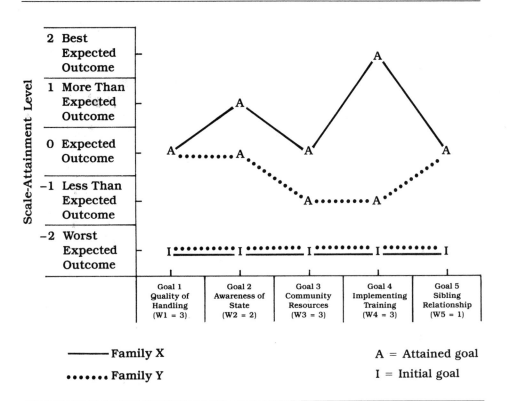

A primary feature is that GAS lends itself to evaluation of intervention effects that may be idiosyncratic from one family to the next. As graphically depicted in Figure 12.3, the two families differ in the change from initial (I) to attained (A) status of goals. The format allows for a common evaluation strategy of various combinations of child and family goals in individualized family interventions. It also lends itself to family involvement in planning and prioritizing goals. Additional features that favor its use as an evaluation tool are the differential weighting of goals to reflect intervention priorities and the derivation of a quantitative index. This index is a *t* score calculated on the basis of the amount of change in goals with the weight, or priority, assigned to the goals. It can be used to compare the progress of one family over time or the progress of two or more families provided with different, individualized interventions. Calculation of the standardized indices (*t* scores) for the values shown in Figure 12.3 yields initial *t* scores of 23 and

28, with an attained *t* score of 54 and 47 at the end of the intervention period for the first and second families, respectively. Given the fact that the standardized index is set to reflect a value of 50 when the expected level of treatment success is attained, it can be concluded that intervention was effective for the first family, for whom expected outcomes was exceeded, whereas the change observed in the second family did not reach the expected level. The flexibility of GAS in handling idiosyncratic information, its emphasis on precise planning, and the derivation of a quantitative index to complement qualitative analysis make it particularly well suited for documenting effects in early intervention. In addition to the formal index of the *t* score, a visual analysis of the change on the goal attainment scale format provides practical documentation of intervention outcome for the program as well as for the parents. This method's application to early intervention settings, however, may be limited by the formality of the process and the fact that the approach is a function of the accuracy and relevance of goal setting. In a review of GAS methodology, Calsyn and Davidson (1978) proposed that it be used not as the sole evaluation approach but in combination with other evaluation strategies. This recommendation makes sense in early intervention programs, because the specification of objectives in individualized intervention plans required in the regulations of Public Law 99-457 could be readily presented in the goal attainment scaling format. In the selection of any evaluation approach, the method of choice is the one that best lends itself to a program's unique orientation and assessment priorities.

SUMMARY

This chapter has stressed the importance of evaluation in terms of accountability, with respect both to ensuring effective interventions for individual families and to using resources effectively at the program level to address a priority in human services. Planning and evaluating interventions should be continuous and complementary processes in a program, with evaluation findings resulting in the revision or refinement of intervention activities. Carefully designed and implemented evaluations can also contribute to more efficient practices in the field of early intervention in that effective interventions can be generalized and implemented with families sharing similar characteristics and needs. An important aspect of evaluation is documenting consumer satisfaction with services. Satisfaction data can complement findings on intervention impact with handicapped children and their families. The evaluation strategies reviewed differ in terms of methodological rigor and the strength of conclusions that can be drawn from their use. A program may be able to choose an evaluation method or that choice may be determined by the needs of oversight or funding agencies. Some evaluation approaches are more demanding than others, both in terms of the time needed to carry them out and in the level of skill required of the evaluator. In any case, every effort must be made to adopt the most comprehensive and rigorous method possible. A practical approach would be to use several methods in combination to achieve both qualitative and quantitative evaluation of intervention effects. The major initiatives being developed on behalf of families with handicapped infants and young children represent a challenging, but as yet poorly researched area of study. An ongoing clinical research approach is needed to advance knowledge about interventions that will be effective and efficient in promoting adaptation and development in families with handicapped children.

REFERENCES

Bailey, D. B., & Wolery, M. (1984). *Teaching infants and preschoolers with handicaps.* Columbus, Oh.: Merrill Publishing Company.

Calsyn, R. J., & Davidson, W. S. (1978). Do we really want a program evaluation strategy based solely on individualized goals? A critique of goal attainment scaling. *Community Mental Health Journal, 4,* 300–308.

Campbell, D. T., & Stanley, J. (1966). *Experimental and quasi-experimental designs in research.* Chicago: Rand McNally.

Casto, G., & Mastropieri, M. A. (1986). The efficacy of early intervention programs: A meta-analysis. *Exceptional Children, 52,* 417–424.

Corey, G. (1986). *Case approach to counseling and psychotherapy* (2nd ed.). Monterey, Calif.: Brooks/Cole Publishing.

Dunst, C. J., & Rheingrover, R. M. (1981). An analysis of the efficacy of infant intervention programs with organically handicapped children. *Evaluation and Program Planning, 4,* 287–323.

Kiresuk, T. J., & Lund, S. H. (1976). Process and measurement using goal attainment scaling. In G. V. Glass (Ed.), *Evaluation studies review manual* (vol. 1). Beverly Hills, Calif.: Sage Publications.

Larsen, D., Attkisson, C., Hargreaves, W., & Nguyen, T. (1979). Assessment of client patient satisfaction: Development of a general scale. *Evaluation and program planning.* Pergamon Press.

Lewis, C. C., Scott, D. E., Pantell, R. H., & Wolf, M. H. (1986). Parent satisfaction with children's medical care: Development, field test, and validation of a questionnaire. *Medical Care, 24,* 209–215.

Meyers, C. E., & Blacher, J. (1987). Parents' perceptions of schooling for severely handicapped children: Home and family variables. *Exceptional Children, 53,* 441–449.

Simeonsson, R. J. (1982). Intervention, accountability, and efficiency indices: A rejoinder. *Exceptional Children, 48,* 358–359.

Simeonsson, R. J. (1986). *Psychological and developmental assessment of special children.* Boston: Allyn & Bacon.

Simeonsson, R. J., Cooper, D. H., & Scheiner, A. P. (1982). A review and analysis of the effectiveness of early intervention programs. *Pediatrics, 69,* 635–641.

Simeonsson, R. J., Huntington, G. S., & Short, R. J. (1982). Individual differences and goals: Multiple problems-multivariate goals. *Journal of the Association for the Severely Handicapped, 5,* 55–72.

Wolery, M., & Bailey, D. B. (1984). Alternatives to impact evaluation: Suggestions for program evaluation in early intervention. *Journal of the Division for Early Childhood, 9,* 27–37.

Author Index

Subject Index